Overcoming Resistance

Albert Ellis, Ph.D., is the founder and Executive Director of the Institute for Rational-Emotive Therapy in New York City. He received his M.A. and Ph.D. degrees in clinical psychology from Columbia University. A former Adjunct Professor of Psychology at Rutgers University and Pittsburgh State College, Dr. Ellis has also been Distinguished Professor of Psychology at the Professional School of Psychological Studies in San Diego. He served as Chief Psychologist of the New Jersey State Diagnostic Center and Chief Psychologist of the New Jersey Department of Institutions and Agencies. He has been a Consultant in Clinical Psychology to the New York City Board of Education and the Veterans Administration, and he has practiced psychotherapy, marriage and family counseling, as well as sex therapy, for over 40 years. He continues this practice at the Psychological Clinic of the RET Institute.

A Fellow of the American Psychological Association, Dr. Ellis has served as President of its Division of Consulting Psychology and as a member of its Council of Representatives. He is a Diplomate in Clinical Psychology of the American Board of Professional Psychology, and a Diplomate of the American Board of Psychotherapy.

Dr. Ellis has published over 500 articles and 49 books, among them *Reason and Emotion in Psychotherapy, Brief Psychotherapy in Medical and Health Practice*, and *A Handbook of Rational-Emotive Therapy*. He has also served as Consulting or Associate Editor of many publications, including the *Journal of Marriage and the Family*, the *Journal of Contemporary Psychotherapy, Journal of Individual Psychology*, and *Cognitive Therapy and Research*.

Overcoming Resistance

Rational-Emotive Therapy
with Difficult Clients

Albert Ellis, Ph.D.

Springer Publishing Company
New York

Springer Publishing Company, Inc.
536 Broadway
New York, New York 10012

85 86 87 88 89 / 10 9 8 7 6 5 4 3 2 1

Library of Congress Cataloging in Publication Data

Ellis, Albert.
   Overcoming resistance.
   Bibliography: p. Includes index.
   1. Resistance (Psychoanalysis)   2. Rational-emotive psychotherapy.   3. Psychotherapist and patient.   I. Title. [DNLM: 1. Physician-Patient Relations.   2. Psychotherapy—methods. WM 420 E470]
RC489.R49E43   1985   616.89′14   85-4728
ISBN   0-8261-4910-3

Printed in the United States of America

Contents

Foreword

When I decided to establish the *British Journal of Cognitive Psycho-therapy* in 1982, one of my major aims was to create a forum where practitioners could share their experiences of problems in practicing cognitive psychotherapy. At that time Paul Wachtel's edited book, *Resistance: Psychodynamic and Behavioral Approaches*, had just been published. This text contained, among others, the views of a number of leading cognitive-behavioral therapists on the topic of client resistance. Although seminal, Wachtel's book was lacking in one important aspect. It did not contain the views of the world's leading authority on cognitive-behavior therapy— Albert Ellis. I decided to rectify this oversight by inviting Dr. Ellis to write a paper on resistance for my new journal. I had felt for some time that the publication of his views on this topic was long overdue. I issued my invitation and not one but four papers on the resistance theme came back. Albert's canny eye for a good text was in focus right from the start and we agreed that he could publish the material in book form at some future date. The present volume is the result.

I am delighted to have the opportunity of writing the foreword to this book, especially since I had a modest hand in its creation. It is an important volume in that it clearly demonstrates the creative aspects of rational-emotive practice. Perhaps for the first time Albert Ellis has committed to print many clinical gems which hitherto only a small cadre of his followers and students have been privileged enough to hear expressed in the confines of his consulting room at the Institute for Rational-Emotive Therapy in New York City.

Dr. Ellis has accomplished much in this book. In it, he clearly outlines the most common forms of client resistance and their particular determinants; in doing so he makes important distinctions between healthy and unhealthy resistance. He enumerates many cognitive, emotive, and behavioral methods that therapists can use to help clients overcome their unhealthy resistance, and he has expanded his ideas on the application of force, energy, and therapeutic efficiency to clients who resist in therapy. Dr. Ellis highlights the differential use of rational-emotive methods with a variety of resistant clients (including the category of borderline clients currently receiving much attention in the clinical literature); included is a healthy dose of clinical realism and pragmatism. While Ellis may prefer methods that are best suited to effect profound philosophic change in his resistant clients, he does not insist on their use. He details a number of 'clever' therapeutic techniques that can help effect change in very resistant clients, but cautions against their routine use. Of importance is a focus on the resistances of therapists that can lead these helping professionals to be their own "most difficult clients".

New clinical formulations are advanced under the heading of 'Rational-Emotive System Therapy,' where he focuses on helping resistant clients to change the disruptive activating events in their lives. This emphasis can sometimes considerably benefit such clients. Finally, a helpful manual to assist RET clients maintain and enhance their therapeutic gains is also provided.

Has Albert Ellis presented the definitive last word on the subject of overcoming client resistance in RET? Not entirely. Since his major purpose is to focus on the resistances of difficult clients, he has not covered extensively the resistances of regular, less disturbed ones. To augment this, I will present briefly a model of the 'working alliance' which I have found useful in understanding the resistances of regular clients (Dryden, 1982). It is a model that I employ in the training and supervision of novice RET therapists (Dryden, 1983) and it is included here both to complement Ellis' work and to organize better those aspects of the alliance that Ellis has covered at various points in the present text.

Bordin's Concept of the Working Alliance

Ed Bordin (1979) has put forward a tripartite reformulation of the old psychoanalytic concept of the working alliance between therapist and client as they strive to help the client overcome his or her problems.

The first component of the alliance is the *bond* between client and therapist. Effective RET is deemed to occur when the two parties form a strong working bond to enable the tasks of therapy to be accomplished in the service of the client's goals. Ellis argues that while relationship factors do not occupy a central role in the theory of RET practice, these had better not be neglected and therapists would be wise to be alert to signs that they and their clients are poorly matched on the bond dimension and to take corrective action. Ellis is also cognizant of the clinical facts of life that strongly suggest that different clients may require the development of different kinds of therapeutic bonds to offset the phenomenon of client resistance. Some clients may benefit from the therapist stressing his or her expertise, some may be helped by the therapist being formal, while others may be aided by therapist informality. Therapists who are unable to vary their 'bonding' behavior may very well induce resistance in some of their clients who seek a different bond than that offered. Furthermore, some clients may prosper with a different bonding relationship at different times in the therapeutic process, and research into the changing nature of bonds in the practice of RET is indicated.

Another feature of the therapeutic bond concerns the degree of understanding of the client's problems shared between client and therapist. Client resistance may be engendered if the two parties differ concerning their definitions of the client's problems. Even if the therapist and client share a common understanding of the latter's problems, they may differ concerning their views of the determinants of these problems. Many a rational-emotive therapy relationship has come to grief because the therapist failed to clearly establish that the client understood and agreed with the former's theory that disturbed emotions and behaviors are determined by irrational beliefs. This is a particular failing of novice therapists.

The second component of the alliance concerns *goals*. Ellis notes in Chapter 10 that resistance may occur due to the therapist and client having different goals with the result that 'parallel tracking' may occur. In this case, the client seeks to pursue goal 'X', while the therapist is working on goal 'Y' and the quality of the ensuing interaction is characterized by the two parties just missing each other due to the fact that they are working on parallel tracks.

Ellis quotes Golden (1983), who has observed that resistance can come about when the client has one or more hidden agendas. In the context of goals, the client states a goal which he or she does not really want, preferring covertly to pursue a goal which remains unstated. This occurs most frequently in couples therapy, to which Ellis alludes, and creative and skillful questioning from the therapist is called for if this situation is to be brought out into the open.

An important concept, that we may also consider, concerns the fact that clients can have a hierarchy of goals, some of which conflict. Therapists would do well to bear this in mind and spend time helping their clients to unravel this complex matrix of goals. In addition, clients sometimes had better be educated into a goal-setting frame of mind if they are to benefit from RET. This is particularly true if they have been previously exposed to more passive forms of therapy. Another area to be emphasized is the notion of the therapeutic contract, a tool which helps client and therapist to be explicit about the former's goals and to which reference can be made when resistance concerning goals occurs.

The final component of the working alliance concerns therapeutic *tasks*. Bordin (1979) has shown that different therapy systems suggest different tasks for each of the participants to carry out in the service of the client's goals. Client resistance can occur when: (1) clients do not understand what their tasks are and thus cannot be expected to carry them out; (2) clients understand what their tasks are but do not understand how executing them will help them achieve their goals; (3) clients understand what their tasks are but do not believe that they are capable of executing them; (4) clients both understand their tasks and believe they are capable of carrying them out, but believe that they should not have to work to change (this is comprehensively covered by Ellis in the present book); (5) clients do not understand their therapists' tasks and/or cannot see the link between their therapists' tasks and their own tasks and goals; (6) clients may in fact be incapable of executing their tasks (e.g., some clients are not intelligent enough to do socratic disputing); (7) therapists do not adequately prepare their clients to understand and execute the latter's tasks; (8) therapists poorly execute their own tasks (i.e., they are poorly skilled on the techniques of RET); (9) therapists compulsively carry out a limited number of tasks (e.g., they often use cognitive techniques but rarely employ behavioral methods); (10) some tasks are not potent enough to achieve the client's goals (e.g., disputing irrational beliefs without exposure is unlikely to help clients with agoraphobic problems (Emmelkamp, Kuipers and Eggeraat, 1978).

In his introduction to the present volume, Ellis hopes the suggestions and hypotheses which he advances will lead to clinical and experimental investigation. One area of study that the 'working alliance' model suggests concerns the pre-therapy preparation of clients for their active and effective participation in the RET treatment process. I would like to see RET therapists develop 'role induction' programs which facilitate clients' successful participation in therapy in each area of the working alliance. It could be that some programs would prevent a substantial degree of client resistance. Another area deserving study concerns client resistance in different therapeutic modalities. Do different types of client resistance occur in individual, marital, family, and group RET?

Ellis hopes that the present book will stimulate further developments in the area of overcoming client resistance. As you can see from the foregoing it has already been successful in my case. I thus join with him and invite you to read this book which is an excellent example of how rational-emotive therapy can be practiced creatively. I am sure that you will find it irresistible!

Windy Dryden, Ph.D.
Editor, British Journal of
Cognitive Psychotherapy
Birmingham, England

References

Bordin, E. S. (1979). The generalizability of the psychoanalytic concept of the working alliance. *Psychotherapy: Theory, Research and Practice, 16,* 252–260.

Dryden, W. (1982, June). The therapeutic alliance: Conceptual issues and some research findings. *Midland Journal of Psychotherapy, 1,* 14–19.

Dryden, W. (1983). Audiotape supervision by mail: A rational-emotive perspective. *British Journal of Cognitive Psychotherapy, 1*(1), 57–64.

Emmelkamp, P. M. G., Kuipers, A., and Eggeraat, J. (1978). Cognitive modification versus prolonged exposure in vivo. A comparison with agoraphobics. *Behaviour Research and Therapy, 16,* 33–41.

Golden, W. L. (1983). Resistance in cognitive-behavioural therapy. *British Journal of Cognitive Psychotherapy, 1*(2), 33–42.

Wachtel, P. L. (Ed.). (1982). *Resistance: Psychodynamic and behavioral approaches.* New York: Plenum.

1
Introduction

Overcoming clients' resistance to therapeutic change is in some ways the most important problem of psychotherapy. For virtually all clients (and other humans) resist changing themselves in one or more important respects: (1) They refuse to admit that they are disturbed enough to come for psychological treatment (or reeducation). (2) When they do come for therapy, they frequently fail to bring up some of their most important—and most "shameful"—difficulties. (3) They often do not listen carefully to what their (well-paid and busy) therapist is saying. (4) They needlessly argue against some of the therapist's observations and teachings. (5) They fail to understand or absorb some of the best therapeutic messages. (6) They agree to carry out homework assignments but then refuse to work at them.

Resistance to therapy often—perhaps almost always—goes still further. For even those clients who listen, understand, learn, and significantly improve in the course of psychological treatment tend to fall back to pre-therapy levels of maladjustment often, and sometimes completely. Once "cured" they sooner or later reexperience severe feelings of anxiety, depression, rage, and self-downing. Once unaddicted to food, cigarettes, alcohol, drugs, gambling, or procrastination, they often become partially or completely readdicted. Once free of the symptoms that drove them into therapy, they frequently develop a different, and sometimes more debilitating, disturbance.

In view of these well-attested realities, we may conclude that to completely and finally cure neurotic and borderline (not to mention psychotic) individuals seems tantamount to changing human nature. For, to say the least, the vast majority of humans appear to be irrational and self-defeating in important aspects of their lives, including the preponderance of psychotherapists (Ellis, 1972e, 1976c, 1977h, 1980c, 1982c, 1983a, 1983b; Gross, 1979; Weinrach, 1973; Zilbergeld, 1983)!

Rational-emotive therapy (RET) was created at the beginning of 1955 largely because I saw that most of my clients stoutly resisted getting better even with the supposedly deepest therapy of them all—psychoanalysis. As I experimented, in the early 1950s, with psychoanalytically oriented psychotherapy, instead of with classical analysis, I got somewhat better but still less than desirable results (Ellis, 1957b, 1962; Ellis & Harper, 1975). Having, as I semihumorously tell my workshop audiences, a gene for efficiency (while Sigmund Freud seemed to have several genes for overgeneralization and inefficiency), I kept experimenting with several non-Freudian methods—including those of Ferenczi (1952), Frank (1975), Herzberg (1945), Horney (1937), Rogers (1951), Salter (1949), Thorne (1950), Watson (1925, 1958), and Wolberg (1948). After welding the best of these methods with ancient and modern philosophy (Dewey, 1922; Epictetus, 1890; Heidegger, 1962; Marcus Aurelius, 1890; Russell, 1950, 1965; Santayana, 1946; Spinoza, 1901; Tillich, 1953), I formulated the principles and practice of RET (Ellis, 1957a, 1958a, 1962; Ellis & Harper, 1961a, 1961b).

Once created, I found RET to be considerably more effective and efficient than the other methods of therapy I had previously employed, but it also had its own inadequacies—some of which I detailed in a final chapter on the limitations of psychotherapy in *Reason and Emotion in Psychotherapy* (Ellis, 1962). Fortunately, however, the failings of RET in particular and of psychotherapy in general have motivated me and other practitioners to keep revising and augmenting RET's formulations (Dryden, 1984; Ellis, 1971, 1973, 1979a, 1980a, in press-a; Ellis & Abrahms, 1978; Ellis & Becker, 1982; Ellis & Bernard, 1983; Ellis & Bernard-in press; Ellis & Harper, 1975; Walen, DiGiuseppe & Wessler, 1980; Wessler & Wessler, 1980).

RET revisions are particularly important in dealing with highly resistant clients, because some of its most effective methods will presently not often work with such individuals (Ellis, 1983c; Young, 1977, in press). Noting this, I decided, at the request of Windy Dryden, editor of the *British Journal of Cognitive Psychotherapy*, to publish a series of articles on the use of RET with therapy resisters. I had intended from the start to turn that series into a book: here is that volume. I have significantly revised and in some cases appreciably expanded the original articles; I have also added and expanded material from three of my other articles, "The Issue of Force and Energy in Behavioral Change" (Ellis, 1979b), "The Value of Efficiency in Psychotherapy" (Ellis, 1980b), and "How to Deal with Your Most Difficult Client— You" (Ellis, 1984b). All told, I think that the material in this book summarizes the most salient theories and practices of RET in regard to resistant clients, and I also believe that it includes important RET material that I have not included in any of my previous books. All the suggestions presented herewith are made tentatively, as potentially revisable hypotheses, and I hope they will lead to considerable clinical and experimental investigation.

2
Common Forms of Resistance

Resistance to personality change—and specifically to psychotherapy, even by those who strongly aver that they want to help themselves change and who spend considerable time, money, and effort in pursuing various forms of therapy—has been observed for many years. Ancient philosophers—such as Confucius, Gautama Buddha, Epictetus, Seneca, and Marcus Aurelius—recognized that people who voluntarily try to alleviate their psychological and behavioral problems often resist their own and their teachers' best efforts. When modern psychotherapy began to develop in the nineteenth century, some of its main practitioners—such as James Braid, Hippolyte Bernheim, Jean-Martin Charcot, Auguste Ambroise Liebault, and Pierre Janet—made the theory of resistance and the practice of overcoming it key elements in their psychotherapies (Ellenberger, 1970; Wick, 1983).

Early in the 20th century, the theory of resistance (particularly compliance) in psychotherapy came into its own with the elucidation of the Freudian concepts of transference and counter-

transference (Freud, 1912/1965b). Freud almost became obsessed
with problems of resistance and expanded his earlier concepts to
include five main varieties: resistance of repression, of transference, and of secondary gain (all stemming from the ego); resistance of the repetition compulsion (arising from the id); and
resistance of guilt and self-punishment (originating in the superego) (Freud, 1926/1965d). Following Freud, psychoanalysts (and
many other kinds of therapists) have also often been obsessed
with problems of resistance.

As several recent writers have aptly noted, views on what
resistance is and how it can best be resolved largely depend on
one's definition of this fascinating phenomenon (Wachtel, 1982;
Weiner, 1982). Personally, I like Turkat and Meyer's (1982, p.
158) definition: "Resistance is client behavior that the therapist
labels antitherapeutic." This is both simple and comprehensive;
and, as its authors suggest, it can also be operationalized to each
client's individual experience and be seen as that specific form of
behavior that is observed when this particular client acts non-
therapeutically according to his or her therapist in these particular situations.

However accurate such a definition of resistance may be, it
is too general to be of much clinical use, and it hardly explains the
main "causes" of resistance, nor what we can preferably do to
help overcome them. Therefore, I shall devote this chapter to
examining, from a rational-emotive therapy (RET) standpoint,
the principal kinds of resistance, in what ways they usually arise,
and what RET (and, hopefully, other) practitioners can do to
understand and help themselves and their clients overcome
therapy-sabotaging blockings.

Healthy and "Normal" Resistance

Some kinds of resistance to personality change and to psychotherapy are "healthy," in that they may actually be helpful to
clients, or they are "normal" in that they are statistically highly
prevalent and are usually to be expected, at least to some degree,
to occur.

Healthy Resistance

Clients sometimes resist change because therapists have their own fish to fry and mistakenly see these clients as having symptoms that they really don't have (e.g., hostility to their parents) or as having their symptoms originate in certain "events" or "facts" (e.g., feelings of lust toward their parents) that the clients view as figments of the therapists' imaginations. Rather than allow these therapeutic "authorities" to lead them up the garden path, such clients refuse to accept their "discoveries" or interpretations and healthfully resist or flee from treatment (Basch, 1982; Ellis, 1962; Ellis & Harper, 1975; Lazarus & Fay, 1982; Wolpe & Lazarus, 1966).

From a rational-emotive view, clients who resist treatment for healthy reasons are explicitly or implicitly telling themselves rational Beliefs (rBs), such as: "My therapist is probably wrong about my having this symptom or about the origins of my acquiring it. Too bad! I'd better ignore his or her interpretations and get another therapist." In the ABC theory of RET, at A (Activating Event) the clients experience their therapists' interpretations and directives (e.g., "You think you love your mother very much but unconsciously you really appear to loathe her"). At B (Belief System), the clients tell themselves the rBs just noted, and at C (emotional and behavioral Consequences) they feel appropriately sorry about their therapists' misperceptions and they actively resist these misperceptions and interpretations. They are consequently acting rationally and sanely and, according to RET, their resistance is self-helping and healthy. The person who has the real problem in these instances—and is "resisting" doing effective treatment—is their therapist!

Resistance Motivated by the Normal Human Condition

As I shall contend throughout this book, resistance that is largely the client's doing is exceptionally common and is often an expected part of the normal human condition (Redl, 1966; Vriend & Dyer, 1973). The real question that, as therapists, we preferably should study is not why so many clients who spend considerable time and money in therapy resist changing themselves, but why so many people, inside and outside psychotherapy, actually do effect significant personality change (Mischel, 1984). Basic self-modification is exceptionally difficult for most people most of the time. When it does occur, it probably stems from special motivating reasons, such as:

1. Many people are so handicapped and miserable because of their disturbed condition—e.g., skid-row alcoholics—that they are driven by this "horrible" condition to make great self-change efforts.

2. Some people change for the "wrong" reasons—for example, to prove how superior and noble they are or to spite others.

3. Some people make a hobby or vital absorbing interest out of growing and changing, and devote a large part of their lives to working (and sometimes very creatively) at this hobby.

4. Some disturbed individuals become devoted or addicted to membership in change-oriented groups or ideologies, such as the encounter movement, est, or religious cults.

5. Some people quite sanely and rationally decide that being emotionally disturbed (like being addicted to smoking or to drinking) is just too painful and self-defeating, especially in the long run, and that therefore they had better fight their disturbance for the rest of their lives.

6. Some individuals try to become leaders or gurus of self-help groups and, to show their good faith and retain their leadership, avidly keep following the self-discipline rules of this group.

7. Some people seem to easily and naturally enjoy the adventure and even the work of changing themselves, and therefore have relatively little difficulty changing.

When clients resist therapy because of their normal human resistance, they are telling themselves (implicitly, consciously, explicitly, or unconsciously) various rBs and irrational Beliefs (iBs). Their main rBs are preferences or desires, such as: "I wish that changing myself and overcoming my personality problems were easier than it seems to be. How unfortunate that it isn't! However, no matter how hard it is, it is so difficult for me to continue the way I am going and to have my feelings of anxiety and depression, that I'd better keep working to overcome these feelings." These rBs will help people resist changing themselves to some extent, but they will also help them go back to the drawing board and keep working at modifying their thoughts, feelings, and behaviors.

In addition to these rBs, however, clients frequently—and, in a statistical sense, normally—have several iBs that partially create or "cause" them to resist changing. These include: (1) "It's not only hard for me to change, but *too* hard! It should not, must not be that hard! How *awful* that it's that difficult. To hell with it, I won't try!" (2) "To try to change myself and fail would be horrible, as I *must* not fail. I *can't stand* failing! I'm an *inadequate, rotten person* if I fail. So I'd better not risk proving how bad I am, and better give up trying." (3) "The people with whom I closely associate—such as my parents, my mate, or my employer—*must* see how hard it is for me to change, and *should* help me change. How terrible that they don't help me as they should! They are no damned good for being so inconsiderate and unfair. I'll be damned if I'll change for bastards and bitches like them!"

Almost all kinds of resistance to change that follow people's wanting to and resolving to work at changing themselves is accompanied by this kind of irrational or *mus*turbatory thinking, as we shall keep seeing in this book. RET, therefore, looks for the iBs that lie behind resistance, including those that tend to create normal human resistance; tries to accurately define exactly what they are; and then (as will be shown many times in these pages) attempts to Dispute, contradict, and challenge them (at point D, the next point in the ABC theory of RET) to help clients give them up.

Resistance Resulting from Severe Disturbance

While virtually all individuals who try to change themselves "normally" resist doing so, at least to some extent, those who are severely emotionally disturbed—such as those who are border-line personalities or are psychotic—have, I hypothesize, an even stronger tendency to resist change. Thus, Rosenbaum (1983) objects to Weiner's (1982) use of the term *impasse* to describe the situation that arises when a client is in therapy for several years and still makes little progress. He indicates—and I think correctly—that many of these clients are exceptionally disturbed individuals, usually diagnosed as borderline personalities, who because of the severity of their problems are "naturally" in for a long therapeutic haul; and that therapists who talk about an impasse with these clients may be misdiagnosing them as "normal" neurotics.

I agree with Rosenbaum, since my long clinical experience has shown me that borderline clients and other severely disturbed individuals will usually, by their very nature, resist any kind of short-term treatment and will almost necessarily have to undergo a fairly long therapy process. They are slow learners, who have put themselves into rigid cognitive and emotional boxes, and they have great difficulty learning how to change, no matter what kind of therapy they undertake. In my opinion, they have a strong biological tendency to be the way they are—and this tendency includes their "normal" resistance to change and their requiring, in most instances, fairly long-term treatment (Ellis, 1976c, 1983c; Giovacchini & Boyer, 1982).

With these kinds of seriously disturbed and rigid clients, RET advocates persistent and strong Disputing of their iBs, as well as the use of a variety of other cognitive, emotive, and behavioral methods. Their treatment is discussed in more detail in Chapter 8 of this book.

Usual Noncompliance or Resistance by Clients

As Lazarus and Fay (1982) indicate, one of the main reasons for resistance is that it partly seems to stem from the individual characteristics of clients. As is only to be expected, clients follow a wide range of patterns of behavior and have a large variety of different characteristics. Some of their traits which appear to notably contribute to their resistance of psychological treatment, even when they ostensibly seek its benefits, include the following:

Resistance Created by Fear of Discomfort

Perhaps the most common, and often one of the strongest, kind of resistance is that stemming from low frustration tolerance or what RET calls discomfort anxiety (Ellis, 1962, 1979a,

1980a). Even psychoanalysts, albeit reluctantly, often recognize this form of resistance. Blatt and Ehrlich (1982) acknowledge it as broad and basic: a fundamental opposition to change and growth. They call it an expression of the basic wish to maintain familiar and predictable modes of adaptation, even though these are uncomfortable and painful in the long run. Dewald (1982) talks about strategic resistance—that is, clients' efforts to seek fulfillment of childhood wishes and to demand unrealistic or impossible goals.

Nonpsychoanalytic therapists also acknowledge discomfort-motivated resistance. Perls (1969) makes avoidance of discomfort a key issue in the creation of neurosis and in efforts to change it. Patterson, a behavior therapist, has shown that as therapy progresses, and clients have to do something to effect change, their resistance significantly increases (Chamberlain, Patterson, Reid, Kavanaugh, & Forgath, 1984; Patterson, 1982). Other behavior therapists—such as Eysenck (1964), Pomerleau (1979), and Yates (1975)—also attribute resistance to lack of compliance resulting from low frustration tolerance (LFT).

In RET this important form of resistance is attributed to short-range hedonism: to clients' short-sighted demands that they achieve the pleasure of the moment even though this may well defeat them in the long run. The main iBs that lead to LFT or discomfort anxiety are: (1) "It's *too hard* to change, and it *must not* be that hard. How *awful* that I have to go through pain to get therapeutic gain!" (2) "I *can't tolerate* the discomfort of doing my homework, even though I have agreed with my therapist that it is desirable for me to do it." (3) "The world is a *horrible place* when it forces me to work so hard to change myself! Life *should be* easier than it is!"

RET shows clients how to dispute these grandiose ideas and to accept the realistic notions that no matter how hard it is for them to change, it's distinctly harder if they don't. It teaches them that there is rarely any gain without pain and that the philosophy of long-range hedonism—or the seeking of pleasure for today *and* for tomorrow—is likely to result in therapeutic change. It shows them how to use their natural hedonistic tendencies by teaching them to reinforce themselves for therapeutic progress (e.g., overcoming procrastination), and to penalize themselves when they refuse to work at therapy (e.g., when they don't do their homework assignments [Ellis & Knaus, 1977; Knaus, 1982]). RET also stresses problem-solving skills that help clients achieve more successful solutions to their difficulties with an expenditure of minimum effort (D'Zurilla & Goldfried, 1971; Ellis, 1962, 1977a; Ellis & Harper, 1975; Ellis & Whiteley, 1979; Goldfried & Davison, 1976; Spivack & Shure, 1974).

Fear of Disclosure and Shame

One of the most prevalent forms of resistance stems from clients' fear of disclosure. They find it uncomfortable to talk about themselves freely (e.g., giving the full gory details of some of the "bad" situations they got themselves into) and to confess thoughts, feelings, and actions that they view as "shameful" (e.g., lusting for their mothers or sisters). They therefore resist being open in therapy and getting at the source of some of the things they find most bothersome (Dewald, 1982; Freud, 1900/1965a, 1926/1965d; Langs, 1981; Rosenbaum, 1983; Schlesinger, 1982; Sullivan, 1956). Freudians tend to insist that resistance consists largely of clients' fear of dredging up material from the unconscious and hold that they therefore resort (unconsciously) to uncompliant tactics (Fenichel, 1945). RET, instead, holds that clients who resist therapy because they are afraid to reveal their "shameful" thoughts and feelings usually do so because they are aware of these feelings or else have them just below their level of consciousness—in what Freud (1965e) originally called their preconscious minds. Thus, RET hypothesizes that if a male client resists talking about sex because of his shame about his incestuous feelings for his mother or sister, he usually (though not always) is conscious of these feelings but deliberately suppresses rather than expresses them.

Clients who resist disclosing and discussing their thoughts, feelings, and behaviors are usually telling themselves iBs such as: "It's wrong to lust after my mother; I *must* not behave that wrongly. I *can't* admit that I do feel that way!" "If I told my therapist that I lust after my sister, he would think I was a sex fiend and wouldn't like me. I have to be liked by my therapist and would be a shit if even he didn't like me."

In RET, we help clients reveal these iBs and—more importantly—to dispute and surrender them. We help them to see that their "shameful" feelings may not even be wrong (for to lust after your mother is hardly to copulate with her); and that even when they are self-defeating (as are continual obsessive thoughts aboout incest), human *behaviors* never make anyone a totally rotten *person*. By helping clients to alleviate just about *all* shame and self-downing, RET shows them how to rid themselves of what Freud would call superego-instigated resistances and to be considerably more open in therapy than they would otherwise tend to be (Bard, 1980; Dryden, 1984; Ellis, 1957a, 1962, 1972c, 1973; Ellis & Grieger, 1977; Ellis & Whiteley, 1979; Walen, DiGiuseppe & Wessler, 1980; Wessler & Wessler, 1980).

Resistance Stemming from Feelings of Hopelessness

A number of clients seem to resist therapeutic change because they strongly feel that they are unable to modify their disturbed behavior—that they are *hopeless* and *can't* change (Ellis, 1957b, 1962; Turkat & Meyer, 1982). These clients sometimes, at first, make good progress; but as soon as they retrogress, even slightly, they irrationally tend to conclude: "My falling back proves that it's *hopeless* and that I'll *never* conquer my disturbance. Because I *must* not be as depressed and incompetent as I now am, and because I am therefore a *complete depressive*, what's the use of my trying any longer to conquer my depression? I might as well give in to it and perhaps kill myself!"

Thoughts and feelings of hopelessness about one's disturbed state are part of what RET calls *secondary symptoms of disturbance*. As I have noted elsewhere (Ellis, 1962, 1979a, 1979g, 1980a), these secondary symptoms tend to validate the RET or cognitive-behavior theory of neurosis. For, on the level of primary disturbance, when people desire to achieve their goals (such as success and approval) and fail to do so, instead of sanely concluding, "It would have been preferable to achieve what I wanted but since I didn't, too bad! I'll try again next time," they sometimes irrationally conclude, "I *should* have achieved success and approval, and since I didn't do what I *must* do, it's awful and I'm no damned good *as a person!*" They then become—or in RET terms *make themselves*—disturbed. But once emotionally upset, they *see* their upsetness and cognize about it in this vein: "I *must* not disturb myself as I am now doing. How *awful*! I am a *total fool* for acting this foolishly, and a fool like me *can't* cope or change. It's *hopeless*!"

RET, through its theory of secondary disturbance (or disturbance *about* being disturbed), shows clients, in particular, how they falsely *invent* their thoughts and feelings of hopelessness and how they can Dispute these and give them up. It uses (as will be indicated later in this book) many cognitive, emotive, and behavioral methods of dispelling feelings of hopelessness that lead to resistance (Ellis, in press-a; Ellis & Abrahms, 1978; Ellis & Whiteley, 1979).

Resistance Motivated by Self-punishment

Freud (1926/1965d) held that resistance often originates in the superego or in our guilt-creating tendencies. Thus, a female client who is jealous of her more accomplished sister and who becomes more conscious of her hatred during therapy may strongly feel that she deserves to be punished for her meanness and may therefore resist overcoming her self-defeating neurotic behavior (such as her overeating or her compulsive handwashing). During more than forty years of clinical practice, I have rarely found this kind of self-punishing resistance among my neurotic clients, though I have found it more often in psychotics and severely borderline individuals.

When resistance motivated by self-punishing tendencies does exist, it seems to stem from clients' overt or covert iBs, such as: "Because I have done evil acts, which I *absolutely should not* have perpetrated, I am a *thoroughly worthless individual* who *deserves* to suffer. Therefore, I *rightly ought* to be punitively disturbed and will make little effort to overcome my handicaps."

If clients actually have these self-punishing philosophies, RET is a highly appropriate form of therapy to show them how to discover and combat their iBs. Psychoanalytic therapies, on the other hand, are often contraindicated because, although they may show clients how self-punishing they are, they rarely teach them how to effectively eradicate the iBs behind their masochistic resistant behaviors (Ellis, 1962, 1972a, 1976a).

Resistance Motivated by Fear of Change
or Fear of Success

Psychoanalytic therapists, from Freud onward, have held that resistance often stems from fear of change, from fear of the future, or from fear of success (Blatt & Erlich, 1982). This is probably true, because many disturbed individuals have a pronounced need for safety and certainty; even though their symptoms make them feel uncomfortable, they are familiar with their negative feelings and behaviors and may be afraid that if they give these up they may experience even greater discomfort. So they prefer to stick with the tried and true discomfort and therefore resist changing and plunging into the unknown.

More importantly, perhaps, many symptoms (such as shyness and fear of public speaking) protect clients against possible failure (such as failing in love or making a laughable speech). To surrender these symptoms would therefore mean risking subsequent failure and disapproval, and a good number of clients would tend to find this more "catastrophic" or "awful" than they find retaining their symptoms.

What has been often labeled "the fear of success" is practically never really that but is, rather, a fear of *subsequent* failure. Thus, if a withdrawn teenage boy stops withdrawing and begins to succeed at school, at sports, and at social affairs, he may (1) lose the comfort and indulgence of his overprotective parents, (2) gain the enmity of his siblings, (3) risk later failure at the activities in which he has now begun to succeed, and (4) be forced to take on much more responsibility and effort than he would like to assume. He may consequently view his academic, athletic, and social "gains" as "dangers" or "failures," and may resist or retreat from continuing to "gain" them. Does he, then, really have a "fear of success"—or one of failure?

When clients do resist psychotherapy because of their fear of changing or their fear of "success," RET looks for their iBs, such as "I *must* not give up my symptoms, since change would be *too* uncomfortable and I *can't stand* such change." "I *cannot* change my neurotic behavior and do better in life because that would be too risky. I might encounter greater failure later, as I *must* not; and if I did, that would be *awful!*" These and similar iBs that underlie the fear of change and fear of "success" are revealed and eliminated during RET, thus minimizing this kind of resistance to change.

Resistance Motivated by Reactance and Rebelliousness

A number of clinicians have observed that some clients react or rebel against therapy because they see it as an impingement on their freedom, and, especially if it is active and directive, they perversely fight it even when they have voluntarily asked for it (Brehm, 1976; Goldfried, 1982; Meichenbaum & Gilmore, 1982). Noting this form of resistance, many therapists have invented or adopted methods of paradoxical or provocative therapy, to try to trick these perversely rebellious clients into giving up their resistance (Dunlap, 1928; Erikson & Rossi, 1979; Farrelly & Brandsma, 1976; Fay, 1978; Frankl, 1960; Haley, 1963, 1984; Watzlawick, Weakland & Fisch, 1974).

When clients resist because of reactance, RET looks for their iBs, such as "I *have to* control my entire destiny, and even though my therapist is on my side and is working hard to help me, I *must not* let him or her tell me what to do." "How *terrible* if I am directed by my therapist! I cannot bear being led by the nose in that manner! I should have *absolutely* perfect freedom to do what I like even if my symptoms are killing me!"

RET reveals and helps clients rid themselves of these types of iBs. It also selectively (and uncavalierly) makes use of humor and paradoxical intention (as noted in detail in Chapter 3). For example, it gives some clients the homework assignment of deliberately failing at encountering others (or at other "dangerous" tasks), to show them that failure is not world shattering (Ellis, 1972c; Ellis & Abrahms, 1978; Ellis & Whiteley, 1979).

Resistance Motivated by Receiving Secondary Gains

Several 19th century and early 20th century therapists noted that many clients receive secondary gains or payoffs from their disturbances and that they therefore are very reluctant to give them up (Ellenberger, 1970; Freud, 1965e). Thus, if a factory worker who hates his job develops hysterical paralysis of the hand, he may resist psychotherapy because if it succeeds he will be forced to return to the work he hates.

Freud (1900/1965a, 1926/1965d) and some of his followers (Berne, 1964; A. Freud, 1946; Fenichel, 1945, 1953) emphasized the unconscious aspects of this defensive process and insisted that if clients can make direct gains by improving, but also have important unconscious secondary gains to maintain by refusing to improve, they will stubbornly resist treatment for deeply unconscious, and often repressed, reasons. Thus, a woman refuses to lose weight and have good sex with her husband because of her underlying hatred of her mother, and receives the strong unconscious payoff of spiting this mother (who wants her to be thin and to have a good marriage).

Although Freudians tend to enormously exaggerate the deeply unconscious (and very dramatic) elements in secondary gains, it seems clear that many clients do resist change because the payoffs they are getting from their disturbances are (or at least *seem* to be) considerable. Goldfried (1982) puts this kind of resistance in behavioral terms by pointing out that when clients change for the "better" they sometimes discover hidden penalties. Women may overcome their unassertiveness, for example, only to find that assertiveness is often ill rewarded in our society. Hence, they may "logically" and "rationally" fall back to being unassertively "neurotic!"

When we analyze secondary gain resistance in RET terms we find that it is often spurred by several iBs, such as (1) "Because my mother *must not* try to make me lose weight, and is a *rotten person* for criticizing me for being overweight, I'll fix her wagon by remaining a fat slob!" or (2) "Because macho men will put me down if I (as a woman) act assertively, I *can't stand* their put-downs; and to avoid being put down by them I'll give up my assertion desires and remain submissive for the rest of my life."

Using RET, we can show clients how to Dispute and surrender these iBs and thereby help them help themselves achieve the greater payoff of losing weight rather than the neurotic one of spiting their mother. And we can encourage women to achieve the primary gain of being assertive rather than the secondary gain of winning the approval of macho men. RET can help resisters determine whether their striving for secondary gains is rational or irrational and whether it is truly worth achieving in the light of their main goals and purposes.

Resistance Stemming from Clients' Hidden Agendas

Golden (1983c) has pointed out that a number of clients enter therapy with "hidden agendas," or with goals that they do not verbalize to their therapist or (in the course of conjoint therapy) their co-therapees. Thus, a husband may have no intention of working on a better relationship with his wife but may push her into therapy so that she can become better prepared to agree to a divorce. Or a teenager may agree to go for steady psychotherapy with no intention of changing herself in the process, but mainly because she wants to manipulate her parents or wants to give herself extra time in which to prepare to run away from home.

Many clients who resist therapy because of their hidden agendas have quite rational Beliefs (rBs), such as: "I wish my wife were sensible and strong enough to work with me toward an amicable divorce, but unfortunately she isn't. So I'll use marital therapy in the hope that she'll become more mature and stronger and then we'll be able to part on better terms." Other resistant clients with hidden agendas, however, have irrational Beliefs (iBs), such as: "My parents are thoroughly *terrible people* and I *can't bear living* with them any longer! I therefore have to lie to my therapist and make her think that I am interested in changing, when actually I'll secretly plan to run away with the married man next door!"

By giving all clients unconditional acceptance and showing them that their therapist fully accepts them as humans even when the client thinks that they are doing the wrong thing, RET provides a therapeutic atmosphere that makes it more likely that resisters with hidden agendas will reveal their real goals to their therapist and will thereby be able to see and to Dispute any iBs that may be involved with their resistance. In one case, for example, I saw a recently divorced woman and her lover for couple counseling because he had discovered her affair with another man, was insanely jealous, and wanted to come with her to resolve this issue. During joint sessions, I worked with him on his jealousy and helped him to be rationally displeased with her sexual infidelity but no longer horrified and enraged at her for engaging in it. She was so impressed with my helping her lover in this respect, and with my noncondemning attitudes toward him, her, and everyone else, that she confessed to me, in a private session, that she had no intention of being sexually exclusive with him or any other man for the present, even though in joint sessions she had been presumably working on her intention of remaining monogamous.

When I accepted this client with her nonmonogamous hidden agenda and helped her surrender her severe guilt about it, she was able to be honest with her lover in our joint sessions and in their relationship outside of therapy, and they worked out an open mating arrangement that was satisfactory to both of them. She expressly indicated, during a joint session at the end of my counseling with this couple, that my consistently displaying the RET-oriented attitude of unconditional acceptance during our sessions was the main reason she was able to bring out her hidden agenda, to work on it with him, and to achieve a satisfactory solution to their relationship and sexual problems.

Resistance to RET and Other Cognitive Therapies

Clients can easily resist all kinds of psychotherapies, for one reason or another; some particularly resist emotive, some resist behavioral, and some resist cognitive therapies. As Epstein (1984) has observed, most individuals show a considerable degree of resistance to awareness of their implicit assumptions that are leading to their emotional-behavioral disturbances. He finds three main reasons for their resistance: (1) In order to become aware of their preconscious or implicit iBs, people have to exert a good deal of self-discipline which they often view as bothersome and sometimes as a threat to their spontaneity. (2) When they become aware of their underlying beliefs, people expose to themselves the degree to which they are self-seeking, manipulative, and rationalizing about their behavior—and they are not eager to acknowledge this degree. (3) When people become aware that their disturbed emotions are not directly instigated by external events but instead are mediated by their own thoughts, and that they are therefore largely responsible for their feelings, they frequently find this discomforting, for they prefer to think of themselves as passive victims of their emotions.

RET has many methods of dealing with resistant clients' lack of discipline or low frustration tolerance, as will be shown later in this book (especially in Chapter 10). It also particularly tries to help people surrender their feelings of shame—including their shame about being disturbed and at being responsible for their own feelings (see Chapter 3). It emphasizes, as will be shown later, clients' secondary aspects of disturbance—their self-denigration for being anxious, depressed, hostile, or self hating. And it teaches clients, over and over again, that although their *symptoms* are unfortunate and handicapping, *they* are never bad or rotten individuals for having such symptoms. It shows them the naturalness and ubiquity of people's upsetting themselves, and of their creating as well as swallowing iBs, and it spends considerable time helping them accept responsibility for their own disordered thoughts, feelings, and actions, and acknowledge that just because they largely instigated such disturbances they have the power to understand and alleviate them.

Other Biological and Neurological Limitations Leading to Resistance

As noted in Healthy and "Normal" Resistance (at the beginning of this chapter), clients may balk at changing themselves and may fail to comply with the teachings and directives of their therapists because they are so severely disturbed—e.g., are borderline personalities or psychotic—that they "naturally" resist therapy. To this category of resisters we may now add those who have other biological and neurological limitations—such as those who are mentally deficient, are neurologically impaired, or are severely diseased and/or physically debilitated (e.g., some individuals with advanced states of multiple sclerosis or cancer).

People with these kinds of biological, neurological, and physical limitations often, as we might expect, resist psychotherapy, even though they may require it more than less debilitated clients do. RET does not have miraculous success with these clients, but it is able to reach some of them and to help them significantly—as shown in the case of Johnson (1981) who made remarkably good use of RET to help overcome his sexual and emotional problems connected with his being afflicted with a most serious disease, scleroderma.

RET shows people who are biologically limited some of their iBs about their limitations, such as "I *must* not be as sorely afflicted as I am! My limitations are *horrible* and prevent me from having virtually any satisfaction whatsoever." It helps them, actively and forcefully, cognitively and behaviorally, to Dispute these iBs (Ellis, 1981b). And it can to some extent be used effectively with mentally deficient and neurologically handicapped individuals who, even if they are not too capable of using RET's disputing of iBs, can learn to repeat to themselves rBs or coping self-statements that may help them to stop resisting therapy and make significant personality changes (Ellis, 1979e, 1979f; R. Lazarus, 1966, 1984; Meichenbaum, 1977). Although RET, I would hypothesize, is the therapy of choice for bright and effective clients who are capable of making profound personality changes, it is also considerably more effective with a wide range of clients who include uneducated, less intelligent, severely handicapped, and biologically limited individuals.

Resistance Connected with Therapist-Client Relationships

Although some of the 19th-century therapists seemed to recognize that therapist-client relationships are often very important in overcoming resistance and in helping clients to change themselves, Freud (1900/1965a, 1912/1965b) pioneered in this respect and encouraged virtually all subsequent psychoanalytic therapists to consider and explore the transference and countertransference relationships between themselves and their analysands. Relationship problems between therapists and their therapees are probably more common in psychoanalysis than in many other forms of psychological treatment, because analysis encourages a long series of sessions (preferably two to five times a

week) and because it particularly explores the feelings of analysands toward their parents, siblings, mates, and other significant
people in their lives—including, naturally, their analyst. However, relationship factors almost inevitably arise in other kinds of
therapy too—even in "objective" and "rational" forms of treatment, such as behavior therapy and RET. These factors frequently appear to abet as well as interfere with clients' therapeutic progress. Some of the main ways in which relationship factors
influence or "cause" resistance will now be discussed.

Resistance Motivated by Client-Therapist Mismatching

Clients are sometimes "naturally" mismatched with their
therapists. They manage to pick or be assigned to a therapist
whom they just do not like—for whatever reasons. Thus, they
may have a therapist who, to their idiosyncratic tastes or preferences, is too young or too old, too liberal or too conservative, too
male or too female, too active or too passive. Because of this
mismatching, they do not have too much rapport with their
therapist and therefore resist him or her more than they would
resist a more preferable therapist.

If this kind of mismatching becomes obvious during therapy
(which it may never), RET tries to discover whether the clients'
prejudices are rational—e.g., a liberal client just does not like
being with a conservative therapist—or whether they are irrational and include iBs, such as: "I *must* have a therapist who thinks
almost exactly the way I do on social issues. This present one is
often conservative and I *can't endure* her views. Even though she
helps me in many ways, unless she becomes much more liberal
she'll destroy me!"

When therapist-client mismatching occurs and appears to
seriously interfere with the therapeutic process, RET-oriented
therapists may try to compensate for what their clients see as
their "flaws," and may succeed in doing so by leaning over
backward to be unusually permissive or hardworking. Or the
clients may naturally overcome their antitherapist prejudices as
the course of treatment intimately proceeds (just as husbands
and wives may become more attached to a physically unattractive
mate as time goes by and they achieve more emotional intimacy).

Or the therapist and client may explore their own iBs that are encouraging them to dislike being with each other, and try to alleviate these iBs. Or the clients and/or their therapists may (often wisely) bring the relationship to a close and aid the client in finding a more compatible helper.

Resistance Associated with Clients' and Therapists' Love-Hate Problems

Psychoanalytic therapists usually assume that love-hate problems between clients and their therapists are invariably sparked by and intimately involved with transference difficulties—that is, stem from their (and especially from the clients') unresolved early family relationships. This is highly questionable. When they have strong feelings of love and hate toward each other, these may be based on reality factors that have little to do with their childhood experiences. Thus, a young female may just happen to have an exceptionally bright, attractive, and kindly therapist who would be an ideal mate for her (or for almost any other woman) if she met him socially, and she may realistically fall in love with him even though he has virtually nothing in common with her father, her uncles, or her brothers. Similarly, her therapist may become enamored of her not because she resembles his mother but because, more than most other women he has met and achieved closeness with in his entire life, she truly *is* charming, talented, and sexy (Ellis, 1959a).

When nontransference, reality-based feelings occur in therapy, and when they lead to intense warm or cold feelings on the part of therapists and/or clients, they can easily foment resistance problems. Thus, a female who intensely loves her therapist may resist improving in order to prolong her therapy, and a therapist who has strong positive feelings for his or her client may also (consciously or unconsciously) encourage resistance to change to ensure that the therapy continues indefinitely.

These nontransference relationship feelings that encourage resistance are sometimes difficult to resolve, because they are reality-based, and therefore both therapists and clients may derive special gains (or pains) from them that may interfere with effective treatment. But they may also include iBs that had better be uncovered and Disputed, such as, "Because I love my therapist and it would be great to mate with him, I *can't bear* leaving therapy and not seeing him any more. So I'll refuse to change! I *must* continue to see him indefinitely!" Or "Because I really care for my client and enormously enjoy the sessions with her, I *must* not help her improve too much and bring these sessions to an end!" Or "Because my therapist really likes me and does her best to help me, but because she does not *really* love me as I love her, I *can't stand* seeing her. It's *too* painful not having sex with her! I *must* discontinue these sessions and get a male therapist for whom I won't care so much and with whom I will not be so frustrated."

When strong nontransference feelings between therapists and clients arise, RET practitioners often live with these feelings and proceed with the therapy. Or they may take mild advantage of them by using clients' positive feelings to encourage them to work harder at therapy (though this is somewhat dangerous, because the clients are then changing themselves for the wrong reason—to please the therapist—rather than for the right reason—mainly to help themselves).

When love-hate feelings between themselves and clients get too involved and begin to encourage client resistance, RET practitioners ferret out the iBs that spark them and work at having the clients change these ideas. When (as occasionally happens) the clients' iBs are linked to their early relations with family members, RET examines and Disputes the self-defeating cognitions that existed during the clients' early life and that to some degree still exist.

As a case in point, I had 22 sessions of RET over a period of eight months with a 35-year-old woman who had had a very close relationship with her father and, from her 7th to her 14th years, had been frequently fondled by him, sometimes when she was almost nude and when he was only scantily clothed. She had nothing but good memories of him and their relationship and became severely depressed for a year when he died of a heart attack when she was 30. She came to see me after five years of previous therapy with a psychoanalyst (who had also died of a heart attack) and she was severely depressed when she came.

At the time I saw this woman, I was 22 years older than she (her father had been 21 years older), and she soon became quite attached to me, had dreams about going to bed with me, and wanted to see me more than once a week (which I, seeing that she was becoming too dependent, refused). She at first resisted RET, partly because she seemed to want to continue in therapy forever, as she had also wanted to do with her previous therapist. Because her feelings toward me seemed to stem from classical transference reactions and because they seemed to be interfering with her treatment, we had several sessions in which we discussed her relations with her father, her previous therapist, and with me.

In the course of these discussions, it became clear that all three intense attachments she had had (and was still having) with older males stemmed from her originally invented, and still strongly held, iBs: "I am a weak, inadequate person who *desperately needs* a strong man to support me, take over my life burdens, and make me feel adequate. When I meet such a man, I *must* win him at all costs, even if it means that I seduce him sexually in order to win his favors. I really don't like sex that much, and have never especially enjoyed it with my husband and the other men I have actually had intercourse with. But when a man pets me and gets aroused with me, I know that he will do almost anything for me. So I *have to* arouse all my potential male saviors, so that they will devote themselves to me, always be available to help me, and make me feel like a worthy person."

We determined, in other words, that the client's incestuous feelings toward her father, and her "transferring" them to her therapists, mainly stemmed from her dire demands for love and support rather than from intense sex feelings, and that she was repeating with me the same kind of dependency needs that she had originated with her father (and had also had with her previous male therapist). Her main "transference" or "repetition compulsion" was not sexual but ideological and emotive, and stemmed from her lifelong belief that she could not make it in the world on her own and accept herself as an independent person: she absolutely required a stronger, older person (preferably a man) to bolster her weaknesses and help her get through life. When, in the course of our RET sessions, we got to her basic iBs and actively Disputed them, and I induced her to take the risks of making her own life decisions and avoid asking "strong" males to help her (which included her cutting down on her therapy sessions), she changed these Beliefs, overcame her resistance, and was able to work through her feelings of depression (which also largely stemmed from her self-deprecating philosophies).

Resistance Sparked by Therapists' Relationship Problems

Like many of their clients, therapists may also have relationship difficulties and may bring them into treatment sessions and thereby encourage clients to resist. Therapists' difficulties in relating to some of their clients may include the following: (1) They may naturally dislike some of their clients, particularly those who are nasty, stupid, ugly, or otherwise unprepossessing, and may act in a negative manner to these clients just as they would if they happened to have social contacts with them. (2) Therapists may have what psychoanalysts call severe countertransference difficulties and may therefore favorably or unfavorably overreact to their clients (Wolstein, 1959). Thus, if a therapist hates her mother and one of her clients looks and acts like this mother, she may (consciously or unconsciously) want to harm rather than to help this client. (3) Therapists may not have personal negative feelings toward their clients but may be insensitive to their clients' feelings and may not know how to maintain good therapeutic relations with them (Goldfried, 1982; Lazarus & Fay, 1982; Meichenbaum & Gilmore, 1982).

If therapists do not like their clients, they can accept themselves and their negative attitudes and may thus be able to focus on suitable helpful procedures and thereby surmount this handicap. In using RET I can almost always focus so well on my clients' problems, and especially on showing them how to correct their iBs and other thinking errors, that it hardly matters that I personally do not like some of them and would never select them as my friends (Ellis, 1959a, 1971, 1973). However, if I continue to feel quite negative toward any of my clients (which is rare), I recommend that they try another therapist or else that they join one of my regular therapy groups, where I have less personal contact with them.

When therapists are insensitive to their clients' feelings and are unaware of methods of maintaining good therapeutic relations with them, RET endorses the methods of other schools of therapy—especially that of Rogers (1942, 1951, 1961)—which help them to be more sensitive and empathic. Thus, RET encourages them to listen carefully and reflectively to clients' difficulties, to be open and honest with them, to give them active encouragement, to deliberately point out their good (as well as some of their self-defeating) characteristics, to go out of their way to give sensitive clients verbal reinforcements, and otherwise to use empathic methods of communication (Crawford, 1982; Dryden, 1982, 1984; Ellis, 1977a; Johnson, 1980; Walen, DiGiuseppe & Wessler, 1980; Wessler & Wessler, 1980; Wessler, 1982). Although giving resistant clients a good deal of positive reinforcement has its distinct dangers (Ellis, 1983a; Turkat & Meyer, 1982), it can also at times be constructively used to overcome resistance.

RET specializes in helping therapists to look at their own countertransference problems by encouraging them to discover and to Dispute the iBs that lie behind their prejudices. Therapists, for example, who hate their clients because they resemble the therapists' obnoxious mothers are irrationally telling themselves ideas like these: "Because my mother treated me badly, I can't stand *any* person who has some of her poor traits!" Or "This client *must not* behave in the obnoxious way in which my mother acted! She's a *horrible person* for acting in this crummy way!" Therapists with negative countertransference may also be telling themselves: "This goddamned client is making it difficult for me! He *shouldn't* give me such a pain in the ass! If he doesn't soon stop that crap and listen carefully to what I am trying to teach him, he *deserves* to keep suffering, and I think I'll let him!"

Irrational Beliefs such as these are fairly easily revealed if therapists use RET to probe their own negative reactions to their clients. And the kinds of overgeneralizations that lead to negative, resistance-inciting countertransference are sought out during RET training and supervision, so that RET practitioners are taught how to find and uproot them (Ellis, 1962; Weinrach, 1973, 1977; Wessler & Ellis, 1980, 1983). (Also see Chapter 9.)

Resistance Related to the Moralistic
Attitudes of Therapists

In addition to the therapist-related resistance just mentioned, a trait that many therapists possess and that blocks them
in helping clients is their moralism: the profound tendency to
condemn themselves and others for evil or stupid acts. Even
though they are in the helping profession, they frequently believe that their seriously disturbed clients *absolutely should not,
positively must not* be the way they are—especially when these
clients abuse their therapists, come late to sessions, refuse to pay
their bills, and otherwise behave obnoxiously. Many therapists
therefore overtly or covertly damn their clients for their wrong-
doings and consequently help these clients damn themselves and
become more instead of less disturbed. Naturally, a number of
such clients tend to resist therapy.

RET practitioners particularly combat this kind of resistance
because one of the key tenets of RET is that all humans, including all clients, merit what Rogers (1961) and Standal (1954)
call unconditional positive regard and what RET calls unconditional acceptance (Ellis, 1962, 1972a, 1973, 1976a). I discuss this
concept in more detail in Chapters 3 and 4. Let me briefly note
here that rational-emotive therapists (RETers) look at their own
(and others') moralism and the iBs that underlie their damning
feelings and behaviors. For example: "My client *should* work at
therapy. She *must* not sabotage my efforts. How *awful* if she does!
I can't bear it!" And RETers work hard at eliminating these iBs
and at giving all their clients, no matter how difficult they are,
unconditional self-acceptance. In this manner—and in the ways
outlined in more detail in Chapters 9 and 10—they help nullify
therapist-encouraged resistance.

Environmental Factors that Lead to Resistance

In his excellent article on resistance in cognitive-behavior therapy, Golden (1983c) lists a number of environmental and other
external factors that motivate people to resist changing themselves when they are in therapy or when they are working on

their own to effect personality transformation. The main environmental interferences that Golden lists are these: (1) Relatives, friends, or associates may deliberately sabotage clients' becoming less disturbed—for example, they may reject or disapprove of the clients when they use therapy procedures to make themselves more assertive or successful. (2) Associates of the clients may inadvertently become "benevolent saboteurs" of therapy—as when a husband fosters his wife's phobias of open spaces or elevators by always accompanying her when she goes out and vainly tries to "help" her but actually reinforces her phobias. (3) Clients may accidentally or willfully acquire disability, welfare, or other monetary benefits for being emotionally disturbed and may thereby lose incentive to eliminate their disturbance. To Golden's list we may add another environmental factor that often helps clients to resist self-improvement: (4) The use of pacifiers, such as alcohol or drugs, which are very common in the clients' social scene and which, when consistently used, prevent them from seeing how disturbed they really are and from doing much to help themselves when they acknowledge their emotional disabilities. Today, in addition, physicians and psychiatrists often cavalierly prescribe psychotropic medication for anyone who is even slightly anxious or depressed; and the steady use of this medication may actually sabotage psychotherapy by taking away clients' incentives to work on themselves (Maultsby, 1984).

RET attempts to help resistant clients to discover and change the iBs that encourage them to give in to environmental factors leading to resistance. Many clients, for example, have iBs like these: "I *must* not change myself too drastically, even when I want to do so, in case others do not approve of me with my new thoughts, feelings, and behaviors." "I *can't stand* giving up my disability benefits and going back to work, even though I would probably be healthier and happier if I did so." "Whenever I get anxious or depressed, it's *awful* and *horrible*, and I must have a drink or take my Valium immediately to avoid this unbearable feeling!" By working against these iBs, and giving *in vivo* homework assignments that undermine them, RET is often effective with people who are encouraged to resist psychological treatment by environmental factors.

As can be seen by the foregoing survey of some of the

common kinds of resistance, clients frequently come to therapy because they are plagued with symptoms of emotional disturbance and yet they stubbornly resist the best efforts of their therapists (and themselves) to relieve their suffering. In many instances, their "resistance" or noncompliance is partly attributable to therapeutic fallibility—to the poor judgment, inept theories, and emotional rigidities of their therapists. But often (perhaps more often) they have their own reasons for resisting the therapist-directed procedures that they voluntarily seek. As noted above, these reasons are varied and wide ranging.

While some aspects of the rational-emotive approach to treating common resistances have just been briefly outlined, the following chapters will discuss RET antiresistance techniques in considerably more detail.

3
Cognitive Methods of Overcoming Resistance

Rational-emotive therapy (RET), together with cognitive-behavior therapy (CBT), assumes that when clients self-defeatingly and irrationally resist following therapeutic procedures and homework assignments, they largely do so because of their explicit and implicit cognitions or beliefs. RET, which tends to be more philosophic and more persuasive than some other forms of CBT (such as those of Bandura [1977], Mahoney [1980], and Meichenbaum [1977]), assumes that resisting clients have an underlying set of powerful and persistent irrational Beliefs (iBs), as well as an innate biosocial tendency to create new irrationalities that frequently block them from carrying out the therapeutic goals and contracts that they overtly agree to work at achieving. Although RET does not agree with psychoanalytic and psychodynamic theory, which holds that client resistance is based on deeply unconscious, repressed thoughts and feelings, it does hypothesize that many—perhaps most—of the iBs that underlie client resistance are (1) at least partially implicit, unconscious, or automatic; (2) tenaciously held; (3) held concomitantly with strong feelings and fixed habit patterns of behavior; (4) to some extent held by virtually all clients; (5) difficult to change; and (6) easily likely to recur once they have been temporarily surrendered (Bard, 1980; Ellis, 1962, 1971, 1973, 1976a, 1979b, 1983a, 1984e; Ellis & Grieger, 1977; Ellis & Whiteley, 1979; Grieger & Boyd, 1980; Grieger & Grieger, 1982; Walen, DiGiuseppe & Wessler, 1980; Wessler & Wessler, 1980).

More specifically, RET assumes that clients who self-defeatingly resist therapy implicitly or explicitly tend to hold three main iBs or philosophies: (1) "I *must* do well at changing myself and I'm an incompetent, hopeless client if I don't." (2) "You (the therapist and others) *must* help me change and you're rotten people if you don't." (3) "Changing myself *must* occur quickly and easily and it's horrible if it doesn't!" Concomitantly with these iBs, resisters feel anxious, depressed, angry, and self-pitying about changing and these disturbed feelings block their forcing themselves to change. Behaviorally, resisters withdraw, procrastinate, remain inert, and sabotage their self-promises to change. RET practitioners are largely concerned with helping resisters (and other clients) make a profound philosophic change so that they adopt a cooperative, confident, determined attitude toward self-change rather than the self-blocking views that they hold. To effect this kind of cognitive restructuring, RET uses a wide variety of thinking, feeling, and activity methods. In this chapter, I shall describe some of the main cognitive methods that RET uses to interrupt, challenge, dispute, and change the iBs that are found to underlie clients' self-sabotaging resistances. These include the following techniques:

Cognitions that Underlie Resistance

Virtually all RET clients are taught the ABCs of emotional disturbance and dysfunctional behavior. Thus, when clients have a neurotic symptom or self-defeating Consequence (C), such as depression and self-hatred, following an unfortunate Activating Event (A), such as rejection by a significant person, they are shown that while A (rejection) probably contributes to and influences C (depression), it does not directly (as they tend to falsely "see" or infer) *create* or *cause* C. Rather, the more direct (and usually more important) "cause" of C (Consequence) is their Belief System (B), which they largely bring to and with which they mainly create or cause C. Although they mistakenly believe that their depression and self-hatred directly and inevitably follow from their being rejected (A), they actually had a *choice* of Bs and Cs, and they foolishly *chose* to make themselves *inappropriately* depressed and self-hating (neurotic) at C, when they theoretically could have *chosen* instead to make themselves feel only *appropriately* disappointed and frustrated (self-helping and unneurotic) (Ellis, 1957a, 1962, 1973, in press-a; Ellis & Harper, 1961a, 1961b, 1975).

According to the ABC theory of RET, when these clients want to be accepted and approved at A (the Activating Event) and are instead unpleasantly rejected, they *can* choose to manufacture or resort to a set of sensible or rational Beliefs (rBs) and *can* thereby conclude, "How unfortunate that So-and-so disapproved of some of my traits and therefore rejected my friendship or love. Too bad! But I can still find significant others to approve of and accept me. Now how do I go about finding them?" If they rigorously created and stayed with these rBs, these clients would, as stated above, feel appropriately disappointed and frustrated— but *not* depressed and self-hating.

Where, then, do their inappropriate and disturbed feelings of depression and self-hatred come from? RET shows clients that these neurotic Consequences (C) mainly or largely (though not exclusively) stem from their iBs. These iBs almost invariably consist of absolutistic, dogmatic, illogical, unrealistic Beliefs. Instead of being expressions of flexible desire and preference (as rBs seem to be), they are inflexible, rigid commands and demands—absolutistic and unconditional shoulds, oughts, musts, and necessities. Thus, feelings of depression and self-hatred (at C) that follow disapproval and rejection (at A) largely result from iBs like: (1) "I *must* not be disapproved of and rejected by a person I deem significant." (2) "If I am rejected, as I *must* not be, it's *awful* and *terrible!*" (3) "I *can't stand* being disapproved of, as I *must* not be!" (4) "If I am rejected by a significant other, as must *never* under *any* condition occur, there has to be something horribly rotten about me, and that rottenness makes me a *despicable, undeserving person!*"

RET, using its cognitively-oriented ABC theory of human disturbance, first tends to show depressed and self-hating clients how they unwittingly (and largely unconsciously) *choose* to *disturb themselves;* how they can therefore *decide* to change their iBs and thereby undisturb themselves; and how they can mainly (though not completely) acquire a realistic philosophy of *preference* rather than an absolutistic philosophy of *necessitizing* and consequently rarely seriously disturb themselves in the future.

In combatting clients' self-defeating resistances, RET puts them into the ABC model and shows them that when they promise themselves and their therapist that they will work at therapy at Point A (Activating Event) and when they act dys-functionally at point C and achieve the self-defeating Conse-quence of resistance, they have both rBs and iBs at point B. Their rBs tend to be: "I don't like working at therapy. It's hard to change myself! But it's hard*er* if I don't; so I'd damned well better push myself, and do this hard work right *now* to make my life easier and better later." If, says the theory of RET, they *only* believed and felt these rBs at B, they would not be especially resistant at C.

No such luck! When clients seriously and self-injuriously resist, they usually *also* create and indulge in iBs such as these: (1) "It's not only hard for me to work at therapy and change myself, it's *too* hard! It *should not, must not* be that hard!" (2) "How *terrible* that I have to work so hard and persistently to change myself!" (3) "I *can't stand* working at therapy that is harder than it *should be!*" (4) "What a *rotten therapist* I have, who makes me work harder than I *should*. And what *crummy methods* he or she inflicts on me! I'm sure there is some easier, more enjoyable method of changing, and until I find it I'll be damned if I'll make myself so uncomfortable with this one!"

These iBs of resistant clients, which mainly consist of a devout philosophy of low frustration tolerance (LFT) or discom-fort anxiety (DA) (Ellis, 1979a, 1980a), can also be supplemented with a philosophy of self-downing or ego anxiety (EA). Resistant clients' iBs then tend to run along these lines: (1) "I absolutely *must* work hard and succeed at therapy." (2) "If I don't change as much and as quickly as I *must*, it's *awful* and *terrible!*" (3) "When I don't make myself change as well as I *must*, I *can't* stand it and life is *intolerable!*" (4) "Unless I do as well as I *must* in therapy, I am an inadequate, hopeless, worthless person!" One might think that these self-blaming iBs would help spur clients to work at therapy and to overcome their resistance. Occasionally, this may be true; but usually these iBs sabotage clients, lead them to feel that they *can't* change, and result in still greater resistances.

RET's primary cognitive technique of combatting resistance, therefore, consists of showing clients that they do not "just" resist and that they do not merely resist *because* they find it difficult to change, but that they *choose* to subscribe to a philosophy of LFT and/or of self-deprecation which, in turn, largely "causes" their resistance. The main cognitive message of RET, of course, is that they can instead choose to *dis*believe and to *surrender* their iBs and can exchange them for rBs that will help them work at rather than resist therapeutic change.

It is interesting to note that even therapists who do not particularly subscribe to RET theories and practices have recognized that when people resist therapy they usually are telling themselves something to create their resistance. Saltmarsh (1976), for example, lists four main ways in which clients may resist therapy and shows how in each case they are telling themselves specific sentences to create these resistances. However, he does not seem to realize the absolutistic shoulds and musts that are crucially implicit in their self-statements. Thus, he points out that clients who are sullenly silent may be telling themselves, "you couldn't possibly understand me," but he forgets to note their implicit philosophy, "as you *must* thoroughly understand and make things easy for me!" Saltmarsh also points out that clients who attack their therapists are often telling themselves, "I'm right and you're wrong," but he does not see that they are probably implicitly believing, "I'm right—as I *must* be—and you're wrong—as you *must* not be!"

Although, then, there are many things that people tell themselves in order to make themselves resist therapy, and although you had better discover these self-statements and work to help the clients change them, keep in mind the most important parts of clients' self-talk: the explicit or implicit demands, commands, shoulds, oughts, and musts that make their reasons for resisting disturbed rather than sensible.

Disputing Irrational Beliefs

The basic disputing techniques of RET can be employed to show clients that the iBs behind their absolutistic shoulds, oughts, and musts—and behind the inferences, attributions, overgeneralizations, non sequiturs, and other forms of crooked thinking that tend to stem from these musts—can be annihilated or ameliorated by vigorous scientific thinking (Ellis, 1958a, 1962, 1971, 1973, in press-a; Ellis & Becker, 1982; Ellis & Grieger, 1977; Ellis & Harper, 1975; Ellis & Whiteley, 1979; Grieger & Grieger, 1982). Thus, resisters are challenged by the therapist and are induced to keep challenging themselves with scientific questions like: "Where is the evidence that I *must* succeed at changing myself?" "Why is it *awful* and *horrible* that it is difficult for me to change?" "Prove that I *can't stand* my having to work long and hard at therapy." "Where is it written that it's *too hard* to change and that it *should not* be that hard?" This kind of scientific disputing is persisted at, by both therapist and clients, until resisters start changing.

After A (Activating Events), B (rational and irrational Beliefs), and C (emotional and behavioral Consequences), RET goes directly (and often quickly) on to D (Disputing). As just noted, D is the scientific method. Science accepts Beliefs as hypotheses, constructs, or theories—not as facts. And scientific theories are not dogmatic, inflexible, absolutistic, or devout. Otherwise they are religious rather than scientific (Ellis, 1983b; Rorer & Widiger, 1983). RET not only tries to be scientific about its own theories and to set them up so that they are precise and falsifiable (Bartley, 1962; Mahoney, 1976; Popper, 1962; Weimer, 1979), but it is one of the few forms of cognitive-behavior therapy that attempts to teach clients how to think scientifically about themselves, others, and the world in which they live. If, RET contends, people were consistently scientific and nonabsolutistic, they would rarely invent or subscribe to dogmatic *shoulds* and *musts*, would stay with their flexible wishes and preferences, and would thereby minimize or eliminate their emotional disturbances (Kelly, 1956, 1966).

RET, therefore, encourages all clients, and particularly resistant ones, to actively and persistently Dispute (at point D) their iBs and to arrive at point E, a new Effect or Effective Philosophy. Where D consists of clients' Disputing their iBs, E consists of the logical and empirical answers they then give to this Disputing. Thus, to perform D and to arrive at E, a client's internal dialogue in regard to his or her resistance would go something like this:

iB I *must* succeed at changing myself during therapy!

D   Where is the evidence that I *have* to succeed?

E   There is no such evidence! Succeeding at changing myself would have several distinct advantages and I'd definitely like to get these advantages. But I never *have* to get what I desire, no matter how much I desire it.

iB If I don't succeed in overcoming my resistance and working at therapy, I am an incompetent, hopeless person who can never stop resisting!

D   Prove that I am an incompetent, hopeless person who can never stop resisting.

E   I can't prove this. I can only prove that I am a person who has *so far* failed to stop resisting but not that I have, nor ever will have, *no* ability to do so in the future. Only my *belief* in my total incompetence to change myself will make me *more* incompetent than I otherwise would probably be!

iB It is *awful* and *horrible* that I have to work at therapy and to change myself.

D   In what way is it *awful* and *horrible* to work at therapy and to change myself?

E   In no way! It is distinctly difficult and inconvenient for me to work at therapy and I'd rather it be easy. But when I label this work *awful* or *horrible*, I mean that (1) it *should not* be as inconvenient as it is, (2) it is *totally* or *100%* inconvenient, and (3) it is *more than* (101%) inconvenient. All these conclusions are wrong, since: (1) It should be as inconvenient as it is—because that's the way it is! (2) It can virtually never be 100% inconvenient—because it invariably could be worse. (3) It obviously cannot be 101%

inconvenient—because nothing can be *that* bad! Nothing in the universe is *awful* or *terrible* or *horrible*, since these are magical, demoniacal terms that go beyond reality and have no empirical referents. If I invent such antiempirical "descriptions" of my experience, I will thereby make my life *seem* and *feel* "awful" when it is only highly disadvantageous and inconvenient and I will then make myself suffer *more* than I would otherwise suffer.

iB I *can't stand* my having to work long and hard at therapy.

D Why can't I stand having to work long and hard at therapy?

E I definitely *can* stand it! I don't *like* working that long and hard and wish that I could change myself easily and magically. But I *can* stand what I don't like, as long as (1) I don't die of it, and (2) I can still in some ways enjoy myself and be happy. Fairly obviously, I won't die because I work at therapy (though I may kill myself if I don't!). And even though this kind of work is often unenjoyable, it leaves me time and energy for other pleasures. In fact, in the long run, it helps me to achieve *greater* life enjoyment. So I clearly *can* stand and *can* tolerate the therapeutic work that I don't like.

iB Because there is no easy way for me to work at therapy, and I'd better uncomfortably persist until I collaborate fully with my therapist and change myself, the world is a horrible place and life is hardly worth living. Maybe I'd better kill myself.

D Where is it written that the world is a horrible place and that life is hardly worth living because there is no easy way for me to work at therapy?

E It is only written in my self-defeating philosophy! It seems evident that because of the way I am and because of the way the world is, I will often have trouble changing myself through therapy. Too bad! Really unfortunate! But if that's the way it is and that's the way I am, I'd better accept (though still dislike and often try to change) the world's limitations and my own fallibility, and I'd better attempt to live and to enjoy myself as much as I can with these undesirable realities. I can teach myself, as St. Francis recommended, to have the courage to change the unpleasant things that I can change, to have the serenity to accept those that I can't change, and to have the wisdom to know the difference between the two.

RET's most famous and popular technique is the one just outlined: that of teaching resistant clients to find their main iBs that significantly contribute to or "cause" their resistances; to actively Dispute (D) these iBs by rigorously using the best logicoempirical tools of the scientific methods; and to persist at this Disputing until they arrive at E, an Effective Philosophy that is self-helping rather than irrational and self-downing. As Kelly (1955) brilliantly noted, humans are natural predictors and scientists. RET, along with other cognitive-behavior therapies, tries to help them be better and more productive scientists in their personal affairs (Bard, 1980; Ellis, 1962, 1973, in press-a; Ellis & Becker, 1982; Ellis & Grieger, 1977; Ellis & Harper, 1975; Ellis & Whiteley, 1979; Friedman, 1975; Grieger & Boyd, 1980; Mahoney, 1974, 1977).

Other Modes of Disputing and of Cognitive Restructuring

The ABCs of RET, which I originally posited in 1955, and which emphasized the influence of iBs on the creation of human disturbance, have been expanded by me and a number of other cognitive-behavior therapists since that time (Beck, 1976; Burns, 1980; Ellis, 1962, 1971, 1973, 1979d, 1984d, 1984e, in press-d, in press-f, in press-g, in press-h; Goldfried & Davidson, 1976; Hauck, 1973; Mahoney, 1974; Meichenbaum, 1977; Novaco, 1975; Phadke, 1982; Walen, DiGiuseppe & Wessler, 1980; Wessler & Wessler, 1980).

In my latest classification of iBs (Ellis, in press-d), I outline them as follows:

Absolutistic Evaluations, Inferences, and Attributions
That Tend to Lead to Self-Defeating (and
Society-Sabotaging) Emotions and Behaviors

Examples: "Because people disapprove of my behavior and presumably of me, and because I *must* act competently and *must* win their approval, it follows that: (1) I am an incompetent, rotten person (overgeneralization). (2) My life will be completely miserable (overgeneralization). (3) The world is a totally bad place in which to live (overgeneralization). (4) I am certain that they will always disapprove of me and that I will therefore always be a worthless individual (overgeneralization, dogmatic certainty). (5) I deserve to have only bad and grim things happen to me (undeservingness, damnation). (6) I deserve to roast in hell for eternity (undeservingness, extreme damnation)."

Common Cognitive Derivatives of Negative
Absolutistic Evaluations (Additional iBs
Stemming From the Basic Irrationalities)

Examples of disturbed ideas: "Because I must act competently and must win people's approval and because I have acted incompetently and/or have lost their approval, it follows that: (1) this is *awful, horrible*, and *terrible!* (awfulizing, catastrophizing). (2) I can't bear it, can't stand it! (I-can't-stand-it-itis, discomfort anxiety, low frustration tolerance). (3) I am a thoroughly incompetent, inferior, and worthless person (self-downing, feelings of inadequacy). (4) I can't change and become competent and lovable (hopelessness). (5) I deserve misery and punishment and will continue to bring them on myself (undeservingness, damnation)."

Other Common Cognitive Derivatives of Negative
Absolutistic Evaluations (Additional iBs)

Examples of logical errors and unrealistic inferences: "Because I must act competently and must win people's approval and because I have acted incompetently and/or lost their approval, it follows that: (1) I will always act incompetently and make significant people disapprove of me (overgeneralization). (2) I am a total failure and am completely unlovable (overgeneralization, all-or-none thinking). (3) People know that I am no good and that I will always be incompetent (non sequitur, jumping to conclusions, mind reading). (4) They will always despise me (non sequitur, jumping to conclusions, fortune telling). (5) People only despise me and see nothing good in me (focusing on the negative, overgeneralization). (6) When they think I am doing well and see me favorably, that is because I am fooling them (disqualifying the positive; non sequitur). (7) Their disliking me will make me lose my job, become friendless, and make everything go wrong in my life (catastrophizing, magnification.) (8) When I act well and people approve of me, that only shows that I can occasionally be right; but that is unimportant compared to my great faults and stupidities (minimization, focusing on the negative). (9) I strongly feel that I am despicable and unlovable; and because my feeling is so strong and consistent, this proves that I really am despicable and unlovable (emotional reasoning, circular reasoning, non sequitur). (10) I am a complete loser and a failure (labeling, overgeneralization). (11) People must be rejecting me for some foolish thing I have done and could not possibly be rejecting me because of their own prejudices or for any other reason (personalizing, non sequitur, overgeneralization). (12) If I somehow get people to stop rejecting me or to like me, I am really a phony acting above my real level, and I will soon fall on my face and show them what a despicable faker I am (phonyism, all-or-nothing thinking, over-generalization)."

Resistant clients (and other people) can learn absolutistic evaluations, inferences, and conclusions from their parents, teachers, and others—e.g., "I must have good luck but now that I have broken this mirror, fate will bring me bad luck and that will be terrible!" But they tend to learn these iBs *easily*, and are prone to hold on to them *rigidly*. They may often be born with a strong tendency to think irrationally. More importantly, resisters often learn family and cultural *rational* standards—e.g., "It is *preferable* for me to treat others considerately"—and then they overgeneralize, exaggerate, and turn these into highly irrational Beliefs— e.g., "Because it is *preferable* for me to treat others considerately, I *have* to do so at all times, else I am a *totally unlovable, worthless person!*"

Even if humans were reared quite rationally, RET hypothesizes that virtually all of them would often take their learned standards and their rational preferences and then irrationally escalate them into absolutistic demands on themselves, on others, and on the universe in which they live (Ellis, 1958a, 1962, 1971, 1973, 1976c, 1984e, in press-a, in press-e; Ellis & Grieger, 1977; Ellis & Whiteley, 1979).

There are almost innumerable ways of Disputing difficult clients' iBs. A simple form of Disputation that can be especially applied, and applied in a persistent and vigorous manner, to the iBs of resisters has been outlined by Phadke (1982). Therapists can break up the D of Disputing into three separate Ds—Detecting, Debating, and Discriminating iBs—and apply these as follows:

Detecting irrational Beliefs. Show clients that whenever they feel seriously disturbed or act self-defeatingly, they most probably have iBs that take the form of absolutistic shoulds, oughts, and musts. Thus, if clients hold irrationalities about themselves, about others, or about the world, you can interpolate and help them see the explicit or implicit *musts* that are included in their convictions. Here, for example, are some common irrationalities and (in parenthesis) the fairly obvious musts that they implicitly include:

1. "I keep failing all the time (because I *must* never fail at important things and if I fail this time, as I definitely *must* not, that means that I will *always* fail)."

2. "People see through me and know that I am a phony (because I *have to* perform better than I do, and even when I seem to act reasonably well, I am far from perfect—as I *must* not be—and they are therefore going to soon find me out and reject me)."

3. "I can't find anything that interests me (because I've *got to* do everything well and if I find something and do it poorly, that's *awful* and I am an *inadequate person*)."

4. "Most people do well (as I *should* do) and lead an enjoyable life (as I *must* lead)."

5. "People treat me unfairly (as they absolutely *must* not!)."

6. "I always fail at important tasks (when I *should* not fail at any of them!)."

7. "She rejected me because of my scarred face (which I

absolutely *must* not have and which would make *any* good woman reject me)."

8. "I am a complete loser (because I *should* practically always win and never get rejected!)."

Debating or Disputing irrational Beliefs. Once the iBs of resistant (and other) clients are clearly delineated, you can actively debate and dispute them by the various techniques outlined in this chapter and in other chapters of this book. You have a wide range of choices and manners here, because iBs can be disputed mildly or strongly, by empirical data or by logic, by direct statements or by analogy, didactically or dramatically, and in many other ways. Many therapists do disputation or debating in a mild, Rogerian manner (Beck, 1976; Glasser, 1965; Johnson, 1980; Lawrence & Huber, 1982; Meichenbaum, 1977; Wessler, 1982). But RET is often done in a more active-directive, vigorous way (Dryden, 1984; Ellis, 1962, 1971, 1973, 1984e, in press-c, in press-h; Ellis & Becker, 1982; Ellis & Harper, 1975). With resistant clients, as shown above and later in this book, I frequently advocate strong disputational methods; but as I also agree with Howard Young (1977, 1984) that disputing can be done in RET in a variety of other ways that emphasize relationship approaches.

Discriminating between rational Beliefs and irrational Beliefs. RET hypothesizes that iBs rarely exist by themselves but are preceded by or associated with rational ones. Thus, clients almost always have preferences or desires—e.g., "I want to pass this examination and get my degree"—along with absolutistic commands or musts—e.g., "Because I want to pass this examination and get my degree, I have to do so, and it would be horrible if I didn't!" In RET, we usually hold that virtually all preferences, even somewhat unrealistic ones, are rational, as long as they are only that—preferences. For if people say to themselves, "I would like very much to have a million dollars right now—*but* if I don't, I don't, and I can still lead a happy life without it," they are not going to seriously upset themselves when they don't have what they'd prefer. But if they tell themselves, "I only want ten dollars right now—*but* I must have it, otherwise I can't get what I want and that would be terrible" they are going to be anxious or depressed even when they have nine dollars and 95 cents.

With resistant (and other) clients, therefore, RET not only shows them that they have explicit or implicit shoulds and musts when they are disturbed and teaches them how to discover and actively dispute these absolutes, but it often shows them that they also have rBs—wishes, values, and preferences—that are distinctly different from their iBs; and it indicates that their rational preferences are almost always legitimate and undisturbing. Indeed, they are generally sane and self-helping for several reasons: (1) They motivate people to continue to live and to look for happiness. (2) They add considerably to human existence. (3) Even when balked, they encourage useful and gratifying learning and growth. (4) Rational preferences can be tested against reality, to see whether people truly like what they thought they would like before their preferences were fulfilled. (5) They aid the discovery of new preferences and new experiences.

RET, consequently, often helps resistant clients to clearly discriminate their rational from their irrational Beliefs. Then, when people recognize their iBs and work at giving them up, they can retain their sensible desires and look for ways of fulfilling them. RET, consequently, has two main aspects: showing people how to give up their self-defeating ideas and actions, and also showing them how they can actualize themselves and lead more pleasant lives. But in order to accomplish the latter goal, you had better help clients determine their rational desires and preferences and then figure out various ways of achieving them. Cognitive therapies are often accused of overfocusing on people's negative outlooks and ignoring their positive orientations. But by concentrating on clients' rBs *and* iBs, RET avoids this dysfunctional emphasis and encourages self-actualization and joy (Bernard & Joyce, 1984; Ellis, 1981c, 1984e, in press-a, in press-f, in press-g; Ellis & Becker, 1982; Ellis & Bernard, 1983).

Rational and Coping Self-statements

RET, following the early leads of Bernheim (1886/1947) and Coué (1923), teaches resistant clients to repetitively say to themselves rational or coping statements and to keep actively auto-suggesting these statements until they truly believe them and feel their effects. Where early advocates of "positive thinking" tended to be overoptimistic and pollyannish, modern beliefs in the power of self-statements are more scientific and originate in the work of Ellis (1957a, 1958a, 1962). Recent scientific advocates of rational philosophies or coping self-statements have been much more realistic, detailed, and down to earth (R. Lazarus, 1966, 1984; Luria, 1976; Meichenbaum, 1977; Meichenbaum & Jaremko, 1983; Novaco, 1975; Vygotsky, 1962).

RET uses two different kinds of coping or rational statements with difficult (and other) clients. First, empirical or realistic statements that counter people's antiempirical or unrealistic beliefs such as: "Now that I've failed with this partner, I'll never be able to succeed in love." And "Because that dog is large, I am sure that it will bite me and rip me to pieces." To contradict these negative, overgeneralized, unrealistic beliefs, RET helps clients work out more sensible and practical ones, such as: (1) "I know it's difficult to succeed in love with a partner I really want, but if I keep trying I will probably eventually do so." (2) "Even though that dog is larger, there is very little chance that he will bite me. Even if he does, I will hardly die of a few dog bites." (3) "If I only keep trying, I think that I definitely can succeed in learning this material and passing this important test." (4) "Many people will reject me when I want them to accept me, but some will also like and accept me." (5) "The world is full of rank injustice, but it also has many just aspects, too." (6) "Even though I get rejected for many jobs, if I keep trying I shall most likely get a fairly good one." (7) "I succeeded this time in not angering myself about what my boss did to me. This shows that I *can* live without anger, even under unfair conditions." (8) "Easy does it! If I just relax, my tension will probably go away and I will then be able to get along better with others."

These kinds of coping statements describe reality much more accurately than the self-defeating, unrealistic statements that people commonly make to themselves and by which they unduly bring on anxiety, anger, depression, and self-hatred. Sometimes they are almost the only kind of new cognitions that resistant clients will accept—particularly when such clients are young, not too bright, highly suggestible, and will not do the more elegant types of rethinking that RET often favors. Unlike autosuggestion and positive thinking, however, RET encourages resisters to think through, and not merely to parrot, rational and coping statements, for otherwise they tend to lose their effectiveness and lead to ultimate disillusionment.

RET also specializes in helping clients construct and repeatedly tell themselves more philosophic self-statements that tend to undo their negativistic *musturbatory* evaluations of themselves, of others, and of the conditions around them. A common absolutistic philosophy, for example, that a large percentage of difficult clients strongly hold is the iB, "I *have to* perform this important task well, and I'm a terrible person if I don't!" A counterattacking self-statement that they can say to themselves and intensively think about many times might be, "I would very much *like to* perform this important task well, but I never *have to* do so. If I do perform poorly, I am a *person who* did badly but never a *bad person!*"

Another common irrationality which many resistant clients hold is, "You treated me inconsiderately and unfairly, as you absolutely *should* not, and I therefore can't stand *you.*" A philosophic, rational, coping statement to contradict this iB could be, "Even when you clearly treat me inconsiderately and unfairly, you have a perfect right, as a fallible human, to act wrongly, and I can stand you and associate with you, though I deplore some of your unjust behavior."

A third irrationality that difficult clients (DCs) often hold is, "Life *should be* much easier than it is and provide me with all the things I really want, just because I want them. A counteracting self-statement can be, "It would be lovely if life were easier, but it never *has* to be. I can take it, even when it is highly depriving, and I can still be a happy human."

Other philosophic, rational, and coping statements that RET helps people to consider and to think about until they see their validity and helpfulness include the following: (1) "*Nothing* is awful or horrible—though many things are highly *inconvenient.*" (2) "I never *need* what I *want*, no matter *how* much I desire it." (3) "When I am addicted to self-defeating behavior, there's rarely any gain without pain." (4) "I am determined to work at changing the undesirable things that I can change, to accept those that I cannot change, and to have the wisdom to see the difference between the two." (5) "Let me try to *be* myself and to *enjoy* myself—not to *prove* myself!" (6) "I predict that I shall always be a highly fallible human (HFH), who will continue to make many important mistakes—and who can always choose to accept myself for making them." (7) "I can rarely change others but can almost always significantly change myself!" (8) "Although I shall often feel sorry and frustrated about the bad things that occur in my life, including those that I make happen myself, I can stubbornly refuse to make myself needlessly ashamed and depressed about anything—yes, anything!"

Because DCs, especially, tend to believe that they should not, must not have to work at changing themselves (but should have someone else magically change them for the better) and because they frequently (and strongly) feel that they *can't* change, RET encourages them to use rational self-statements that will notable attack these ideas and help them to get on with their lives. These include coping statements about therapy, such as: (1) "Therapy doesn't *have* to be easy. I can, in fact, *enjoy* its challenge!" (2) "Sure it's hard to work at changing myself. But it's much *harder* if I don't!" (3) "Too bad if I am often inept at changing myself. That only proves that I am still, and will continue to be, a highly fallible person. I can still accept myself *as* fallible—and then work like hell to be *less* fallible. (4) "Therapists do the best they can to help me. They, too, have their problems and limitations. Tough! Now how can I experiment with the suggestions they make to me and do my damnedest to help myself?"

Let me repeat: RET hypothesizes that reasonably bright and well-educated clients, including some of the most difficult ones, had better not do mild or occasional Disputing of their iBs but preferably should do so (as shall be noted later) in a strong, vigorous way. It holds that such individuals can thereby achieve elegant rather than inelegant solutions to their problems. But it also gives them a choice of rational, coping statements that they can repeat to themselves and finally internalize. And it sees these two methods—logicoempirical disputing of iBs and steady restating of rBs—as being consistent with each other. Resistant clients (and other people with emotional difficulties) can keep using both these techniques to good effect, and effective therapists can actively and persistently (as well as encouragingly) teach them how to do so.

Referenting

RET uses the general semantics method of referenting (Danysh, 1974) and teaches resistant clients to make a comprehensive list of the disadvantages of resisting and the advantages of working at therapy and to keep regularly reviewing and thinking about this list (Ellis & Abrahms, 1978; Ellis & Becker, 1982; Ellis & Harper, 1975). Thus, under disadvantages of resisting, clients can list: "(1) It will take me longer to change. (2) I will keep suffering as long as I resist changing. (3) My refusing to change will antagonize some of the people I care for and will sabotage my relationships with them. (4) My therapy will become more boring and more expensive the longer I take to change myself. (5) Continuing to afflict myself with my symptoms will make me lose much time and money. (6) If I continue to resist, I may well antagonize my therapist and encourage him or her to put less effort into helping me. (7) My refusing to work hard at therapy and thereby continuing to remain irrationally fearful and anxious will force me to forego many potential pleasures and adventures and make my life much duller." Similarly, using this referenting technique, clients are shown how to list the advantages of working harder at therapy and thereby abetting their own personality change. By reviewing and examining these disadvantages of resistance and these benefits of nonresistance, they are helped to resist considerably less.

RET often forcefully brings to clients' attention not only present but later probable disadvantages of resisting therapy. Thus, the RET practitioner can remind the client, "Yes, you don't have to work right now at overcoming your low frustration tolerance, since your parents are still around to help support you economically. But how are you going to earn a decent living after they are gone, unless you prepare yourself to do so now?" "Of course, you may be able to get away with your drinking and staying up late at present, but won't it eventually sabotage your health? And do you really want to keep making yourself fat, tired and physically ill?"

Challenge of Self-change

RET tries to sell some resistant clients on the *adventure* and *challenge* of working at changing themselves. Thus, it gives clients the homework exercise of Disputing Irrational Beliefs (DIBS) which helps them debate their iBs and to reframe some of the difficulties of therapy by asking themselves questions like, "What good things can I feel or make happen if I work hard at therapy and still don't succeed too well?" (Ellis, 1974a; Ellis & Harper, 1975). Rational-emotive therapists also prod resistant clients with questions like, "Suppose you pick the wrong therapy technique and work hard at it with little good results. Why would that be great for you to do?" By these paradoxical questions, they hope to help resisters see that (1) trying something and at first failing at it is usually better than not trying at all; (2) striving to change leads to important information about oneself that may result in later success and pleasure; (3) action can be pleasurable in its own right, even when it does not produce fine results; (4) trying to change oneself and *accepting* delayed results increases one's frustration tolerance; (5) the *challenge* of striving for therapeutic change (like the challenge of trying to climb Mt. Everest) may be exciting and enjoyable in its own right.

Although ego-enhancing methods of therapy are seen by RET as having their distinct dangers (since if clients are led to think of themselves as good or worthy individuals when they succeed at therapy they will also harmfully view themselves as bad or worthless individuals when they fail), some elements of verbal reinforcement can be used to combat resistance. Thus, therapists can show clients that *it* is good and desirable (and not that *they* are good or worthy) if they use their energy and intelligence to work at therapy. This technique can be combined with the challenging method. For example, the therapist can say to the client, "Yes, many people are prone to sit on their asses and to stupidly resist changing themselves. But anyone who fortunately has *your* intelligence, talent, and ability, *can* overcome this kind of resistance and show how competent he or she is at changing. Not that you *have to* use your innate ability to change. But wouldn't you get much better results if you did?"

Proselytizing Others

One of the regular RET cognitive techniques that can be especially helpful with resistant and difficult clients consists of inducing them to use RET methods with others (Bard, 1980; Ellis, 1957a; Ellis & Abrahms, 1978; Ellis & Harper, 1975; Ellis & Whiteley, 1979). If you have clients who resist giving up anger, you can try to get them to talk others—relatives, friends, or employees—out of *their* anger. If your clients refuse to do their RET homework, you can try to induce them to give homework assignments to others and to keep checking to see if these people actually do their homework.

Thought Stopping

RET generally takes a skeptical view toward the efficacy of direct suggestion and of a therapist's authoritatively telling clients what to do, when they are either in a conscious or in a hypnotic state. Although it acknowledges that such authoritarian commands often work, it holds that they usually only have a temporary effect, that they lead mainly to symptom removal rather than elegant philosophic change, and that they often help make clients more dependent on outside authorities than on their own thinking and changing abilities. The main purpose of RET is *self*-change rather than submission to outside influences or reinforcement (Ellis, 1983a).

Similarly, RET does not enthusiastically endorse thought stopping (Rimm & Masters, 1974; Wolpe, 1958, 1982), because when people vehemently tell themselves to *stop* thinking obsessive thoughts, they often temporarily succeed; but they tend to later revert to obsessive thinking again and therefore have only temporarily given themselves relief. In the case of resistant clients, however, and especially those who are severely bothered by obsessive thinking, thought stopping can sometimes be effective. Johnson, Shenov, and Gilmore (1983) have presented a case where a Vietnam veteran was plagued with vivid hallucinations and obsessional ruminations about his shooting a Vietcong soldier, was severely depressed, and had great difficulty overcoming his obsessions. They employed Rimm and Master's (1974) fourfold thought-stopping technique of (1) having the therapist interrupt the client's overt thoughts, (2) having the therapist interrupt his covert thoughts, (3) having the client overtly interrupt his own covert thoughts, and (4) having him covertly interrupt his own covert thoughts. They instructed the client to practice this thought-stopping procedure at least three times a day by generating his own obsessional thoughts and utilizing the technique with any spontaneously occurring ruminations. In conjunction with an anger-induction technique, this procedure worked.

When some of my own clients resist giving up their obsessive thoughts and their compulsive actions, I say to them, "I believe you when you report that you spontaneously, against your will, keep thinking these thoughts and feel driven to act compulsively. I doubt whether you are deliberately trying to bring on these symptoms, and agree that you get overwhelmed with them from time to time. But I still think that you, to some extent, willfully indulge in *retaining* this behavior. You *do* have the power to stop doing what you have spontaneously started doing. It is enormously difficult for you, sometimes, to do so; but you still have a good degree of choice in stopping yourself. To exert this choice, you can forcibly—yes, and forcefully—tell yourself *stop* when you find yourself obsessively ruminating. And you can also forcibly and forcefully tell yourself to *stop* carrying out some of your compulsions. This kind of thought stopping and compulsion stopping may well not work forever. You may fall back into the old obsessive-compulsive behaviors. But you can at least temporarily stop them if you strongly try to do so. And by doing this, you will be able to see that you *do* have a much greater degree of control over your thoughts and your actions than you often think that you do. Moreover, you don't have to stop there. Once you get yourself to stop thinking an obsessive thought, you can then work at seeing what you are telling yourself to create it, such as, 'I *must* not think this thought! I *have to* stop thinking it!' If you look for the absolutistic shoulds and musts that are leading to your obsessive worries or to your anxieties *about* your obsessions, and if you show yourself powerfully that it is *desirable* but not *necessary* that you stop worrying, you will then undermine the *mus*turbatory philosophy that creates and sustains your obsessions (and your compulsions), and you will be able to thereby minimize them."

With difficult and resistant clients, then, I sometimes use thought stopping and compulsion stopping in conjunction with RET anti*mus*turbatory disputing of their iBs, and I find that this combination is more effective than mere thought stopping itself. Controlled studies of this combined RET procedure have not yet been done, but I have some clinical evidence in its favor. So you can experiment with using it with your resistant clients.

Cognitive Distraction

Cognitive distraction is frequently used in RET to divert clients from anxiety and depression (Ellis, 1973, 1984d, in press-a, in press-e; Ellis & Abrahms, 1978; Ellis & Whiteley, 1979). Thus, clients may be shown how to relax (Jacobsen, 1942), how to meditate (Ellis, 1984f), how to do yoga exercises, and how to use other forms of distraction when they upset themselves and do not want to obsess about the things they upset themselves about or do not want to obsess about their feelings.

On the one hand, distraction is often not too useful with resistant clients because it only temporarily diverts them from their rebellious and defensive persistence with their disturbed behavior—and they therefore soon return to this behavior. On the other hand, severely disturbed and resistant clients who refuse to use some of the more elegant techniques of RET because of their abysmal low frustration tolerance may only tend to work with distraction methods (which they can easily learn and fairly easily apply). Therefore, when you encounter such clients you may decide to settle for some of the popular distraction techniques instead of urging these clients to apply more thoroughgoing methods that, if they used them, would give them more long-run benefits. Preferably, you can use both distraction techniques and more elegant disputational methods of RET—*if* you can induce clients to use both.

One particularly effective form of distraction that works well with resistant clients, if you can persuade them to use it, is the kind of vital absorbing interest that Robert Harper and I espouse in *A New Guide to Rational Living* (Ellis & Harper, 1975). Thus, if you can help them become absorbed in writing a book, in becoming an active member of a self-help group, or in volunteering to help others in some ongoing manner, they can sometimes find such a high degree of constructive enjoyment in this vital interest that it minimizes their tendency to become negatively addicted to alcoholism, drug taking, stealing, or other serious self-defeating behavior.

Cognitive distraction, then, has advantages and disadvantages when used with seriously disturbed, resistant clients. Employ it experimentally and try to tailor it to individual clients, in accordance with their observed tendencies to use or abuse it.

Use of Humor

Many resistant clients have little sense of humor, and that is precisely why they find it so hard to see how they keep defeating themselves and how absurd are their thoughts and behaviors. Some, however, in spite of their severe disturbance, do have a good sense of humor that you can use to interrupt and interfere with their resistance. Remember, in this regard, that emotional disabilities do not consist of taking things seriously and giving meaning to them—for that, Viktor Frankl (1966, 1975) has shown, is a healthy aspect of humans—but of taking them much *too* seriously. Properly used humor, therefore, shows how ridiculous and far-fetched iBs often are, and it can serve as an important antidote to giving *exaggerated* significance to the events of people's lives (Ellis, 1977b, 1977c, 1981a; Farrelly & Brandsma, 1977; Fay, 1978; Greenwald, 1984).

With many of my resistant clients, I highlight the irony of how they are thinking and acting against their own interests.

Thus, I kept showing one of my stubborn clients how ironic it was that she railed and ranted against cold weather, and thereby made herself suffer *more* when it was cold. I showed another of my resistant male clients that the more he angered himself about the inefficiencies created by some of the people with whom he was working, the less he was able to devote time and energy to correcting their inefficiencies.

I also frequently tell my resistant clients, "If the Martians ever come to visit us and they're really sane, they'll die laughing at us Earthians. For they'll see bright people like you vainly insisting that they absolutely can do something that they can't do—such as change the ways of their parents—while simultaneously insisting that they can't do something that they almost invariably can do—such as change themselves. The poor Martians probably won't be able to understand this and may well fly back to Mars convinced that humans are completely crazy!"

One of the main RET techniques that I created in 1975, when I gave a paper, "Fun as Psychotherapy" (Ellis, 1977b) at the American Psychological Association Convention in Washington, D.C., is the use of rational humorous songs. These songs are actually cognitive, emotive, and behavioral. Cognitively, they usually satirize and attack a major iB. Emotively, they are musical and rhythmical, since they consist of humorous lyrics to well-known popular songs, and they have a distinct evocative and dramatic impact. Behaviorally, they are designed to be sung again and again by disturbed individuals until they internalize their rational meaning and tend to automatically think and feel the way the song is oriented, so that they do not upset themselves seriously in the first place, or are fairly easily and quickly able to unupset themselves in the second place, once they find that they are anxious or depressed.

I have found that some of my most difficult clients, with whom many other RET methods failed to work for a long time, are able to use these rational-emotive humorous songs and to frequently jolt themselves out of severe awfulizing or horribilizing feelings. One of the most popular RET songs, for example, that you can use with clients with severe low frustration tolerance is this one:

WHINE, WHINE, WHINE!

(To the tune of the Yale Whiffenpoof Song
by Guy Scull—a Harvard man!)

I cannot have all of my wishes filled—
Whine, whine, whine!
I cannot have every frustration stilled—
Whine, whine, whine!
Life really owes me the things that I miss,
Fate has to grant me eternal bliss!
And since I must settle for less than this—
Whine, whine, whine!

(Lyrics by Albert Ellis, copyrighted 1977 by the
Institute for Rational-Emotive Therapy)

Another anti-low frustration tolerance song is this one:

BEAUTIFUL HANGUP

(To the tune of "Beautiful Dreamer"
by Stephen Foster)

Beautiful hangup, why should we part
When we have shared our whole lives from the start?
We are so used to taking one course
Oh, what a crime it would be to divorce!
Beautiful hangup, don't go away!
Who will befriend me if you do not stay?
Though you still make me look like a jerk,
Living without you would take so much work!
Living without you would take too much work!

(Lyrics by Albert Ellis, copyrighted 1980 by the
Institute for Rational-Emotive Therapy).

One of the anti-perfectionist RET humorous songs is this one:

PERFECT RATIONALITY

(To the tune of "Funiculi, Funicula" by Luigi Denza)

Some think the world must have a right direction
And so do I! And so do I!

Some think that, with the slightest imperfection
They can't get by—and so do I!
For I, I have to prove I'm superhuman,
And better far than people are!
To show I have miraculous acumen—
And always rate among the Great!
Perfect, perfect rationality
Is, of course, the only thing for me!
How can I ever think of being
If I must live fallibly?
Rationality must be a perfect thing for me!

(Lyrics by Albert Ellis, copyrighted 1977 by the
Institute for Rational-Emotive Therapy)

One of the RET anti-depression songs that often goes over
well with difficult clients is this one:

I'M DEPRESSED, DEPRESSED!
(To the tune of "The Band Played On" by Charles B. Ward)

When anything slightly goes wrong with the world,
I'm depressed, depressed!
When any mild hassle before me is hurled, I
feel most distressed!
When life isn't fated to be consecrated, I can't
tolerate it at all!
When anything slightly goes wrong with the world,
I just bawl, bawl, bawl!

(Lyrics by Albert Ellis, copyrighted 1980 by the
Institute for Rational-Emotive Therapy)

An RET song that helps people be more realistic about
themselves and others is this one:

GLORY, GLORY HALLELUJAH!
(To the tune of "The Battle Hymn of the Republic")

Mine eyes have seen the glory of relationships
that glow
And then falter by the wayside as love passions
come—and go!

I've heard of great romances where there is no
        slightest lull—
But I am skeptical!

Glory, glory hallelujah! People love you till
        they screw ya!
If you'd cushion how they do ya, then don't
        expect they won't!
Those who say they madly love you often put all
        else above you
And at times they push and shove you!—So don't
        expect they won't!

(Lyrics by Albert Ellis, copyrighted 1977 by the
Institute for Rational-Emotive Therapy)

A song that helps difficult clients zero in on their secondary
symptom (their depression about their depression) is:

WHEN I AM SO BLUE

(To the tune of Johann Strauss,
"The Beautiful Blue Danube")

When I am so blue, so blue, so blue
I sit and I stew, I stew, I stew!
I deem it so awfully horrible
That my life is rough and scarrable!
Whenever my blues are verified,
I make myself doubly terrified,
For I never choose to refuse
To be blue about my blues!

(Lyrics by Albert Ellis, copyrighted 1980 by the
Institute for Rational-Emotive Therapy)

An RET humorous song to combat the dire need for approval (or what I often call love slobbism) as well as anger is:

LOVE ME, LOVE ME, ONLY ME!

(To the tune of "Yankee Doodle")

Love me, love me, only me or I'll die without you!
Make your love a guarantee, so I can never doubt
        you!

> *Love me, love me totally; really, really try, dear;*
> *But if you must rely on me, I'll hate you till I*
> *die, dear!*
> *Love me, love me all the time, thoroughly and*
> *wholly;*
> *Love turns into slushy slime 'less you love me*
> *solely!*
> *Love me with great tenderness, with no ifs or*
> *buts, dear:*
> *For if you love me somewhat less I'll hate your*
> *goddamned guts, dear!*

(Lyrics by Albert Ellis, copyrighted 1977 by the
Institute for Rational-Emotive Therapy)

Another shame-attacking and anti-low frustration tolerance
rational-emotive humorous song for use with resistant clients,
and one that can be used to combat resistance to working at
therapy, is this one:

I WISH I WERE NOT CRAZY!
(To the tune of "Dixie" by Dan Emmett)

> *Oh, I wish I were really put together—*
> *Smooth and fine as patent leather!*
> *Oh, how great to be rated innately sedate!*
> *But I'm afraid that I was fated*
> *To be rather aberrated—*
> *Oh, how sad to be mad as my Mom and my Dad!*
>
> *Oh, I wish I were not crazy! Hooray, hooray!*
> *I wish my mind were less inclined*
> *To be the kind that's hazy!*
> *I could agree to try to be less crazy;*
> *But I, alas, am just too goddamned lazy!*

(Lyrics by Albert Ellis, copyrighted 1977 by the
Institute for Rational-Emotive Therapy)

Paradoxical Intention

With highly resistant and negativistic clients—as Erikson (Erikson & Rossi, 1979), Frankl (1960, 1975), Haley (1963), and others
have shown—paradoxical intention sometimes works and is

therefore a potentially effective cognitive method of rational-emotive and cognitive-behavioral therapy (Ellis & Whiteley, 1979). Thus, you can tell depressed clients to loudly wail and moan about everything that occurs in their lives. Or you can have highly anxious people take the assignment of only allowing themselves to worry from 8:00 to 8:15 A.M. every day. Or you can insist that resistant clients refuse to do *anything* you tell them to do—such as refuse to come on time for their sessions and refuse to do any homework assignments. Perversely, resisters may then stop resisting. But don't count on this, since paradoxical intention is a shocking but limited method that tends to work only occasionally and under special conditions.

Suggestion and Hypnosis

You may use strong suggestion or hypnosis with some difficult clients even though these sometimes prove to be inelegant techniques that may interfere with clients' independent thinking. Resistant clients who *believe* that hypnosis works may allow themselves to change with hypnotic methods when they would not allow themselves to do so without hypnosis. RET has included hypnosis methods from its inception (Ellis, 1958b, 1962, in press-c); and many therapists who use RET have combined it with hypnotic procedures (Araoz, 1982; Golden, 1983a, 1983b; Stanton, 1977; Tosi & Eshbaugh, 1978; Tosi & Henderson, 1983; Tosi & Marzella, 1977; Tosi & Reardon, 1976).

The special method which I usually use to combine RET with hypnosis involves first putting clients in a light trance or state of relaxation, employing a modification of Jacobsen's (1942) method, and then giving them strong suggestions to use RET in their regular posthypnotic life. I give the details of this method in an article, "The Use of Hypnosis With Rational-Emotive Therapy (RET)," in Dowd and Healy's book, *Case Studies in Hypnotherapy* (Ellis, in press-c). In this article, I describe the case of a 33-year-old unmarried borderline female who had a 20-year history of being severely anxious about her school, work, and love and sex performances, and who became classically anxious about her anxiety, had a severe case of phrenophobia, and was sure that she would end up as a bag lady without any friends, lovers, or money. After having 13 sessions with this severely anxious woman, I saw that at times she used the main message of RET—that you largely feel the way you think—and notably decreased her feelings about falling in love, about sex, and about business. But a few weeks later she would fall back again and make herself exceptionally upset—especially about her anxiety itself. After hearing that one of her friends was helped to stop smoking by hypnotherapy, she asked me if I used it along with RET and I said that I sometimes did, but that I often didn't encourage clients to resort to it because they thought of it as a form of magic and used it instead of working at the RET. I agreed, however, to try it with her and used it once, but (as I usually do when I hypnotize people) made a recording of the session and asked her to listen to it every day for at least 30 days thereafter.

In the first part of the session, I put this client in a light trance state with Jacobsen's relaxation technique. Then I continued as follows:

> *You're only focusing on my voice and you're going to listen carefully to what I'm telling you. You're going to remember everything I tell you. And after you awake from this relaxed, hypnotic state, you're going to feel very good. Because you're going to remember everything and use what you hear—use it for you. Use it to put away all your anxiety and all your anxiety about your anxiety. You're going to remember what I tell you and use it every day. Whenever you feel anxious about anything, you're going to remember what I'm telling you now, in this relaxed state, and you're going to fully focus on it, concentrate on it very well, and do exactly what we're talking about—relax and get rid of your anxiety, relax and get rid of your anxiety.*

> *Whenever you get anxious about anything, you're going to realize that the reason you're anxious is because you are saying to yourself, telling yourself, "I must succeed! I must succeed! I must do this, or I must not do that!" You will clearly see and fully accept that your anxiety comes from your self-statements. It doesn't come from without. It doesn't come from other people. You make yourself anxious, by demanding that something must go well or must not exist. It's your demand that makes you anxious. It's you and your self-talk; and therefore you control it and you can change it.*

> *You're going to realize, "I make myself anxious. I don't have to keep making myself anxious, if I give up my demands, my musts, my shoulds, my oughts. If I really accept what is, accept things the way they are, then I won't be anxious. I can make myself unanxious and tense by giving up my musts, by relaxing—by wanting and wishing for things, but not needing, not insisting, not demanding, not musturbating about them."*

You're going to keep telling yourself, "I can ask for things, I can wish. But I do not need what I want; I never need what I want! There is nothing I must have; and there is nothing I must avoid, including my anxiety. I'd like to get rid of this anxiety. I can get rid of it. I'm going to get rid of it. But if I tell myself 'I must not be anxious! I must not be anxious! I must be unanxious!' then I'll be anxious.

"Nothing will kill me. Anxiety won't kill me. Lack of sex won't kill me. There are lots of unpleasant things in the world, that I don't like, but I can stand them; I don't have to get rid of them. If I'm anxious, I'm anxious—too damn bad! Because I control my emotional destiny—as long as I don't feel that I have to do anything, that I have to succeed at anything. That's what destroys me—the idea that I have to be sexy or I have to succeed at sex. Or that I have to get rid of my anxiety." In your regular life, after listening to this tape many times, you're going to think and to keep thinking these things. Whenever you're anxious, you'll look at what you're doing to make yourself anxious, and you'll give up your demands, and your musts. You'll dispute your ideas that, "I must do well! I must get people to like me! They must not criticize me! It's terrible when they criticize me!" You'll keep asking yourself, "Why must I do well? Why do I have to be a great sex partner? It would be nice if people liked me, but they don't have to. I do not need their approval. If they criticize me, if they blame me, or they think I'm too sexy or too little sexy, too damn bad! I do not need their approval. I'd like it, but I don't need it. I'd also like to be unanxious but there's no reason why I must be. Yes, there's no reason why I must be. It's just preferable. None of these things I fail at are going to kill me.

"And when I die, as I eventually will, so I die! Death is not horrible. It's a state of no feeling. It's exactly the same state as I was in before I was born. I won't feel anything. So I certainly need not be afraid of that!

"And even if I get very anxious and go crazy, that too isn't terrible. If I tell myself, 'I must not go crazy! I must not go crazy!' then I'll make myself crazy! But even if I'm crazy, so I'm crazy! I can live with it even if I'm in a mental hospital. I can live and not depress myself about it. Nothing is terrible—even when people don't like me, even when I'm acting stupidly, even when I'm very anxious! Nothing is terrible! I can stand it! It's only a pain in the ass!"

Now this is what you're going to think in your everyday life. Whenever you get anxious about anything, you're going to see what you're anxious about, you're going to realize that you are demanding something, saying, "It must be so! I must get well! I must not do the wrong thing! I must not be anxious!" And you're going to stop and say, "You know—I don't need that nonsense. If these things happen, they happen. It's not the end of the world! I'd like to be unanxious, I'd like to get along with people, I'd like to have good sex. But if I don't, I don't! Tough! It's not the end of everything. I can always be a happy human in spite of failures and hassles—if I don't demand, if I don't insist, if I don't say, 'I must, I must!' Musts are crazy. My desires are all right. But,

again, I don't need what I want!" Now this is what you're going to keep
working at in your everyday life.

You're going to keep using your head, your thinking ability, to focus, to
concentrate on ridding yourself of your anxiety—just as you're listening and
concentrating right now. Your concentration will get better and better. You're
going to be more and more in control of your thoughts and your feelings. You will
keep realizing that you create your anxiety, you make yourself upset, and you
don't have to, you never have to keep doing so. You can always give your anxiety
up. You can always change. You can always relax, and relax, and relax, and not
take anyone, not take anything too seriously.

My client used the recording of her hypnotic RET session
once or twice a day for the next 45 days and reported a significant decrease in her anxiety level, especially in her anxiety about
her anxiety. She stopped being phrenophobic, convinced herself
that if she had a breakdown and went to the mental hospital it
would be highly inconvenient but not horrible or shameful, and
then hardly thought at all about going crazy. When she did, she
was able to feel comfortable within a few minutes by strongly
telling herself, "So I'll be crazy. Tough! I'm sure I won't stay that
way very long—and if I do, that will just be tougher. But not
shameful! No matter how crazy I am, I'll never be a turd for
being that way!"

If you, then, know how to do hypnosis and want to combine
it with RET, you can consider using the way I used it with this
client. Or you can use other forms of hypnosis combined with
RET as described in the writings, cited above, of Araoz, Golden,
Stanton, and Tosi and his associates.

Philosophy of Effort

The usual practice of RET is to explain to clients, right at the
beginning of therapy, that they have enormous self-actualization
powers (as well as self-defeating tendencies), and that with hard
work and practice they will be able to fulfill these powers (Ellis,
1962; Grieger & Boyd, 1980; Grieger & Grieger, 1982; Walen,
DiGiuseppe & Wessler, 1980; Wessler & Wessler, 1980). Clients
are also shown that they can easily fall back to old dysfunctional
patterns of behavior and that they therefore had better persistently keep monitoring themselves and keep working to change.

With resistant clients this realistic message is often repeated with the aim of both prophylaxis and cure. A favorite RET slogan is: "There's rarely any gain without pain!" This philosophy is steadily promulgated to combat the low frustration tolerance of resisters (Ellis, 1977d, 1979a, 1979b, 1980a).

Working with Clients' Expectancies

As Meichenbaum and Gilmore (1982) have shown, clients bring cognitive expectancies to therapy and may see what is helping in their sessions with the therapist as disconfirming these expectancies. Consequently, they may resist changing themselves. If so, you can accurately and emphatically perceive and share your clients' expectancies, make sense out of their unproductive resistant behavior, and thereby help them overcome resistance. Using RET, you might well go one step further and, as you help your clients explore and understand the reasons for their resistance (and the iBs that often underlie this resistance), you can actively push, encourage, and persuade them to surrender their persistent ideas and behaviors (Ellis, 1979b, in press-a; Ellis & Whiteley, 1979).

Irrational Beliefs Underlying Primary and Secondary Resistance

Clients frequently have both primary and secondary resistance. Primary resistance stems largely from their three main musts: (1) "I *must* change myself quickly and easily and I'm an incompetent person if I don't!" (2) "You *must* not force me to change, and I'll fight you to death if you do!" (3) "Conditions *must* make it easy for me to change, and I won't try to help myself if they don't!"

Once humans resist changing themselves for any of these three reasons, they sometimes *see* that they resist and have another set of iBs about this resistance, such as: (1) "I *must* not incompetently resist change and I'm a pretty worthless person if I do!" (2) "I *must* not hostilely or rebelliously resist change and it's *awful* if I do!" (3) "I *must* not have a low frustration tolerance that makes me resist change, and I can't stand it if I do!" Their

secondary disturbances—that is, their guilt or shame *about* resisting—tend to tie up their time and energy and incite *increased*
resistance. In RET, therefore, we look for and try to eliminate
secondary as well as primary resistances: we do so by showing
clients their primary and secondary iBs and by Disputing both
these sets of iBs just as we would Dispute any other irrational
Beliefs. By helping them to first undo their disturbances *about*
their resistance, we show them how to remove these secondary
problems and then how to get back to changing the ideas and
feelings that constitute the primary resistance.

Disputing Irrational Beliefs Underlying Avoidance of Responsibility

Resistance may sometimes stem from clients' trying to avoid
responsibility for change and from their deliberately (though
perhaps unconsciously) fighting the therapist's efforts to help
them change. This form of childish rebelliousness can arise from
ego irrationalities ("I must thwart my therapist and 'win out' to
show what a strong independent person I am.") or from low
frustration tolerance irrationalities ("I must not have to work too
hard at therapy, because if I assume full responsibility for changing myself life becomes too rough and unsatisfying."). When
avoidance of responsibility and concomitant rebellion against the
therapist or against working at therapy result in resistance, RET
tries to show clients the iBs behind this kind of avoidance and
rebellion and it teaches them how to combat and surrender these
iBs.

Use of Quick and Active Disputation

Although RET therapists may sometimes help create resistance
by actively and quickly Disputing their clients' iBs, they may also,
by this "poor" technique, promptly smoke out clients' resistances,
see exactly what kind of DCs (difficult customers) these clients
are, and promote more efficient and effective therapy methods.
Active Disputing, though risky, may uncover resistances rapidly,
save therapists and clients considerable time and effort, lead to

vigorous countermeasures by the therapist, and sometimes lead to a suitable quick (and inexpensive!) end to therapy.

Some cognitive-behavior therapists—e.g., Meichenbaum and Gilmore (1982)—recommend that resistance be overcome by graduating the change process into manageable steps and by structuring therapeutic intervention so that the therapist maximizes the likelihood of success at each stage. This will sometimes work, but also has its dangers with those who resist because of abysmal LFT. For with these individuals gradualism may easily *feed* their LFT and help them believe that it is *too* hard for them to change and that they *must* do so in a slow, gradual manner (Ellis, 1983a).

Disputing Impossibility of Changing

When clients contend that they *can't* change, RET can show them that this is an unrealistic, antiempirical view not supported by any facts (which merely show that *it is difficult* for them to change). But RET therapists cannot only use this realistic, scientific refutation, but also employ the more elegant anti*mus*turbatory form of Disputing. For clients usually tell themselves, "I can't change," because they start with the basic proposition, "I *must* have an ability to change quickly and easily, and I'm incompetent and pretty worthless if I don't do what I *must*." RET Disputes this *mus*turbatory, absolutistic thinking by showing them that they *never* have to change (though changing would be highly desirable) and that they are *people who act incompetently* rather than *incompetent people*. This Disputing of the idea, "I can't change" may be more profound and more elegant than the simple antiempirical Disputing of Beck (1976), R. Lazarus (1966), Meichenbaum (1977), Maultsby (1975), and other proponents of CBT.

Helping Clients Gain Emotional Insight

RET often shows resistant clients that they falsely believe they are working hard to improve and to overcome their own resistance, when they really aren't. Thus, they frequently say, "I see that I am telling myself that therapy should be easy, and I see that that is wrong." They then mistakenly think that because they have *seen* how they are resisting and have *seen* the error of their ways, they have worked at changing this error and thereby *overcome* their resistance. But they have usually done nothing of the sort. Their "insight" has not been used to help them *fight* the idea that therapy should be easy. Using RET, you can now show them that they'd better see and fight this idea—that is, Dispute it by asking themselves, "*Why* should therapy be easy," and by vigorously answering, "There's *no* damned reason it should be! It often is—and *should* be—hard. Because that's the way it is—*hard!*"

RET tries to distinguish clearly between so-called intellectual and emotional insight (Ellis, 1963). Resistant clients often say, "I have intellectual insight into my hating myself but this does me no good, since I still can't stop this self-hatred. What I need is emotional insight." What these clients mean is that they see that they hate themselves and may even see the irrational self-statements they make to bring about this feeling (e.g., "I must always succeed at important tasks and I am worthless when I don't"), but they do not know how to change their iBs or they know how to change them but refuse to do the *persistent* and *strong* Disputing that is required to give them up.

In RET we try to show clients—particularly resistant ones— three main kinds of insight:

Insight No. 1. The understanding that they mainly disturb themselves rather than get upset by external conditions and events.

Insight No. 2. The understanding that no matter when they first started to upset themselves (usually in childhood) and no matter what events contributed to their early *disturbance*, they *now*, in the present, continue to make themselves upset by *still* strongly subscribing to iBs similar to those they held previously. And they now keep their old disturbance alive by continually reindoctrinating themselves with these iBs.

Insight No. 3. Since people are born with the tendency to accept iBs from others and to create many of their own; since they consciously and unconsciously reinstill these iBs in themselves from early childhood onward; and since they easily, automatically, and habitually actualize these ideas in their feelings and actions and thereby powerfully reinforce them over long periods of time; there is usually no simple, fast, easy, and complete way to change them. Only considerable work and practice—yes, *work and practice*—to challenge and Dispute these iBs, and only long, concerted *action* that contradicts the behavioral patterns which accompany them will be likely to minimize or extirpate them (Ellis, 1962, in press-a).

RET, then, teaches clients that insights No. 1 and 2 are important but not sufficient for profound philosophic and behavioral change; and that they had better progress to the most important insight of all—Insight No. 3.

More specifically RET shows resistant clients who say that they have intellectual insight into their symptom (such as self-hating) but can't give it up because they don't have emotional insight, that they usually only have Insight No. 1—and even that, often, only partially. Thus, a young woman may say, "I see that I hate myself," but may not see what she is irrationally believing to create her self-hatred (e.g., "Because I am not as competent as I *must* be, I am a thoroughly *inadequate person*"). Even when she sees what she is believing to create her self-hatred, she has only achieved Insight No. 1, and she may falsely believe that she obtained her self-hating belief from her parents and *that* is why she now hates herself.

In RET, we would therefore help her achieve Insight No. 2— "No matter how I got the iB that I *should* be more competent and am an *inadequate person* if I'm not, *I* now continue to indoctrinate myself with it so that *I* am fully responsible for believing it today; and therefore *I* had better give it up."

RET doesn't stop there—since she still might be left with only mild or "intellectual" insight—but pushes her on to Insight No. 3: "Since *I* keep actively believing that I *should* be more competent and am an inadequate person if I'm not, and since *I* tend to keep recreating and newly inventing similar iBs (because it is my basic nature to do so), I had better keep steadily and forcefully *working and practicing*—yes, keep *working and practicing*— until I no longer believe this. For mainly by continually disputing and challenging this belief and by *forcing myself* to keep acting against it will I be able to finally give it up and replace it with rBs and effective behaviors."

Insight No. 3, plus the determination to act on this level of understanding, is what RET calls "emotional" insight or "will-power." And it is this kind of cognitive restructuring or profound philosophic change which RET particularly employs with resistant clients. (Also see Chapter 5.)

Bibliotherapy and Audiotherapy

RET employs bibliotherapy with resistant clients and encourages them to read RET-oriented pamphlets and books—such as *Reason and Emotion in Psychotherapy* (Ellis, 1962), *A New Guide to Rational Living* (Ellis & Harper, 1975), *Feeling Good* (Burns, 1980), *Humanistic Psychotherapy: The Rational-Emotive Approach* (Ellis, 1973), *A Guide to Personal Happiness* (Ellis & Becker, 1982), *I Can If I Want To* (Lazarus & Fay, 1975), and *Overcoming Procrastination* (Ellis & Knaus, 1977). RET practitioners also give a good many talks, courses, workshops, marathons, and intensives that help clients understand the theory and use the techniques of RET. I have especially found that some RET cassette recordings, films, and TV cassettes are useful with resistant clients who are urged to listen to them many times until the presentations on these materials sink in. Notably useful in this respect are the cassette recordings, *Conquering the Dire Need for Love* (Ellis, 1977e), *Conquering Low Frustration Tolerance* (Ellis, 1977d), *Overcoming Procrastination* (Knaus, 1974), *I'd Like to Stop, But . . .* (Ellis, 1974b), *Self-Hypnosis: The Rational-Emotive Approach* (Golden, 1983b), *Twenty-one Ways to Stop Worrying* (Ellis, 1972b), and *How to Stubbornly Refuse to be Ashamed of Anything* (Ellis, 1972c).

Imaging Methods

One of the main modes of human cognition is imagery, and RET frequently employs imaging methods. These are sometimes especially useful with resistant clients, since some of them resist because they see and feel things more incisively through pictorial than through verbal means (Coué, 1923; A. Lazarus, 1978, 1981). Consequently, when they block on or find difficulty with verbal self-statements and philosophic disputing of iBs, they can sometimes be reached more effectively by imagery methods. To this end, RET—following Coué (1923) and a host of his disciples—can teach resisters to use positive imagery to imagine themselves doing things that they negatively contend that they can't do (e.g., successfully giving a public talk); and it can help them imagine bearing frustrating conditions that they normally think they absolutely can't bear. Also, as noted in the next chapter, RET frequently employs Maultsby's technique of rational-emotive imagery (Maultsby, 1975, 1984; Maultsby & Ellis, 1974), by which resistant (and other) clients are shown how to imagine one of the worst things that could happen to them, to implode their disturbed feelings about this happening, and then to work at changing these to more appropriate negative feelings.

Modeling Techniques

Bandura (1969, 1977) pioneered in showing how modeling can be used to help disturbed individuals; and RET has always used such methods (Ellis, 1962, 1971, 1973, in press-a; Ellis & Abrahms, 1978; Ellis & Whiteley, 1979). In the case of resistant and difficult clients, RET practitioners not only teach them how to unconditionally and fully accept themselves no matter how badly or incompetently they behave but they also model this kind of acceptance by displaying firm kindness to these clients and showing by their attitudes and demeanor (as well as their words) that they can fully accept such clients even when they fail to do their homework, and when they otherwise stubbornly resist the therapist's efforts (Ellis, 1962, 1973, in press-a; Ellis & Whiteley, 1979). RET also sponsors public workshops—such as my famous Friday-night workshops that are given regularly at the Institute for Rational-Emotive Therapy in New York—where live demonstrations of RET are given for large audiences, so that the members of the audience can see exactly how RET is done and can model their own self-help procedures after this model. Resistant clients who serve as volunteer demonstratees at these workshops are often particularly helped by the public session they have with me (or other RET therapists) and by the feedback and the comments they receive from 15 to 20 members of the audience.

Recorded Playback of Therapy Sessions

Carl Rogers (1942) pioneered in using recordings of therapy sessions to help therapists understand exactly what they are doing and how to improve their techniques. RET, beginning in 1959, pioneered the use of audiotapes for two other purposes: (1) To show therapists throughout the world exactly how RET is done, so that they can model their own use of it after the practices of its originator and other RET practitioners (Dryden, 1981; Ellis, 1959c, 1966a, 1966b; Elkin, Ellis & Edelstein, 1974; Wessler & Ellis, 1980). (2) To give clients recordings of their own sessions so that they can listen to them several times and thereby hear and internalize some of the therapeutic messages that they would otherwise miss or forget. This second use of recordings, which also can be done with video equipment if this is available, has been found very useful with resident clients, since if they are given homework assignments of listening to their own taped sessions (and sometimes of the tape sessions of others), they often get across to themselves some of the elements of RET that they otherwise easily miss (Ellis, 1979b, in press-a; Ellis & Abrahms, 1978; Ellis & Whiteley, 1979). One of my borderline clients, for example, who argued vigorously against almost every point I made about his needlessly upsetting himself, often accepted these same points when he listened to a cassette recording of each session several times during the week following this session.

The Use of Cognitive Homework

RET has always specialized in the use of activity homework assignments, because my early experiments on myself, when I was 19 years old (and not even interested in becoming a psychologist or psychotherapist) largely consisted of forcing myself to do the things I was afraid of doing (especially, public speaking and encountering females in whom I was sexually interested), as well as convincing myself that failing at important tasks and being rejected by others for failing was hardly the end of the world and that I could still survive and be happy (Ellis, 1972g, 1983d). But RET has also always used cognitive homework, because I realized, as I first began to use it, that even if people begin to dispute and change their iBs and wind up by creating for themselves a new effective philosophy of everyday living, they easily fall back to the old irrational ideas that they have held from early childhood onward, and they thereby vitiate their therapeutic progress. This seems to be especially true for resistant clients— who often agree, from the start, with the rBs that their therapist is helping them arrive at and think through, but who very frequently then fall back to their old irrational thinking and seriously disturb themselves again.

RET therefore almost always employs some precise, repetitive forms of cognitive homework, including: (1) having clients write down and look for their iBs whenever they see that they are emotionally disturbed; (2) encouraging them to actively dispute these iBs, both in their heads and on paper; (3) getting them to make diaries or other records of their common dysfunctional thoughts, feelings, and behaviors; and (4) using various kinds of rational self-help forms to dispute their iBs until they significantly change them and wind up with appropriate feelings and behaviors (Burns, 1980; Ellis, 1969b, 1970b, 1974a; Ellis & Harper, 1975; Maultsby, 1971a, 1975, 1984; Sichel & Ellis, 1984). Because cognitive homework is as much an active behavioral as a thinking technique, I shall discuss it in more detail in Chapter 6.

As can be seen from the material just presented, RET cognitive methods, when carefully selected and employed with resistant and difficult clients, can often be effective. In the next chapter I shall consider in more detail some of the main emotive procedures that RET practitioners can use with resisters.

4
Emotive Techniques of Overcoming Resistance

The previous chapters on RET approaches to overcoming resistance have mainly considered RET's cognitive methods. This chapter will summarize some of RET's main emotive methods and will particularly apply them to resistant clients.

Although some critics of RET assume that it was almost entirely cognitive when I first created it in 1955 and that it later jumped on the emotive and behavioral bandwagons that started rolling in the 1960s, this is not true. RET has always been what Schwartz (1982) calls a unified-interaction approach to psychotherapy as well as what A. Lazarus (1981) calls a multimodal form of therapy that includes cognitive, emotive, and behavioral techniques and that rarely omits any of these modalities when used with an average client. Multimodal methods are an integral part of RET because, as stated in my first presentation at the American Psychological Association meetings in Chicago in 1956 (Ellis, 1958a) and as repeated in Chapter 2 of my seminal book, *Reason and Emotion in Psychotherapy* (Ellis, 1962), RET theorizes that "human thinking and emotion are *not* two disparate or different processes, but that they significantly overlap and are in some respects, for all practical purposes, essentially the same thing. Like the two other basic life processes, sensing and moving, they are integrally integrated and never can be seen wholly apart from each other. . . . Instead, then, of saying 'Smith thinks about this problem,' we should more accurately say that 'Smith senses-moves-feels-THINKS about this problem'" (Ellis, 1962, pp. 38–39).

In Chapter 2 of *Reason and Emotion in Psychotherapy*, I also make clear: that emotional disturbances, such as anxiety and hostility, largely *but not competely* stem from distorted perceptions and irrational thinking; that many emotive methods—such as catharsis and dealing with the relationships between the therapist and client—help to change clients' unrealistic cognitions; that not only straight thinking but also effective *action* are required to overcome anxiety, depression, and other disturbed feelings; and that RET follows several ancient philosophers—especially Zeno of Citium, Epictetus, and Marcus Aurelius—who clearly noted interrelationships among cognitions, emotions, and behaviors.

RET, then, stresses cognitive or philosophizing methods of therapy more than virtually all the other major cognitive therapies—including those of Adler (1927/1968), Beck (1976), Dubois (1907), Goldfried and Davison (1976), Guidano and Liotti (1983), Kelly (1955), Mahoney (1974), Meichenbaum (1977), and Raimy (1975). But it also, as its very name shows, is highly emotive, evocative, and dramatic (Ellis, 1962, 1969a, 1971, 1972c, 1973, 1977a, 1977b, 1979b, in press-a; Ellis & Abrahms, 1978; Ellis & Becker, 1982; Ellis & Grieger, 1977; Ellis & Harper, 1975; Ellis & Whiteley, 1979). In regard to overcoming resistance, RET frequently employs the following emotive methods:

Unconditional Acceptance of Clients

RET gives *full* or *unconditional* acceptance to resistant clients— meaning that it fully accepts them as humans no matter how execrable or self-defeating their behavior is (Ellis, 1962, 1972a; Miller, 1983). If you use RET, you can do this *even* with difficult

customers—including psychotics, borderlines, and sociopaths—
by showing them that you never damn or condemn them, even
when they act badly in therapy. You can strongly show them (as
noted previously in this book) that their behavior is immoral or
foolish but that *they* are never *rotten people* or *total fools*. This kind of
RET-favored unconditional acceptance sets the stage and permits
you to get after resistant clients very strongly because they
realize that you still fully accept *them* (Ellis, 1984b, 1984j).

One of my 35-year-old male clients, a drug addict and borderline personality, was quite obnoxious to his wife and children
and equally annoying as a client. He broke appointments without
due advance notice, was very delinquent in paying the Institute's
clinic, and continually plagued me about how little I was helping
him and how bad a therapist I was. Though I firmly kept getting
after him about his drug taking and his annoying behavior, I was
virtually never angry at him and steadily showed him that I felt
that he could change and improve even when he insisted that he
was hopeless. After a year and a half of his behaving badly in
therapy and in his outside life, he finally saw that I fully accepted
him, though not his poor behavior, and his attitude toward me
completely changed. He acknowledged his failings, stopped putting himself down, withdrew from all drugs cold turkey, worked
hard to make some extra money to pay off his debt to the
Institute, and during the last ten years has given away about a
hundred copies of *A New Guide to Rational Living* (Ellis & Harper,
1975) and referred about 30 people to the Institute for therapy
and workshops. As he said during one of his final sessions with
me,

> I know that you have always disliked many of the things I do but I have always
> been impressed with your lack of hostility and your great faith in me. I am sure
> that, if I continue to behave the way I have done in the past, you would never want
> to be anything like a friend. But you have really proved to me, by your manner
> and tone, that you follow the philosophy of acceptance that you keep writing
> about in your books.

In this case, at least, my *accepting* this difficult client, in spite of his
obnoxious behavior, finally paid off.

Encouragement

RET, along with Adlerian individual psychology, endorses active encouragement of clients, and particularly of those who are resistant (Ellis, in press-a; Ellis & Abrahms, 1978; Losoncy, 1980). As an RET practitioner, you can show resisters that you have real faith in their ability to change and that you know and *feel* that they can do so. Coaching and pushing clients to change are a regular part of RET and are especially useful for working with difficult individuals.

With the 35-year-old drug addict I mentioned in the previous section of this chapter, I was very encouraging, even though he kept falling back to drugs and to negativistic behavior. While almost everyone in his community kept telling him what a hopeless louse he was, I showed him that it was very hard for him to change but that he could *still* do it and could raise himself by his boot-straps—which he finally virtually did.

Strong Language

Strong, and sometimes "obscene" language is often used in RET—especially with delinquents and sociopaths. When you employ such language, your clients may see that you are not pro-authority and not too conventional, and therefore they are likely to be less resistant. Other difficult clients are sometimes jolted or jarred by direct, powerful language and thereby moved to change. They often reveal their "shameful" thoughts, feelings, and behaviors more quickly and fully, and are again helped to give these up. As shown in more detail in Chapter 5, such clients speak to themselves powerfully and directly and can often be reached when you employ the kind of self-talk they themselves employ.

One of the most successful of the rational humorous songs that I use with resistant clients and that I get them to sing over and over to themselves is "Maybe I'll Move My Ass," sung to the tune of Charles K. Harris' "After the Ball":

> *After you make things easy and you provide*
> *the gas;*
> *After you squeeze and please me, maybe*
> *I'll move my ass!*
> *Just make life soft and breezy, fill it*
> *with sassafras!*
> *And possibly, if things are easy, I'll*
> *move my ass!*

An even more forceful rational humorous song that I effectively employ with D.C.'s (difficult customers) is this "obscene" ditty:

I AM JUST A FUCKING BABY!

(To, Kerry Mills' "Meet Me in St. Louis, Louis")

> *I am just a fucking baby, drooling*
> *everywhere!*
> *How can my poor life OKAY be if you*
> *do not care?*
> *If you tell me No or Maybe,*
> *You will quarter me and slay me!*
> *For I am just a fucking baby—*
> *Please take care, take care!*

RET, however, does not necessarily include strong or obscene language and can be effectively done, even with resistant clients, without it (Johnson, 1980; Wessler, 1982).

Group Methods of RET

RET group therapy is particularly effective with many resistant clients because in group they have their childish and rigid ideas disputed by several other group members, and not merely by one therapist, and they are therefore more likely to surrender them. They also frequently observe other group members effectively using RET methods and consequently are encouraged to use these themselves. When the group gives them homework assignments they are also more likely to perform them than if these are given by an individual therapist (Ellis, 1973, 1982a).

One of the most difficult clients I have ever had was a 42-year-old manic-depressive male who had been continually in therapy since the age of 20 and had been hospitalized four times. Although a brilliant professor of physics, he had never been reached by his previous therapists and still enraged and depressed himself almost every day about trivial frustrations—such as his students coming late to class or not turning in their assignments. I reached him more than all his previous therapists by using very vigorous RET disputing of his demands to have everything go well in school and by showing him that he had damned well accept Murphy's law—"Anything that can be fucked up, will be!"—or else suffer. But he edited out many of my arguments by insisting that I was only a therapist paid to help him and that therefore I would naturally try to argue against his irrational Beliefs (iBs). I finally, against his initial desire, induced him to join one of my regular therapy groups. Only after he had been in three of these groups (because his available nights kept changing so that he was forced to switch to a new group), and only after he saw that all the members of the group argued just as vigorously against his nonsense as I did, was he able to accept some of the scientific principles of RET disputation and to surrender his rage-creating and depression-producing iBs.

Pleasurable Pursuits

Many resistant clients are anhedonic (Ellis, 1962; Meehl, 1962) and have difficulty enjoying themselves in normal ways. You can sometimes help such clients by suggesting constructive pleasures (e.g., sports, massage, acting, or music) and by showing them how to engage in such activities. A list of potential pleasures is included in *A Guide to Personal Happiness* (Ellis & Becker, 1982).

I have seen literally scores of clients, who were anhedonic and/or depressed and who resisted therapy for a long period of time, who mainly seemed to change because I finally helped them to commit themselves to a vital absorbing interest (Ellis & Harper, 1975), such as a social or political cause, writing a book, or becoming an auxiliary therapist. Self-help groups like Alcoholics Anonymous and religious groups like the Zen Buddhists are able at times to help some exceptionally disturbed individuals, partly because they not only provide these people with a new philosophy of life but also provide them with a cause to devote themselves to and to fight for. If you can help your difficult clients to become similarly absorbed, you can sometimes appreciably help them.

Emotive Confrontations

Emotive confronting can be used to jolt and move recalcitrant clients. RET practitioners can use powerful evocative confrontation, such as that used by Casriel (1974) and Mowrer (1964). As shown in Chapter 5, sometimes only by "breaking down" some sociopaths and other resistant clients in these highly confronting ways is their resistance likely to be eliminated (Ellis, 1959a, 1962, 1984e, in press-a). Although RET rarely uses confrontation for purely abreactive or cathartic reasons, it does actively use it to get at and to help change resistant and defensively employed cognitions.

   For example, if you have a female client who denies saying anything to herself when very angry at her lover, you may at times say something like, "Bullshit! I never heard of anyone as angry as you who was not commanding and demanding that her lover *should* not, *ought* not act the way he does. Now let's be honest, when you almost threw that knife at your lover, were you not telling yourself, indeed shouting to yourself, something like, 'You lousy bastard! You *shouldn't* be lying to me like this!'? Weren't you *insisting*, in your mind, that he *ought* to tell you the truth?" By confronting resistant clients in this manner, you often smoke out their iBs—though, of course, you had better be careful not to *give* them beliefs that they don't actually have.

Rational-Emotive Imagery

RET often employs rational-emotive imagery (Maultsby, 1975, 1984), especially when done in an implosive and evocative

manner that I adapted (Maultsby & Ellis, 1974). Thus, you can
assign resistant clients to imagine vividly that they keep failing
and keep getting criticized and thereby induce in them extreme
feelings of inadequacy. Then you can get them to change their
feelings *only* to those of regret and disappointment instead of
worthlessness; and when they do so (mainly by changing some of
their self-berating cognitions), you can recommend that they
practice this process for 30 or 60 days in a row until they train
themselves to automatically feel regretful and disappointed (and
not self-downing) when, in imagination or in real life, they thereafter experience failure and criticism.

Rational-emotive imagery is actually another form of Disputing—but, unlike Disputing, it is an evocative, imaginative, and
behavioral mode of helping clients to see and change their iBs
and thereby to change their inappropriate and self-defeating
emotions to appropriate and self-helping feelings.

Shame-attacking Exercises

RET shame-attacking exercises (Ellis, 1969a, 1972c; Ellis &
Abrahms, 1978; Ellis & Becker, 1982) are often especially effective with resistant clients. You can encourage these clients to
perform in public some "shameful," "embarrassing," "humiliat-
ing," or "silly" act—such as wearing an outlandish costume,
borrowing money from a stranger, or shouting out the stops in a
train or bus. If they will do these acts many times and work on
their feelings so that they do *not* feel ashamed or self-downing,
they will be able to conquer some of their powerful self-immolat-
ing feelings that they often contend they are "absolutely unable"
to conquer.

Oddly enough, though some resistant clients will not work
at monitoring and changing their irrational thinking that makes
them embarrassed—e.g., the iB, "If people see me in this garish
outfit they will all laugh at me and thus make a perfect fool out
of me!"—some of them will fairly easily do the shame-attacking
homework assignments that will undermine and eliminate these
Beliefs. On the other hand, some resistant clients will do their
cognitive homework fairly well, but will refuse to do shame-

attacking assignments and will therefore "see" that, as RET teaches, nothing is really shameful—but will never really *accept* this rational philosophy. Particularly for resisters, therefore, you had better stress *both* cognitive homework and *in vivo* shame-attacking assignments.

Dramatic Anecdotes and Stories

Dramatizing new ideas and behaviors to clients is a regular part of RET and may be especially used with clients who are resistant to less dramatic methods. Thus, as a therapist, you can tell dramatic stories about some of your other clients or friends who used RET techniques. You can use material from your own life and can theatrically show how you helped yourself with therapy.

With resistant clients, for example, I frequently tell the story I narrate in *How to Master Your Fear of Flying* (Ellis, 1972d) which shows how I managed to get over my anxiety when I was in a storm-battered plane on my way to the Kinsey Institute for Sex Research in Bloomington, Indiana. After at first only *mildly* convincing myself that it wouldn't be terrible—but only highly inconvenient!—to die in a plane crash, and therefore not really undoing my panic state, I finally *strongly* said to myself, "If I die, I die! Fuck it!—So I'll die!" and then my panic entirely vanished.

Relationship Emphasis

RET does not stress relationship factors as much as do many other forms of therapy, but it does acknowledge that building a close or trusting relationship is often important with difficult and resistant clients (Dryden, 1984; Ellis, in press-b, in press-f, in press-g; Young, 1977, 1984). I have gone out of my way, ever since I started practicing RET in 1955, to show adolescent delinquents and older psychopaths that they can trust me to understand them and appreciate how badly the world has often treated them. They also quickly see, by my language and demeanor, that I am hardly a conventional member of the bourgeoisie and that I myself am somewhat socially rebellious. Consequently, they usually trust me from the start and feel that I will give them a fair therapeutic deal and will honestly try to help them help themselves. Howard Young, who worked with many delinquents, blue collar workers, and Christian fundamentalists, developed some unusual methods of relating to them and of using their prejudices to relate well to them and to convince them of more rational ideas and behaviors (Young, 1977, 1984).

Even, therefore, if you do not ordinarily relate closely or warmly to most of your run-of-the-mill clients, you can consider making special efforts in this regard with some of your most resistant ones. Your achieving what they deem to be an unusually trusting relationship with them may be almost the only way that you will be able to reach out and help them.

Forceful Self-Dialogues

Several years ago, when trying to help one of my borderline clients overcome his extreme feelings of anger toward gum chewers and smokers, I asked him to record a ten-minute dialogue between his rational and his irrational self with the latter strongly holding that these public enemies be drawn and quartered and his rational self just as powerfully—or *more* powerfully—arguing that they were fallible humans who could be forgiven for their sins. At first, he only used his cassette recorder to state a mild essay forgiving these offenders, but he still remained very angry at them after he made and listened to this recording (and had me and his therapy group listen to it).

I assigned him to make another recording and this time he made a very powerful one that included this kind of dialogue between his rational and irrational voice.

IRRATIONAL   That goddamned boy who kept cracking bubble gum
VOICE   in my ears in a jam-packed subway train—he is a
              thorough louse and should have his cock cut off! That
              would fix him!

RATIONAL   Don't you think that's a little too harsh? After all, he
VOICE   probably didn't even know he was bothering you.
              Can't you forgive him?

IRRATIONAL VOICE	No! Gum cracking like that is absolutely unforgivable! All people like him should be drawn and quartered!
RATIONAL VOICE	Really? Isn't that extreme punishment for such a mild crime?
IRRATIONAL VOICE	No! Nothing is bad enough for such scums of the earth!

As you can well imagine, this client was even angrier after making this tape and some members of his therapy group were actually scared by his vehemence and the apparent severity of his disturbance—especially the gum chewers in the group! So I had him make a recorded self-dialogue for the third time—but this time concentrate on making his rational voice much stronger. He did so, and finally got his rational self to say very powerfully on the tape, "I don't care how inconsiderate this gum-chewing boy is. He's still a very *fallible* human. And he has a *perfect right* to his goddamned fallibility! His *behavior* stinks, but he is still a valid, screwed up, unstinking *person*! And if I hate *him*, rather than his bad *act*, then I have a very serious problem, too!"

Because he presented his rational arguments very strongly on this third tape, my client finally lost his anger—and thereafter became less angry toward other gum chewers. Since then, I often get my resistant clients to make recorded self-dialogues in which they very strongly try to talk themselves out of their bigoted views. As a variation on this method, I role play their irrational views and they vehemently try to talk me out of these irrationalities. My impression is—though this question is not as yet confirmed by research studies—that strong disputing of irrational beliefs in these dialogues is significantly more effective than mild-mannered disputing.

Emotive and evocative methods like those just described are almost a necessity to overcome the resistance of many clients. The issue of force and energy in therapy is so important that the next chapter will consider it in more detail.

5
Force and Energy
in Overcoming Resistance

As was seen in the previous chapter, RET makes a special issue of force and energy in effecting behavioral change. From the start, it pointed out that what we call emotion largely consists of strong, vehemently held cognitions, while "pure," dispassionate thought leads to behavior but not usually to what we call intense or disordered feeling (Ellis, 1958a, 1962). As RET developed, it emphasized the *strength* of ideas even more strongly, and it began to use even more emotive-cognitive methods than it used during its first few years (Ellis, 1969a, 1971, 1972c, 1973, 1977b, 1977c; Ellis & Abrahms, 1978; Ellis & Harper, 1975).

The issue of cognitive strength is particularly relevant to resistant clients, because they seem to use a great deal of force and energy in devising and maintaining their self-defeating behaviors, and RET has therefore always held that highly active-directive, confronting, and forceful therapist demeanors may be desirable (and sometimes almost necessary) if therapeutic movement is to be achieved. This aspect of effective therapy is so important that I shall discuss its theory and practice in some detail in this chapter.

What I call the issue of force and energy in behavioral change is one that has been sadly neglected over the years. Although hundreds of psychotherapists utilize a great many forceful and energetic methods (Burton, 1969), they frequently do not acknowledge the concept of forcefulness in what they do, and sometimes they even deny it. The Freudians, for example, vigorously force their clients to fit themselves into the procrustean bed of their oedipal complexes, and they manipulate the "transference" relationship with these patients so that they become very dependent on the analysts. Yet they often speak and write as if psychoanalysis mainly appeals to the scientific and reasoning aspects of humans and as if it finally wins out through the pure voice of reason (Freud, 1965e). Other therapists, such as the Rogerians (Rogers, 1961) and the Gestalt therapists (Perls, 1969), consciously employ highly emotive methods with their clients, but they rarely talk about the *force* or *vigor* of their unsubtle techniques.

When the concepts of force or energy are employed in behavioral change, they are more commonly (and usually unscientifically) related to hypotheses about the central forces or energies of the universe. People are told that (1) such forces indubitably exist, (2) you can get in touch with them by various transpersonal and mystical approaches, (3) you can thereby tap these universal forces and use them to your own personal ends, and (4) you can consequently overcome virtually all your emotional problems and enormously increase your potential for actualizing yourself. This kind of devout belief in universal forces and of the human ability to tap these forces and acquire immense personal power from zeroing in on the "energies" of the universe has been with us for literally thousands of years, but it is unfortunately becoming much more widespread in recent times. Innumerable books and articles state or imply that cosmic forces are there for the asking and that we can easily commune with them and thereby increase our own power of coping with ourselves and life (Albin & Montagna, 1977; Campbell, 1975; Ferguson, 1980; Harrell, 1976; Houston, 1982; Ingalls, 1976; Krippner, Davidson & Peterson, 1973: Ostrander & Schroeder, 1974; Pulvino, 1975; Schutz, 1971; Smith, 1976; Stewart, 1981; Targ & Puthoff, 1977; Tart, 1975; Weil, 1973). Protesting against this mystical trend in psychology and psychotherapy have been relatively few recent writers, including Alperson (1976), Duffy (1975), Ellis (1972e, 1977a, 1977h, 1980c, 1982c, 1983b, 1984a, 1984k, in press-e), Flew (1976), Kurtz (1976).

The Basic Issue of Force and Energy in Behavioral Change

The real or basic issue of force and energy in behavioral change seems to have little or nothing to do with the mystical or trans-personal hogwash that presently abounds in the literature. It concerns the following question: Assuming that certain ideas or cognitions help individuals to change their basic personality struc-ture (and diminish certain psychological symptoms or distur-bances), is it important that these ideas be conveyed by the therapists, or by the clients, to themselves, in a pronounced, vigorous, forceful, and dramatic manner? And if it is important that certain health-promoting ideas be forcefully invoked in therapy, what are some of the most effective ways of doing so?

As noted, little consideration has been given in the past to this particular problem of behavioral change. Many therapeutic writers have talked about intellectual insight and emotional in-sight and have held that the latter will lead to significant person-ality change while the former will not (Alexander & French, 1946; Hobbs, 1962; Wolberg, 1967). Unfortunately, they have not been very precise in their definitions. I (and a certain number of other writers who have followed my lead) have defined emo-tion as largely consisting of "a certain kind—of biased, preju-diced, or strongly evaluative kind—of thought" (Ellis, 1962, p. 41), and I have consequently discussed the problem of changing behavior by utilizing powerful, vigorous thinking processes (Ellis, 1957a, 1962, 1971, 1973, 1977a, 1980b; Ellis & Grieger, 1977; Ellis & Harper, 1975). A few psychotherapists, such as Finney (1972), have not particularly discriminated between vigorous and blander thinking but have used what could be called vigorous counterpropagandizing methods in their therapy.

All told, however, surprisingly little has been done in this respect, in spite of the fact that methods of propaganda and counterpropaganda have been studied, mostly by social psy-chologists, for many years and that, in the course of these studies, considerable attention has been paid to the powerful or less powerful ways in which persuasion has been promulgated (Hovland & Janis, 1959). So I think that we might safely conclude that although therapists frequently *use* vigorous persuasion or "brainwashing" methods in their encounters with clients, they have not been particularly keen on thinking about the concept of forcefulness or energeticness in their procedures; in fact, to some extent, they may have even deliberately and defensively avoided this area of discussion and research.

The Problem of Intellectual and Emotional Insight

Clinical observers, as noted, have for many years noted the difference between intellectual and emotional insight and have pointed out that when clients are intellectually aware of their problems and understand the sources of these problems, they frequently make minor or minimal personality changes: when they have emotional insight into these same problems, however, they frequently make much more major changes. Unfortunately, the literature in this respect is quite vague as to what the real difference between emotional and intellectual insight is and as to why the former is presumably more effective than the latter.

I gave fairly careful thought to this problem some years ago and came up with what I think is at least a partial solution to these questions (Ellis, 1963). First, I tried to define emotional and intellectual insight more precisely. In so doing, I noted that what we usually call emotional insight has several important characteristics.

1. Clients have some degree of intellectual insight—that is, admit that they are disturbed and that their behavior is irrational or self-defeating. Without this "intellectual" acknowledgment of admission, emotional, or "fuller" insight will probably not occur.

2. Clients usually realize that their present behavior has some antecedent causes and does not magically spring from nowhere. It does not "just" occur, but has tended to occur for quite a long period of time, and it occurs in conjunction with certain activating experiences or stimuli.

3. Clients assume some kind of responsibility for the dysfunctional or self-defeating behavior and realize that they have something to do with originating it and carrying it on. In rational-emotive therapy's A-B-C model of personality, the client realizes that A (an Activating Experience or Activating Event) does not directly or mainly cause C (an emotional or behavioral Consequence, such as anxiety or depression). Instead, B (the client's own Belief System) directly causes the feeling and the behavioral Consequence, and the client is partly responsible for having and carrying on this Belief System.

4. Clients realize that even if they were significantly helped, usually during early childhood, to have certain irrational Beliefs (iBs) and to create self-defeating emotions with these Beliefs, they *choose* to keep these Beliefs right now, in the present, and to keep affecting themselves by them.

5. Clients clearly and strongly "see" or "acknowledge" that they can now do something *to change* their iBs and thereby to change the habitual disturbed feelings and disordered behaviors that spring directly from these Beliefs. These client Beliefs are firm or strong and are solidly held much of the time.

6. Clients feel determined to work at (yes, *work* at) changing their iBs—to accept their falsity, acknowledge that they do not conform to empirical reality, to see their illogical or contradictory aspects, and to keep striving, because of the poor results they bring, to give them up and not return to believing them again. Working at changing Beliefs includes the clients' (a) forcefully and repetitively disputing and challenging them, (b) forcing themselves to go through the pain and trouble of steadily contradicting these ideas, (c) practicing feeling differently about them or their results (e.g., practicing feeling happy about giving up smoking instead of clinging to the idea that it is awful to go through the pain of giving it up), (d) directly and vigorously acting against the iBs or against the actions to which they self-defeatingly lead (e.g., forcing oneself to put the lit end of a cigarette in one's mouth every time one takes a puff at the other end of it).

7. Clients not only feel determined to work at challenging their iBs but actually do this kind of work and do it often and vigorously. Thus, if a woman has a swimming phobia, she had better keep convincing herself, over and over again, that swim-

ming is not terribly dangerous, and also repeatedly plunge into a swimming pool until she gets rid of the idea that it is.

8. Clients fully realize that their emotional disturbances are usually under their own control and that they can continue to think and act their way out of them whenever they recur. This means continual determination and action, whenever a new emotional upset occurs, to conquer it as quickly as possible and to become convinced of some general Beliefs that will tend to prevent many kinds of future disturbances, such as, "Nothing is awful or terrible," "I can always accept myself, no matter what faults I have," "Many things are hassles but not horrors," and "All humans, including myself, are incredibly fallible and will keep making fairly serious mistakes forever, and that is unpleasant and inconvenient but hardly the end of the world!"

9. Clients keep admitting that there seems to be no better way to become and to remain undisturbed except by their continually working and practicing, in theory and action, against whatever disturbances they create.

The preceding rules may be partially summarized by saying that people who have intellectual insight see how they create their own disturbances and what they can do about uncreating them, but tend to see these things lightly, occasionally, and weakly; those who have emotional insight see the same things intensely, often, and strongly. More to the point, people with emotional insight tend to work hard, often, and powerfully at giving up their self-defeating Beliefs and acting against them, while people with intellectual insight do this kind of work mildly, seldom, and weakly. Resistant clients sometimes have intellectual but not emotional insight but sometimes have neither. In RET we do not usually find it too difficult to help them attain the former, but (like most psychotherapists), we often have trouble helping them achieve emotional—or effective or powerful—insight.

False Issues in Utilizing Force and Energy

If what I have just said about intellectual and emotional insight tends to be true, the main issue in utilizing force and energy to bring about behavioral change seems to be work and practice more than it is an issue of mere insight or resolve to change. New Year's Resolutions are easy to make—but proverbially hard to keep. "Willpower" is easy to invoke—but difficult to put into practice. Concepts such as motivation, determination, will, intention, and resolve are all important in behavioral change, and it is possible that very little effective change takes place without people having a good degree of these "feelings." But just as bread is not enough for most people to live on and enjoy life, so willpower is not enough to incite and induce basic personality change unless we include, under willpower, not merely the resolve and determination to modify one's traits and behaviors but also the action, work, and labor that one had better apply in order to back up this resolve.

That is why the transpersonal or mystical solutions are usually false solutions. They assume the existence of general forces and energies as a central part of the universe, which probably has at least some partial validity, since human life seems unviable apart from a basic source of energy, such as the sun. But they also assume some mass of energy or force in some special or central place that humans can easily tap and put to their own use—including their own psychological use. This hypothesis seems very questionable, especially when it assumes that we can *directly* zero in on universal forces and use them, at will, for our own pleasures and our own straighter thinking.

Perhaps the most foolish part of this hypothesis is that *anyone* can *easily*, with a few simple mystical or religious instructions, focus on the universal reservoir of Mighty Energy and can use it for immediate personal satisfaction. This utopian view probably stems from the feelings of low frustration tolerance (LFT) that many people have and that constitutes one of their major disturbances! The idea that "I must have things easy, and the universe must provide me quickly and effortlessly with immediate and immense gratification" is one of the most asinine *must*urbatory ideas with which humans victimize themselves and, as one would well imagine, it leads them far astray from the work and practice that they almost always require to bring about profound behavioral changes (Ellis, 1971, 1973, 1977a, 1979a, 1980a).

Ironically, some religious and mystical sects, such as the Zen Buddhists, refuse to take this easy way to the heaven of vast resources of Universal Energy. Instead, they teach their members that they must discipline themselves, often in exceptionally rigorous and overzealous ways, if they are to get "in touch with the infinite," attain "higher consciousness," or otherwise acquire those Great Forces. Even though, as noted, such Energies and Forces probably do not exist, nor are they connected with human psychic abilities, the disciplined procedures that these sects advocate *do* often have a salutary effect on mental health. It is extremely difficult to maintain one's LFT when one is deliberately following rituals such as rising early in the morning, meditating in uncomfortable positions for hours on end, fasting a great deal of the time, and wearing reasonable facsimiles of hair shirts!

Although, therefore, the utopian, spiritualistic philosophies of these mystical sects are unverifiable and probably filled with arrant claptrap, the disciplined procedures that supposedly lead to "nirvana," "universal fulfillment," "higher consciousness," or what you will, may themselves provide the kind of work and practice that help the devotees of these religions to achieve that aspect of emotional insight that includes forceful activity. In other words, if you foolishly believe that when you rigorously diet, exercise, and give up smoking, some archangel will reward you by permitting you to enter the pearly gates of Heaven, and you actually do consistently diet, exercise, and refrain from smoking in accordance with this silly hypothesis, you may, first, achieve better physical health than you otherwise would achieve, and, second, learn how to discipline yourself and acquire confidence in your own self-controlling talents. These two beneficial results may occur in spite of the nonsense that you believe, but this nonsense may motivate you to follow some sensible procedures that will help you emotionally.

The following questions still remain, of course: How can you engage in the same kinds of useful self-discipline *without* believing devoutly in the mystical (and disturbance-creating) nonsense that goes with it? How can you validate the results of your high frustration tolerance in its own right, to discover in what ways it is advantageous and disadvantageous, so that you (and others) become more sensibly disciplined (disciplined not for the sake of discipline itself or for the sake of some imagined deity)?

An Operational Definition of Force and Energy in Behavioral Change

RET hypothesizes that emotional insight (or intellectual insight backed by the individual's determination [will] to change and consistent hard work and practice at the process of actual change), frequently results in pronounced and "elegant" modification of important personality traits and behaviors. It also theorizes that when elegant cognitive or philosophic restructuring occurs, people not only tend to minimize or lose their disturbed symptoms, but also maintain increased emotional health in the future (Bard, 1980; Ellis, 1962, 1971, 1973, 1977a, in press-a; Grieger & Boyd, 1980; Grieger & Grieger, 1982; Lembo, 1976; Morris & Kanitz, 1975; Walen, DiGiuseppe & Wessler, 1980; Wessler & Wessler, 1980).

Assuming that these hypotheses have some validity, or that they are at least worth checking out, the following question arises. How many people, and particularly resistant clients, forcefully and energetically change their disturbance-creating or irrational Beliefs so that they achieve a high degree of "emotional" insight? To answer this, let me first try to define operationally the concepts of force and energy in psychotherapy or behavioral change, so that I thereby accurately present what individuals had better *do* to employ it.

To be more precise in this respect, I will start with the example of a very typical iB that many people seem to have and that leads them to feel anxious, depressed, needlessly inhibited, and inadequate. This is the Belief that "I *must* perform adequately or well in this task and *have to* win the approval of others by doing so; if I significantly fail in these respects, it is *awful,* I *cannot stand* it, and I am a *rotten person (RP)* for behaving badly and for gaining the disapproval of others." Let us assume that one of your resistant clients has this iB and that it leads to anxious and depressed feelings and to dysfunctional behaviors. How, using an operational approach to defining force and energy, can you help him or her vigorously and effectively surrender this set of iBs and change these self-defeating emotions and behaviors?

Let me list some specific things you may instruct your clients to try to achieve emotional insight or elegant philosophic reconstruction. Some of the following tasks overlap with each other, but each may be important in its own right for the resister to work at:

1. You had better actively and strongly Dispute (at point D in RET) your iBs *quite often*. To do this you would *frequently* challenge and question these Beliefs, using the logicoempirical methods of science, and ask yourself nonrhetorical queries such as: "Where is the evidence that I *must* perform adequately or well in this task? Why do I *have to* win the approval of others by doing so? What proof exists that it is *awful* (and not merely highly inconvenient) if I fail in these respects? Where is it written that I *cannot stand* failure and rejection? What data exists to show that I am truly a *rotten person* (instead of a person who may have *acted rottenly* on this occasion) if I fail and get rejected?"

Gaining emotional and not intellectual insight (or gaining *more complete* instead of *partial* insight) into the irrationality of your self-defeating Beliefs consists of your winding up with the new rational Effect (E in RET) or new empirically based philosophy more *commonly*, more *frequently*, and more *consistently* than you have done before. Even when you strongly or emotionally believe that you *must* perform well and win others' approval, you do not believe this 100% of the time. You *mostly* or *often* believe it. And if you get emotional or *forceful* insight into your iBs and their self-destructive qualities, you will come to believe this drivel only *occasionally* or *less often* than you do now. Therefore you had better actively Dispute and surrender these crazy beliefs *quite often*.

2. You had better acquire a *more total* or *more prevailing* belief that you don't have to perform well and win others' approval and that you can fully accept yourself (i.e., your aliveness and potential for happiness) if you perform badly. Again, as a human you rarely believe anything *totally* or *completely*, but have conflicting views about innumerable things. Thus you probably believe that overeating is bad for you, but you also believe that it is somewhat good for you. You may believe that it is horribly unfair when people treat you unjustly, but you also believe that that is the way the world is and that you can bear their unjust treatment.

Disturbance-creating beliefs, such as the idea that you *have to* perform well and be approved by others, tend to be totalistic. You devoutly and fully believe them, at least at the moment when you feel depressed about performing badly and gaining others' disapproval. You do not believe them in a complete or 100% manner, but you tend to believe them in a basic, underlying, and 80 or 90% way. To *really* or *basically* disbelieve them, therefore, you had better keep working at believing them in a much less totalistic and less prevailing manner. Thus, if you have a 95% belief that the world is round and a 5% belief that it is flat, you will probably not get into any serious trouble and can take a long trip with minimum qualms. However, if you have a 95% belief that it is flat and a 5% belief that it is round, your travel will tend to be highly restricted or you will travel in an exceptionally anxious state! In the latter case, your problem is to work on your 95% belief that the world is flat until you make it into a 5% or less belief.

3. You had better believe your rational Beliefs(rBs) more strongly, intensely or powerfully than your irrational Beliefs. Thus you can, if you wish, lightly or weakly believe that, "I must perform well and win others' approval," but you had better more strongly and intensely believe that, "I really don't *have* to perform well and win others' approval, although it would be highly preferable if I did." Exactly *how* you can measure the intensity of your beliefs is not entirely clear, since it overlaps with believing them often and totally, especially with the latter. But there does seem to be a power or intensity to beliefs, as Osgood (1971) has shown, and it is somewhat different from believing something often or totally.

Thus you can lightly or weakly believe, "I had better not eat a lot of food," and believe in a stronger manner that, "It would be better if I did eat a lot of food." If so, you would tend to *act* on the latter instead of the former belief. But there are probably also other indications of the strength of a belief, such as your having, when you hold a strong or powerful belief, an intense feeling about its truth or (in more cognitive terms) an intense conviction that it is true and that you had better act as if it were true.

A strong belief, in other words, is one that you tend to hold (a) with firm conviction, (b) in a relatively fixed and unchanging manner, (c) with a high degree of probability or certainty, (d) without cavil or qualification, (e) dogmatically, (f) wholly or totally, (g) almost all of the time, and (h) absolutely, even when empirical evidence tends to disconfirm it. Rationally, you may hold a strong belief because virtually all the evidence that you have seems to support it; irrationally, you may hold it because you "feel" that it is true, even though there is little evidence to support it and much to refute it. In either instance, you tend to feel that the belief is quite true or valid, and you tend to act on it.

To make a strong iB weak and a weak rB stronger, you can do several things. If, for example, you take the iB that, "I must perform well and be approved by so-and-so," you can try to weaken it in these ways: (a) Ask yourself, "Where is the empirical evidence that I *must* act in this manner and get these results?" Answer: "There is no such evidence, since I obviously *can* (or have the ability to) perform badly and win disapproval." (b) Ask yourself, "Does it seem likely that a universal law exists that commands my performing well and winning the approval of others?" Answer: "Obviously not, since if the law existed I would always and only have to perform well and win others' approval, and clearly I am able to perform badly and gain disapproval." (c) Ask yourself, "What horror or disaster will probably or possibly occur if I don't perform well and win the approval of others?" Answer: "No horror or disaster! I will probably be quite inconvenienced if I act badly and others don't like me, but I will still be able to live and enjoy my life in various ways." (d) Ask yourself, "Will I be a truly or totally rotten person if I do not perform well and get others' acceptance?" Answer: "No, of course not. I will then be a person with, at worst, a rotten trait, a poor performance, and a poor result—others' nonacceptance. But I will not be thoroughly rotten and can perform quite well in many other ways." (e) Ask yourself, "Will some force in the universe define me as undeserving and damn me, during my lifetime or some hypothetical afterlife, if I do not act well and get others' approval?" Answer: "Not that I can see or prove! It is most unlikely that some force in the universe is personally interested in me, will spy on my poor performances and my unacceptability to others, and will utterly damn me and make me undeserving of any joy in the here and how or in some hypothetical afterlife if I behave poorly." (f) You can vigorously and powerfully try to interrupt your iBs and replace them by rBs. Thus you can ask yourself, in a vehement manner: "Why the hell *must* I perform well and where is the goddamned evidence that I *have to* win others' approval?" And you can answer, with equal vigor: "There's *no* damned reason, no reason whatsoever why I must perform well! And if I do not win others' approval, hell, I do not! It will not kill me!" (g) You can dogmatically (and somewhat *irrationally!*) keep reindoctrinating yourself with a counterbelief that effectively gets you to give up your irrational, self-defeating Belief, for example: "I am a perfectly lovely, special *person*, who deserves everything good in life just because I am I! Therefore I do not have to perform well, but am still noble and special. And if others disapprove of me, that is their problem, and they hardly deserve my acquaintance of friendship anyway. To hell with them!"

You can use still other methods of strongly uprooting your irrational Beliefs and coming to more rational Beliefs: (a) Deliberately work at changing your Beliefs, from time to time, so that virtually none of them remains fixed and invariant. (b) Get yourself to believe, for instance, that "I must perform well (or had better perform well) only in certain unusual situations, as when my life depends on it or I will truly cause some disaster to happen to me by performing poorly. I need others' approval only in special cases, as when I depend on them for life and limb." (c) Constantly interrupt your iBs and replace them with rBs. (d) Work against your general absolutistic tendencies to believe devoutly in anything whatever and see that you only accept things skeptically, tentatively, and with a willingness to believe in the opposite. Practice keeping yourself open to new or contradictory beliefs.

4. Realize that having an iB will not necessarily make you act on it (although it will distinctly help you to do so) and that determination to think, feel, and act against it will tend to get you to surrender it. See that you can be firmly determined, mildly determined, or not determined to think or do something and work at being firmly or strongly determined to give up your iBs and to act against them. Along these lines, talk to yourself as follows: "I am utterly determined to accept myself even if I perform badly and people do not approve of me. If it is the last thing I do, I will work hard at unconditional self-acceptance. Knowing that I can live and enjoy myself no matter what others think of me is probably the most important view that I can ever have, and I *will* have it, I *will*, I *will*, I *will!*"

5. Strongly and determinedly push yourself into actions

that will contradict your tendency to hold irrational Beliefs and will reinforce your tendency to have rational ones. Thus you can (a) risk failing at certain important tasks, instead of avoiding them, (b) deliberately fail at certain tasks to show yourself that you will not die of failure, (c) tell significant people bad things about yourself in order to risk their disapproval, (d) use rational-emotive imagery (Maultsby, 1975, 1984; Maultsby & Ellis, 1974; Ellis, 1977a; Ellis & Harper, 1975) to imagine yourself failing and to make yourself feel only disappointed and sorry instead of panicked and depressed when you imagine this.

6. Keep working against your iBs, feeling appropriate rather than inappropriate emotions (e.g., disappointment and sorrow instead of depression and feelings of worthlessness) when you fail, and acting in a risk-taking manner. Realize that it normally requires constant practice to make yourself *really* and *strongly* believe sane ideas and to act on them and that it requires still more practice, to some extent for the rest of your life, to get yourself to the point where you retain rational thinking and appropriate behaviors once you have initially attained them.

7. Accept the near inevitability of falling back to your iBs. As has been noted on several occasions (Ellis, 1962, 1973, 1976b, 1976c, 1977a; Ellis & Grieger, 1977; Ellis & Harper, 1975), humans not only have a strong tendency to think crookedly but to fall back to their crooked thinking once they temporarily overcome it. So, in all probability, do you! Accept the fact, therefore, that you most probably will return at times to silly ideas and self-defeating behaviors and that this is too bad, but not horrible. You are not a lesser person for falling back. At these times, merely focus on your behavior and how to change that instead of on your you-ness and how to condemn that. You can learn by most of your retrogressions, and you can have fewer and fewer of them as the years go by. But you most probably will not reduce them to zero, not as long as you are still human!

8. Accept the fact that no matter how many times you fall back to dysfunctional ways of thinking, emoting, and behaving, you can give them up again and return to more satisfying ways. You can work at strongly determining that you *will force yourself* to uproot your self-defeating behaviors and go back to less defeating pathways. Determine to keep rehabituating yourself to more

efficient and more satisfying ways of living. Work at this determination and at the actions required to actualize it.

9. Do not be afraid, at times, to use temporary or palliative techniques of changing yourself. You can, for example, learn relaxation methods (Benson, 1975; Jacobsen, 1942; Lazarus, 1981), various kinds of pleasurable diversions (Ellis, 1976b; Masters & Johnson, 1970), Yoga and meditation techniques (Shapiro & Walsh, 1984), physical and body exercises (Lowen, 1970), emotive methods (Casriel, 1974; Janov, 1970; Lazarus, 1981), and other diversionary methods. You can also take tranquilizers, alcohol, marijuana, and various other types of drugs to help yourself be temporarily distracted and relaxed. But recognize that these methods usually do not lead to profound philosophic change, and sometimes interfere with it. They help you feel better but not get better. We might say, therefore, that they are often among the most dramatic forms of unforceful, unenergetic therapy, and that is why they tend to be so palliative, and tend to leave you with an underlying shame-creating and hostility-instigating philosophy that will later rise to smite you. If you use distraction methods with the full knowledge that they usually bring temporary results, and that they sometimes put you in a mood where you can *then* vigorously and determinedly work to change your underlying disturbance-creating assumptions—fine. If, however, you employ them "curatively," they may well give poor results, and ultimately lead you to more harm than good (Ellis, 1972f).

Force and Energy in the Treatment of Resisters

Scientists are becoming more and more aware of the enormous importance of human perception, cognition, and intention in world affairs. Psychotherapists have essentially said this for years (Adler, 1927/1968; Ellis, 1957a, 1962, 1971, 1973, 1977a; Ellis & Harper, 1975; Maslow, 1962; Rogers, 1961). Now biological and physical scientists are also beginning to say it (Sperry, 1977).

When you want to have significant effect, however, on your own life as well as the universe around you, your thinking clearly and rationally is often not enough—unless under the heading of rational we also include an emotive factor and acknowledge that efficient thinking involves a forceful, energetic, and determined element. Mild-mannered thinking (the kind that you do when you merely observe that smoking or overeating has disadvantageous elements and that it would probably be better if you did not engage in such behavior) may be a necessary but not sufficient condition for basic personality change. It had better be accompanied or followed by a more vigorous, dramatic kind of thinking that goes one step further to include the determination to act, and the actual action that backs up this kind of change-oriented cognition.

The theory of RET says that resistant clients are indeed forceful and energetic in their thinking, emotion, and behaving. They powerfully and rigidly believe absolutistic nonsense. Therefore, you had better help them to undermine this with strong Disputing and challenging of their antiscientific dogmas. At times, you can also help them figure out appropriate positive philosophies—e.g., "I *can* control my emotional destiny!"—and to repeat them solidly and persistently: not pollyannaish and utopian slogans, but realistic observations and maxims.

Overgeneralized or mystical-minded concepts of a universal force or energy, and of how humans are to get in touch with and utilize such forces are, again, not enough. In fact, they can be pernicious and reactionary as far as instigating basic personality change is concerned. It therefore behooves social scientists to specify more operationally and practically the kinds of force or vigor that we can inculcate in our attempts at rationality and with which we can effectively implement these attempts. Peculiarly, little attention has yet been given to this problem in psychology or psychotherapy: this chapter is an attempt at specifying some of the more important elements in forceful, energetic thought and action and at harnessing some of these elements in the process of personality change. It is also an attempt to set up some hypotheses that can be experimentally investigated and either validated or rejected. Important therapeutic progress may well come out of such *forceful* and *energetic* thinking and acting!

6
Behavioral Techniques of Overcoming Resistance

Just as it is invariably emotive as well as cognitive, so is RET highly behavioral. Resistant individuals especially require active-directive and usually *in vivo* homework assignments. In fact, one of the main reasons I abandoned psychoanalysis and created RET was because one of my attractive, highly intelligent female clients refused to meet eligible males, even though she was highly desirous of forming a permanent relationship, and though I helped her gain all kinds of insight into why she was inhibiting herself, yet she still refused to act on her desires. I finally gave her the ultimatum of returning to see me for therapy only after she had made real attempts to encounter several eligible males. Three months later, after acting on this assignment, she returned to therapy—and from that time onward her problem of shyness began to be resolved.

Noting this and successfully trying similar methods with several other inhibited and withdrawn clients helped me to reject psychoanalytic therapy almost entirely and to begin actively developing RET. So from the very start, RET has included active-directive behavioral methods. Some of the most useful of these with resistant individuals include the following methods which you can use with your own clients.

101

Courting Discomfort

Resisters frequently have abysmal low frustration tolerance (LFT) and therefore will not follow the RET rule that there is rarely any gain without pain. Consequently, it is sometimes wise to forcefully bring their LFT to their attention and to insist that unless they deliberately and often court discomfort they have virtually no chance of changing or of benefiting from therapy.

As an example of this, I recently said to one of my 50-year-old clients, an accountant who has always worked below his level of competency and would now like to go into selling because it is "too difficult" for him to keep up with the other accountants with whom he works, "You want to know what 'inner sickness' keeps you from being satisfied at work. Well, I'll tell you what it is. It's called *two-year-oldism*—your demand that the world treat you like a two-year-old and do everything for you and let you *easily* get what you want. Technically, it's called low frustration tolerance. But it's really two-year-oldism—that is, childish demandingness. And as long as you have it and keep watering it, you'll whine and scream, as you are now doing, about working on your new job. But when you admit that that's the real diagnosis—two-year-oldism—you'll then stop your whining and push your ass to do the best you can on this job. And you'll finally do quite well, because you are bright and competent enough to do so. But not at first! At first, you'll be very uncomfortable—because it *is* hard learning this new job. But if you push and push and push yourself, as you would have to do at playing the piano or at any sport you want to excel at, you'll *finally* find it easy and enjoyable. Not at first—but *finally*! So *make* yourself do the work you dislike, *force* yourself to do it and do it. Deliberately *push* yourself to be *un*comfortable—yes, *un*comfortable—until you finally find the work easy and comfortable. And even, at times, enjoyable. By courting and courting *dis*comfort, and by that hard route alone, you'll *later* become comfortable. Not right away—*later*."

Although this client fought me for most of this session and often talked over me so loudly that he couldn't hear anything I said, I strongly persisted, and at last got through to him. He admitted that his "fear" of his new job was mainly discomfort anxiety or LFT, and not ego anxiety as he had previously loudly claimed. And he accepted the homework assignment of forcing himself to work hard at his new job until it finally became more comfortable. Within two weeks, he showed that my prediction came true and that he actually did find the new job easy and enjoyable—and had lost all fear of not being able to do it well.

So if you keep after resistant clients many times, and quite forcibly, until they do what they are irrationally afraid of or what their LFT stops them from attempting, you may help them to see that many situations are not "horrible" or "terrible" but only inconvenient—and even, ultimately, enjoyable.

Reinforcement Methods

RET often makes use of both reinforcers and penalties to help clients change (Ellis, 1972c, 1977a, in press-a; Ellis & Abrahms, 1978; Ellis & Whiteley, 1979). With recalcitrant clients, you can encourage them to give themselves highly satisfying reinforcers—e.g., special foods or the pleasure of masturbating—only *after* they have done the therapeutic homework that they have promised themselves to do but that they keep avoiding.

The problem with resisters, of course, is that they promise to do their homework and then do it irregularly and/or meagerly, or else do not do it at all. RET has some special methods of ecnouraging them to follow through with their homework assignments:

1. When clients fail to do homework they agree, as noted above, to use the pleasurable reinforcers. Only after they have done it.

2. When they still avoid homework and nonetheless indulge in stipulated pleasures—e.g., eat their favorite foods when they have *not* engaged in the activities they have promised themselves to do—you can ask them, "When you didn't do the homework, what did you tell yourself to make you avoid doing it?" The usual answer is: "It was hard to do it and I told myself it was *too* hard. It shouldn't *be* that hard! How *awful* that it's that hard! I *can't stand* doing it!" You then show these clients how to dispute these irrational Beliefs (iBs) and how to get to Effective rational self-statements (Es), such as "Yes, it's hard doing this homework, but

it's not *too* hard. And it's harder, in the long run, for me *not* to do it. No matter how hard it is, it *should* be that hard—because that's the way it is! It's not *awful*, but only damned *inconvenient*, to do it—and *more* inconvenient if I don't! And although I may never *like* doing this homework, I definitely *can* stand it—and had better if I want to change!"

3. When resistant clients engage in pleasurable pursuits noncontingently, even though they *don't* do their homework, you again can help them see the iBs that drive them to the reinforcers, such as: "I *need* this enjoyable food even though I have not done my homework to 'earn' it. I *can't bear* giving it up! I *should* be able to enjoy it and not have to forego it when I don't do my homework." If you can get resistant clients to clearly see these philosophic underpinnings of their LFT, and then to actively dispute and surrender these iBs, they will then have a much easier time using the principles of reinforcement to help them do their homework.

4. If resisters still resist, they can be given a monitor—such as a mate or a close friend with whom they live—who will monitor their homework and their reinforcements. Thus, if Jones says that he will only listen to music after he has exercised for 20 minutes, his mate or roommate can watch him to see if he actually does exercise before he allows himself to listen to music and can report to the therapist when he is enjoying the music without doing the exercise.

5. You, as therapist, can monitor difficult clients' reinforcement by checking to see how they use it and by sometimes precluding it when they don't do their homework. Thus, if a client agrees to go on a vacation only after she has dieted for two months, you can hold the money she is going to send to the travel agency and not give it to her to send until she has shown that she has actually dieted.

Penalizing Methods

For many years, as a result of my own experience with what I call DCs (difficult customers), RET has used penalties as well as reinforcers to encourage people to do their homework assignments. As I frequently tell my lecture and workshop audience throughout the world, many of the experiments that supposedly validate Skinner's theory of operant conditioning and that presumably prove that reinforcement is better than penalization to help people change their behaviors are really untrustworthy—because they are often done with children as subjects. Children—being, of course, crazy!—will do anything for M & M's. But adults, and particularly adult DCs, often won't. To help difficult adult clients change, RET often uses stiff penalties in addition to (but not necessarily instead of) reinforcements.

To this end, you can have your resistant clients agree to penalize themselves severely every time they promise themselves to perform some homework assignment and then refuse to carry out that promise. But what kinds of penalties are effective? Many kinds are, depending on what your individual client finds penalizing—such as burning a 20-dollar bill, contributing it to a cause they loathe, cleaning a toilet for an hour, visiting a boring friend or relative, or doing unpleasant paperwork.

For example, one of my female clients agreed to stop smoking but kept smoking two whole packs of cigarettes a day no matter how many times one of my therapy groups showed her what she was telling herself to enhance her smoking and no matter what reinforcements she employed (such as food and music) to help her stop. She finally agreed to kiss one of her male suitors whom she considered ugly and unsexy every time she smoked more than five cigarettes a day. From that time onward, her cigarette smoking dropped to two or three a day and only went back to a pack or two when she temporarily withdrew this penalty, wrongly believing that she could easily keep down her cigarette consumption without it.

In difficult cases, then, you can encourage clients to give themselves stiff penalties whenever they fail to carry out their promised homework. Don't make the mistake here of confusing penalties with punishments. RET teaches people never to punish—meaning, castigate, damn, or down—themselves when they do badly, since it opposes all forms of self-rating (Ellis, 1962, 1972a, 1973, 1976a, 1977a). But it encourages them to penalize *without* damning themselves when immediate penalties would help them do homework assignments that, in the long run, would be to their distinct advantage. So try to see that your clients who use penalties, use them *without* using self-damnation.

In the case of penalties, as in that of reinforcement, if your DCs say that they will use them and then actually cop out, you can (1) help them to see and to dispute the iBs that they tell themselves to make themselves cop out, (2) arrange for some person close to them to monitor them and to see that they really use the penalties they say they will use, and (3) you yourself can act as a monitor and can burn their 20-dollar bills or mail them to a cause they consider obnoxious when they fail to enact the promised penalty.

Modeling Activity

To help clients *act* on (and not merely talk to themselves about) changing themselves, RET encourages therapists to be highly active and directive and thereby serve as behavioral role models. Resistant clients, in particular, may benefit by your becoming an unusually *active* role model. Thus, if you are distinctly active during therapy sessions; if you do your own homework and prepare properly for these sessions; if you indicate to your clients that in your personal life you rarely procrastinate and that you concertedly work at the things you promise yourself to do; and if you display this kind of active-directive, life-involved behavior during and outside of therapy, you may present a helpful model to your resistant clients that will encourage them to take some real *action* to change themselves.

In Vivo Desensitization

Resistant clients notably avoid discomfort and will do behavioral assignments that are relatively easy and comfortable—such as reading bibliographic material, listening to therapeutic tape recordings, or engaging in Wolpe's (1982) systematic desensitization procedures. But they often will not converse with strangers, engage in public talks, or stop their compulsive activities. RET therefore has always specialized in homework assignments that include *in vivo* desensitization and response prevention (Ellis, 1962, 1969b, 1970a, 1972c, 1973, 1977a, in press-a).

Frequently, you will simply not help resisters to change unless and until you get them, as noted above, to stay in unpleasant situations until they become more comfortable; and, in addition, you will not help them to give up their self-defeating fears unless you induce them to keep repeating, *in vivo*, acts that they irrationally fear (e.g., dancing or talking in public). By hook or crook, therefore, using your best persuasive and exhortatory methods, you had often better push them into desensitizing activities.

As a case in point, I saw a 38-year-old male who had never even petted with a woman, let alone had intercourse, even though he was obsessed with heterosexual fantasies and had masturbated (using these fantasies) daily for 25 years. It took six months of active-directive RET to get him to make a single date and another four months to induce him to make any sexual overtures to the woman he began dating. After giving him literally scores of homework assignments about talking to, dating, and making overtures to women, and after getting him to burn 800 dollars as penalties for not carrying out these assignments, he finally got going in his 11th month of treatment, and within the next year was so unfearful of dating and copulating that he had intercourse with 45 women—and began incessantly looking for new conquests. I finally had to work with him on his obsessive-compulsive dating and to convince him that there are other things in life besides sex! Without my strongly persisting at encouraging him to do *in vivo* desensitization, it is most doubtful (as we both agreed) that he would have ever got over his extreme fears of sexual rejection.

Similarly, I saw a woman who washed her hands at least 20 times on every occasion that she urinated or defecated, out of extreme fear that if even minute amounts of urine or feces remained on her hands she would be hopelessly contaminated. By persistently showing her that she had virtually no chance of giving up her lifelong need for certainty and its concomitant feelings of overwhelming anxiety unless she forced herself, however painfully, to refrain from her handwashing, I helped her to decrease her hand washing by ten percent every week until she was able, at the end of ten weeks, to wash her hands only once every time she went to the bathroom. For the first several weeks, she was extremely anxious every time she left the bathroom. But as she kept vehemently telling herself, "I *don't* need certainty! If I get contaminated, tough—I'll still live and be happy!" her anxiety went away. Eleven years of previous psychoanalytic therapy had hardly affected this woman, and may have been iatrogenic. But in ten weeks of RET-oriented *in vivo* response prevention she improved remarkably. As her handwashing and her anxiety steadily decreased, she also became much less shy and inactive and began to have a fuller social life, whereas she had for many years been a recluse. In her case, as in that of many of the people I induce to do *in vivo* desensitization and response prevention, my convincing her that unless she deliberaterly courted and lived through her current anxiety she would probably have to suffer with it forever seemed to significantly help her deliberately institute present pain to achieve future gain.

Implosive Desensitization

Although graduated desensitization exercises to remove irrational fears have been favored by behavior therapists for many years (Jones, 1924a, 1924b; Watson & Reyner, 1920; Wolpe, 1958, 1982), they have their disadvantages and limitations (Ellis, 1983a), especially when used with resistant clients. For one thing, such clients can build up renewed fears in the intervals between the gradual desensitizing procedures. Perhaps more importantly, difficult clients usually have abysmal low frustration tolerance (LFT) and if they are encouraged to surrender their self-defeating behaviors *easily* and *gradually* this kind of procedure implies that they *have to* avoid pain and in some ways it may sustain or even increase their LFT philosophy.

Consequently, you may often find it advantageous to have your resistant clients desensitize themselves implosively with massed instead of graduated practice (Marks, 1972; Stampfl & Lewis, 1967). To illustrate, I frequently tell the story of a 45-year-old accountant who had suffered from an elevator phobia for more than 30 years and who went to great lengths (sometimes walking up and down more than 20 flights of stairs) to avoid riding in them. He refused to do the graduated desensitization homework assignments which I and his therapy group gave him, even though three other members of the group gradually went in elevators and overcame their long-standing phobias of doing so. He came to me one day for a special session of individual therapy and said, "I'm getting desperate. I could get several better jobs than the one I have but all of them are on the upper floors of tall buildings and I would have to get over my elevator fears to take them. What shall I do? How can I overcome my phobias?"

Knowing this man's great resistance to graduated homework, I said to myself, "Nothing will probably do any good as far as getting him to go through the anxiety of riding in elevators, but what have we got to lose? I think I'll be very strong and see what happens." So I said to him, very powerfully and with all the sincerity I could muster, "Well, seeing what your record of resistance has been so far, not only to RET but to the 15 years of therapy you had before I saw you, I would say that you only have two good possibilities to overcoming your self-indulged fear of elevators."

"What are those two possibilities?" he anxiously asked. His voice was quavering and his hands were waving around in a clearly distraught manner.

"One," I said, "get in those damned elevators at least 20 times a day every single day for the next 30 days. Yes! At least 20 times a day for the next 30 days! Or—" I deliberately paused dramatically, knowing what my next highly significant sentence was going to be.

"Or what?" he asked.

"Or suffer enormously for the rest of your life! Yes, s-u-f-f-e-r—*suffer*! Forever! Which of these two will you choose?"

My client's face blanched and his lips compulsively clamped. I thought he would almost have a fit, but he grimly and silently held his facial muscles in check. A few minutes later he left my office, and I was convinced that he would still do nothing about getting into elevators.

Well, I was wrong. As he reported to the next group session five days later, that very afternoon he forced himself to ride in 22 elevators. The next day he took 21 rides, the third day 24 rides, and so on for the next few weeks. By the eighth day of his implosive *in vivo* therapy he had overcome over 80% of his fear of elevators. On the tenth day he forced himself to ride an elevator in New York City's World Trade Center Twin Towers, the highest elevator buildings in the world, on a day so windy that the building was shaking somewhat (as tall buildings do on windy days) and workmen were fixing some of the elevators. Nonetheless he took the express elevator to the 98th floor of the building—and experienced virtually no feelings of anxiety.

This does not mean that if you use implosive therapy with your difficult clients it will always work—hell, no! Frequently they won't carry it out—or they'll do it only briefly, then stop. But if you keep after them, and strongly convince them that no matter how hard it is to do, implosive *in vivo* assignments frequently work much better, and especially more quickly, to overcome their irrational fears, you will sometimes be able to help resisters to use them—and thereby help themselves enormously. In the case of my accountant client, once he overcame his elevator phobia, he clearly and cognitively *saw* that several of his other fears—especially his fear of talking to strange women and of going on job interviews—were quite unfounded, and he began to fearlessly talk to women, to go on interviews, and to do several other social and business tasks that he had been paralyzed to do previously. But, once again, this does not mean that implosive therapy always or even usually works. When used discriminately in selective cases, and vigorously pushed, however, it can induce some resisters to overcome emotional and behavioral problems that they otherwise might never surmount.

Skill Training

RET often includes skill training—that is, showing clients how to change their Activating Events (A) and their disturbed Beliefs (B) and Consequences (C) by learning communication, assertion, sex, problem solving, and other skills (Ellis, 1956, 1962, in press-a; Ellis & Becker, 1982; Grieger & Boyd, 1980; Lange & Jakubowski, 1976; Paris & Casey, 1983; Walen, DiGiuseppe &

Wessler, 1980; Wessler & Wessler, 1980; Wolfe, 1977; Wolfe & Fodor, 1975). Many resistant clients who will not go along with RET Disputing or other cognitive methods will often be amenable to learning practical skills that will help them perform better and enjoy life. Through such skill training they can sometimes be helped to change their behaviors and even, ultimately, to work at changing some of their iBs.

As a case illustration, I saw a 59-year-old woman who had suffered from painful intercourse and vaginismus all her life with her husband (to whom she had been married 30 years) and with four previous lovers. All the men in her life had been blue-collar workers who saw sex mainly as intercourse and who had only tried to satisfy her with penile-vaginal copulation; and she had unassertively let them do as they would and had consequently only had painful sex and highly incomplete intromission. Yet a recent gynecological examination had shown that there was nothing wrong with her vaginally or sexually.

I had a very hard time at first trying to help this woman see that sex was not shameful and that she had a perfect right to talk to her impatient husband about her sex problems and to get him to arouse her fully before intercourse and to satisfy her non-coitally if she didn't experience orgasm during coitus.

Being anxious for her husband's approval and ashamed of sexual discussion, this woman at first resisted sex therapy, and also refused to bring her husband into conjoint therapy, so that I could educate him as to some of the sexual facts of life. Seeing that I was not getting very far with this client, I used RET assertion training with her (Alberti & Emmons, 1982; Ellis, 1975a; Lange & Jakubowski, 1976; Paris & Casey, 1983; Wolfe, 1977; Wolfe & Fodor, 1975, 1977). I showed her, in social and business affairs, how to be much more assertive. I also had her read several sex manuals, including *The Art and Science of Love* (Ellis, 1965), *Sex and the Liberated Man* (Ellis, 1976b), *The Intelligent Woman's Guide to Dating and Mating* (Ellis, 1979c), and *The Joy of Sex* (Comfort, 1972).

As she acquired assertive and sex skills, this woman became more confident of her own abilities for the first time, saw that she *could* enjoy herself sexually, forced herself to speak up to her husband after 30 years of verbal shilly-shallying, and overcame her shame and guilt about going after what she really wanted in bed. The anti-shame and self-accepting philosophy that RET teaches people helped her significantly. But without the assertion-training skills and the sex information that were also provided to her in the course of therapy, the Disputing of her iBs may not have taken hold and been effective.

RET, therefore, often includes information giving, role playing, and other elements of active skill training. If you use this type of RET-oriented assertion training, communication training, sex training, and other types of skill training with your DCs, you will often help them considerably.

Behavior Rehearsal and Role Playing

A good many resistant clients avoid doing their therapeutic homework and cannot easily be monitored by mates, relatives, or friends to see that they do it. With some of these clients, behavior rehearsal or role playing within individual or group RET sessions will serve as a temporary substitute for *in vivo* homework and may get these clients, ultimately, started on doing such homework.

For example, I had a 40-year-old teacher in one of my therapy groups for a year and a half and she still would not stand up to her pupils, fellow teachers, and principal as the group kept urging her to do. Her overweening fear of others' disapproval always interfered with her being more assertive and prevented her from carrying out her *in vivo* homework assignments. Finally, spurred on by one of my RET trainees, who was assisting me in group and who liked the technique of role playing, I started to use this method regularly with this client.

Every week, for a period of about 20 weeks, I got this teacher to play herself while one of the group members played someone in school with whom she was having difficulty (e.g., a surly pupil or an intimidating supervisor). In doing this kind of role playing, we quickly brought out the client's feelings of anxiety and inadequacy and were able to show her what she was telling herself to create these feelings. Thus, she kept insisting to herself that she couldn't stand others' raised voices; and we helped her see that she damned well *could* stand them and did *not* have to put herself down when she heard them.

By constant behavior rehearsal, moreover, we were able to help this resistant client acquire a repertoire of adequate verbal and motor responses to her "persecutors" at school and, as she rehearsed these responses, she became more able to use them in practice and to start doing the *in vivo* homework assignments that we had previously given her in vain.

Systematic Desensitization

I have rarely used Wolpe's (1958, 1982) famous method of systematic desensitization (SD) in RET because I think it usually inferior to *in vivo* desensitization and to courting discomfort (mentioned above). However, with some resistant clients who will not engage in *in vivo* homework assignments, I and other RETers sometimes first use SD in an effort to loosen them up.

Thus, I saw a 36-year-old computer programmer who had only kissed a man lightly twice in her life and who had refrained from all petting and other sex acts. She now wanted to get over her fear of sex because she wanted to relate to a man she cared for but who would have nothing to do with her unless she at least petted with him. I gave her several homework assignments to force herself to kiss this man passionately and to do some mild petting with him, but she refused to do any of them. I then used systematic desensitization with her and got her to imagine herself petting with her inamorato and to relax and think of him being affectionate (but not sexual) with her every time she became anxious. After she did this several times, and thereby reduced her sexual anxiety, she was able to start doing *in vivo* petting assignments and finally have intercourse with the man she cared for, and did so in an enjoyable, nonanxious manner. Without the preliminary use of SD, she might have quit therapy without ever doing the *in vivo* petting.

As can again be seen from the above material, RET often employs a variety of behavioral techniques, in addition to many cognitive and emotive methods, with resistant clients. Rarely, if ever, does it compulsively stick to one favored method. In fact, the more resistant a client is, the more cognitive, emotive, and behavioral methods are usually employed. RET is designed to be not only effective but efficient and therefore to solve clients' problems as quickly as feasible, utilizing minimal therapist time and effort (see Chapter 7). With average clients who are not resistant, it can therefore often employ a relatively small number of techniques and can help these clients to improve significantly in a fairly short period of time. It invariably uses *some* cognitive, emotive, and behavioral modalities but doesn't have to compulsively utilize many of them, as is sometimes done in multimodal therapy (Lazarus, 1981) or in holistic psychotherapy. With resistant clients, however, RET is often done more comprehensively and intensively because that is what such clients sometimes require.

The Use of Cognitive Homework

As noted at the end of Chapter 3, RET has always specialized in the use of cognitive homework and, especially, in using various kinds of rational self-help forms to help clients dispute their irrational Beliefs (iBs) until they significantly change them and until they get themselves to wind up with strong rational Beliefs (rBs) and a more effective philosophy of life (Burns, 1980; Ellis, 1969b, 1970b, 1974a; Ellis & Grieger, 1977; Ellis & Harper, 1975; Maultsby, 1975, 1978, 1984; Sichel & Ellis, 1984). Resistant clients particularly require cognitive homework, because (1) they tend to rigidly hold their iBs; (2) they often do not see that they hold them, even after their therapist has pointed them out several times; (3) they tend to insist that their iBs are really rational; (4) they temporarily give them up but then go back to strongly believing them again; and (5) when urged by the therapist to keep looking for and then Disputing their unrealistic and absolutistic ideas, they fail to do so or they do so sporadically and sloppily when they had better do so consistently and precisely.

It is therefore often desirable to assign specific cognitive homework—including the filling out of self-help report forms—to resisters and to check on them to see that they keep working at them, bringing them in for discussion, learning to correct them, and then getting into the habit of using them on a steady basis. At the Institute for Rational-Emotive Therapy in New York, we have experimented over the years with different kinds of self-help forms and have found just about all of them to be highly useful, but have also found that if they are too complicated and require too much work on the part of the clients, they tend to be used only sporadically. Dr. Joyce Sichel and I have therefore taken the form we have used for the last decade (Ellis, 1970b) and have modified and simplified it (Sichel & Ellis, 1984). We have used this new Self-help Report Form for two years and find that it is more useful than the previous version and is much more likely to be steadily filled out by our clients, and particularly by our resistant clients (see Figure 1). This form also includes a typical set of responses to it by a resistant client.

Another self-help item that we have found helpful with many clients, and again particularly with resistant ones, is Disputing Irrational Beliefs (DIBS) (Ellis, 1974a). Using DIBS, you encourage your resistant clients to write down, as precisely as they can, one of their main iBs, and then to ask themselves a series of questions about it and to write down their answers until they change the belief and tend to keep it changed.

For example, one of my borderline clients, a 32-year-old male who devoutly believed that he must never make any kind of serious mistake at his job (claims adjuster), filled out DIBS as follows:

What irrational beliefs do I want to dispute and surrender: I must never make a serious mistake at work.

Is this belief true? No, it is not true; it is obviously false.

Why is this belief false? Because: (1) If I *must* not under any conditions make a serious mistake at work, then that would be a law of the universe and I could not make one. But obviously I can and do make mistakes, so that law does not exist. (2) I obviously have made many serious mistakes at work and (a) I am still around to make more of them, and (b) nothing terrible has happened and my firm is still in business. (3) Everyone else I know who works for my firm, including several of my superiors, keep making serious mistakes and they do not get fired and manage to survive quite happily.

Is there any evidence that my belief is true? No, there doesn't seem to be any. It is true that if I make serious mistakes at work it will be unfortunate and I may be penalized—I may lose salary in-

FIGURE 1. RET Self-Help Form. Copyrighted 1984 by the Institute for Rational-Emotive Therapy.

RET SELF-HELP FORM

Institute for Rational-Emotive Therapy
45 East 65th Street, New York, N.Y. 10021
(212) 535-0822

(A) ACTIVATING EVENTS, thoughts, or feelings that happened just before I felt emotionally disturbed or acted self-defeatingly: _____
My boss yelled at me in front of three people I supervise

(C) CONSEQUENCE or CONDITION—disturbed feeling or self-defeating behavior—that I produced and would like to change: _____
(1) Anger (2) Humiliation

(B) BELIEFS—Irrational BELIEFS (IBs) leading to my CONSEQUENCE (emotional disturbance or self-defeating behavior). Circle all that apply to these ACTIVATING EVENTS (A).	**(D) DISPUTES** for each circled IRRATIONAL BELIEF. Examples: "*Why MUST I do very well?*" "*Where is it written that I am a BAD PERSON?*" "*Where is the evidence that I MUST be approved or accepted?*"	**(E) EFFECTIVE RATIONAL BELIEFS (RBs)** to replace my IRRATIONAL BELIEFS (IBs). Examples: "*I'd PREFER to do very well but I don't HAVE TO.*" "*I am a PERSON WHO acted badly, not a BAD PERSON.*" "*There is no evidence that I HAVE TO be approved, though I would LIKE to be.*"
1. I MUST do well or very well!	*Why must I?*	*I don't have to, but it would be better if I did.*
2. I am a BAD OR WORTHLESS PERSON when I act weakly or stupidly.	*Where is the evidence that I am worthless?*	*Only in my head! At worst, I am a person who acted stupidly this time & can change.*
3. I MUST be approved or accepted by people I find important!	*Really?*	*No. I'd like my boss's approval but I don't need it.*
4. I am a BAD, UNLOVABLE PERSON if I get rejected.	*Why am I?*	*Only because I foolishly tell myself I am!*
5. People MUST treat me fairly and give me what I NEED!	*Where does the universe command this?*	*It doesn't! People have the right to treat me unfairly! And they will use it!*
6. People who act immorally are undeserving, ROTTEN PEOPLE!	*Is my boss really a thoroughly rotten person?*	*No. He has many good traits even if he treated me rottenly this time.*
7. People MUST live up to my expectations or it is TERRIBLE!		
8. My life MUST have few major hassles or troubles.		
9. I CAN'T STAND really bad things or very difficult people!	*In what way can't I stand my boss's unfairness?*	*I can stand it and still be a happy person!*

(OVER)

116

FIGURE 1. *(continued)*

10. It's AWFUL or HORRIBLE when major things don't go my way!	*Why is it awful?*	*It's not! It's only damned inconvenient!*
11. I CAN'T STAND IT when life is really unfair!		
12. I NEED to be loved by someone who matters to me a lot!		
13. I NEED a good deal of immediate gratification and HAVE TO feel miserable when I don't get it!		
Additional Irrational Beliefs:		
14. *I shouldn't have foolishly upset myself about this.*	*Where is it written that I must not upset myself?*	*Only in my nutty philosophy! It's foolish to upset myself but I am a fallible human who should at times act foolishly.*
15.		
16.		
17.		
18.		

(F) FEELINGS and BEHAVIORS I experienced after arriving at my EFFECTIVE RATIONAL BELIEFS *(1) Displeasure at my boss's behavior (2) Regret at my supervisee's, Seeing him yell at me.*

I WILL WORK HARD TO REPEAT MY EFFECTIVE RATIONAL BELIEFS FORCEFULLY TO MYSELF ON MANY OCCASIONS SO THAT I CAN MAKE MYSELF LESS DISTURBED NOW AND ACT LESS SELF-DEFEATINGLY IN THE FUTURE.

Joyce Sichel, Ph.D. and Albert Ellis, Ph.D.
Copyright © 1984 by the Institute for Rational-Emotive Therapy.

100 forms $10.00
1000 forms $80.00

creases. So this evidence shows that it is highly *desirable* that I don't make serious mistakes at work. But because it is highly *desirable* hardly proves that it is *necessary* that I don't make serious mistakes—that I *must* not make them. No matter how desirable any of my actions is, there doesn't seem to be any proof that I therefore *must* act desirably. It is good and proper that I do act that way—but hardly *necessary*.

What are the worst things that could actually happen to me if I keep making serious mistakes at work? (1) I could get criticized by my superiors. (2) I could lose raises and promotions. (3) I could possibly be fired. (4) If I were fired, I might find it very difficult or impossible to get a job that is equally good. (5) At the very worst, I might not be able to get any other job and might have to go on welfare. But even if any or all of these *worst* things came to pass, it would only mean that I would be highly inconvenienced, and not that I would starve and die. And even if I never got another job as good as this one, I could still be reasonably happy at a lesser one—or, for that matter, if I were on welfare. I wouldn't *like* any of these things to happen, but there is no reason why, if worse came to worse and they did happen, I could still not live a fairly enjoyable existence.

What good things could happen or could I make happen if I keep making serious mistakes at work? (1) I could learn from my mistakes and therefore do better in the future. (2) I could give myself unconditional acceptance in spite of my mistakes—accept myself as a *fallible* human who will always make some serious blunders, just because I am human. (3) I could discover that some of the people with whom I work, including some of my supervisors, actually *like* my making mistakes—because it makes them feel better about their work and their fallibility. (4) Even if some people in my office began to dislike me for making serious mistakes, I could convince myself that I do not *need* their approval, although it would be very nice to have it, and that I could be a happy human without their liking me. (5) By continuing to make serious mistakes at my job—and at other things I do in life—I can accept the *challenge* of seeing myself as an okay individual even if I am criticized, even though I make less money, and even if my job never turns out too well. (6) If I keep making a good many serious mistakes after I have calmed myself down and have stopped castigating myself for making them, I may discover that this is really not the right job for me, and I may be able to find another kind of work where I make fewer errors and I feel happier about working.

After this client had filled out DIBS in this manner, and after he had filled out a number of other DIBS sheets on doing poorly in his social life, he became much less anxious and depressed about his work and about his social relations, and he then began to perform better in both these areas. With the help of these DIBS sheets and by using our other Self-help Report Form (Sichel & Ellis, 1984), he began to accept himself with his failings for the first time in his life, and although he did not solve all his emotional problems he felt that he had significantly improved. I still see him from time to time at one of my regular Friday night Problems of Living workshops at the Institute for Rational-Emotive Therapy, and he tells me that he is doing much better but that he successfully uses our Self-help Report Form, and especially DIBS, whenever he temporarily falls back into a state of anxiety or depression.

Helping Clients Strengthen and Maintain Therapeutic Progress

As noted in the previous section, virtually all psychotherapy clients, and particularly resistant ones, tend to fall back either temporarily or permanently after they have made significant progress in changing themselves. According to RET theory, this largely stems from the human condition: the propensity of men and women (not to mention children!) to see what they are doing badly, to work at doing better, and then to fairly easily fall back into their old, sloppy, lazy habits of emotional disturbance and behavioral malfunctioning (Ellis, 1962, 1976c).

Must we then feel hopeless about achieving and maintaining therapeutic change? Not quite! RET faces this challenge by being notably behavioral (as well as cognitive and emotive) and by stressing what it calls Insight No. 3 (see Chapter 3): that there is normally no way but work and practice—yes, *work and practice*—for disturbed individuals to make themselves and keep themselves less disturbed. To this end, RET stresses, especially for resistant clients, that they keep working to achieve and to maintain their gains over their emotional and behavioral problems. To help them do this, it encourages them to read the RET-oriented literature and to listen to audiocassettes (as noted in Chapter 3), and to keep doing so (going over this kind of material) many times.

One of the pamphlets published by the Institute for Rational-Emotive Therapy in New York and used with all its clients, and notably with its resistant clients, is the following one, "How to Use RET to Maintain and Enhance Your Therapeutic Gains" (Ellis, 1984g). This handout gives cognitive behavioral instructions for working at the maintenance of progress in therapy:

How to Use RET to Maintain and Enhance Your Therapeutic Gains

If you work hard at using the principles and practices of rational-emotive therapy (RET), you will probably significantly change your self-defeating thoughts, feelings, and behaviors and feel much better than when you start therapy. Good! But you will also, at times, fall back—and sometimes far back. No one is perfect and virtually all psychotherapy clients take one step backwards to every two or three steps forward. Why? Because that is the nature of humans: to improve and to retrogress.

How can you (imperfectly!) retard your tendency to fall back and how can you maintain and enhance your goals? Here are some methods.

How to Maintain Your Improvement

1. Try to see exactly what thoughts, feelings, and behaviors you changed to bring about your improvement. For example, if you were severely depressed when therapy started and now you feel little or rarely depressed, you may discover that (a) you stopped telling yourself you are worthless and that you couldn't even succeed in getting what you want, that (b) you got yourself involved in a love relationship that is satisfying, and that (c) you forced yourself to go on job interviews instead of avoiding them.

2. Keep thinking, thinking, and thinking rational Beliefs (rBs), such as, "It's great to succeed but I can fully accept myself as a person

even when I fail!" Keep actively Disputing and challenging your irrational Beliefs (iBs), such as, "I *have* to succeed in order to be a worthwhile person!" Do this, as soon as feasible, whenever you return to your iBs; but also do it preventively, at least several times every week.

3. Seek out, unfrantically but persistently, personal pleasures and enjoyments—such as reading, entertainment, sports, hobbies, and vital interests.

4. Whenever you feel *in*appropriately depressed, anxious, or self-downing, make yourself, instead, feel *appropriately* sorry, concerned, disappointed, and annoyed, and don't stop working on changing your inappropriate to appropriate feelings until, at least temporarily, you succeed. Preventively use rational-emotive imagery to practice appropriate feelings in advance of things going wrong.

5. Keep risking and doing things that you irrationally fear—such as riding in elevators, socializing, job hunting, or creative writing. Once you have overcome one of your irrational fears, keep acting against it on a regular basis and don't allow any prolonged avoidance of it if your discomfort returns.

6. Avoid self-defeating procrastination. Do unpleasant tasks fast—today! Only allow certain rewards (for example, eating, vacationing, reading, socializing) *after* you have performed difficult tasks that you easily avoid.

7. Accept the active *challenge* of maintaining your emotional health and feeling reasonably happy no matter how unfortunate are some of your life events. Steadily and determinedly see that you almost always have some *choice* of how you think, feel, and behave.

8. Remember—and use—the three main insights of RET. *Insight No. 1:* You largely *choose* to disturb yourself about the unpleasant events of your life, even though you may be encouraged to do so by external happenings and by social learning. You consciously or unconsciously *select* certain iBs and self-defeating behaviors. *Insight No. 2:* No matter how or when you acquired your irrational ideas and self-sabotaging habits, you now, in the present, choose to maintain them—and that is why you are *now* disturbed. *Insight No. 3:* There is rarely any other way than persistent *work and practice*—yes, *work and practice*—to change your iBs, inappropriate feelings, and self-destructive behaviors.

How to Deal with Backsliding

1. Accept your backsliding as a normal, almost inevitable condition. See it as part of your human fallibility. Evaluate *it* as bad and unfortunate, but (as we teach *ad nauseam* in RET) pigheadedly refuse to rate *you*, your *self* or *being*, as a bad or incompetent person.

2. Put your recurring symptoms and problems in the usual ABC framework of RET. Assume that your renewed anxiety (or feelings of hostility or depression) is a Consequence (C) of some Activating Event (A) interacting with some set of your Beliefs (B) and especially of some of your irrational beliefs (iBs).

3. Just as you originally used Disputing (D) to challenge and surrender your iBs, do so again—but immediately and persistently. For example, if you have the iB, "I *must* win So-and-so's approval to be happy with myself," keep Disputing: "*Where is the evidence* that I *must?*" "*Prove* that I *have to.*" "Though winning So-and-so's approval may be highly desirable, what *law of the universe says* that I *absolutely need it?*" Continue Disputing your iB until you really see and feel that you have changed it.

4. Very strongly and vigorously say to yourself—and *convince* yourself of—rBs, such as: "I do not *need* what I *want!*" "*Nothing* is awful or terrible—only inconvenient!" "I *can* stand what I don't like!" "*No* human is damnable and worthless—including me!"

How to Generalize from Working on One Emotional Problem to Working on Other Problems

1. Show yourself that most (perhaps all) emotional and behavioral problems are mediated by your (and others') iBs and can be alleviated by your strongly and persistently changing these iBs.

2. Recognize that there are three major kinds of irrationalities that lead to disturbance and that the symptom you are working to alleviate thus falls under one, two, or three major headings: (a) "I *must* do well and be approved by significant others!" (b) "Other people *must* treat me fairly and nicely!" (c) "My conditions of living *must* be easy and *have to* give me what I want (and *need!*) when I want it."

3. Recognize that when you employ one of these absolutistic *musts*, you easily and naturally make other irrational conclusions, such as: (a) "It is *awful* to fail and be disapproved (as I *must* not be)!" (b) "I *can't stand it* when I fail and am disapproved of (as I *must* not be!*)" (c) "I am an inferior person for failing and being disapproved of (as I *must* not be)!"

4. Recognize and think carefully about the hypothesis that just about all your present and future disturbances, like the present ones on which you are working, are *also* related to the three major iBs posited by RET and by their main illogical and antiempirical derivative irrationalities. Figure out (many times!) that it is almost impossible for you to disturb yourself in *any* way if you rigorously stay with your *desires* and *preferences* and rationally surrender your absolutistic, dogmatic, devout musts.

5. Profoundly acknowledge that you can change your iBs by using the scientific method—by taking your iBs as hypotheses (not as facts) and by logically and empirically Disputing them until you prove to yourself that they are untenable. Observe that flexible thinking and scientific challenging is incompatible with iBs that lead to emotional-behavioral disturbance and that the scientific method can almost invariably be employed—if you will *work* at using it—to alleviate needless disturbance.

7

The Value of Efficiency in Helping Resistant Clients

The issue of value in psychotherapy is exceptionally important, and the existential therapists in particular may be credited with highlighting this importance (Adler, 1968; Frankl, 1966; May, 1969). Some psychotherapeutic values, however, have often been neglected and I shall stress in this chapter one of these: namely, efficiency, which I think is somewhat different from the value of effectiveness. Usually, we test the "effectiveness" of a given form of therapy by showing that, in both controlled experiments and in clinical practice, it results in significant gains for clients when therapized groups are compared to placebo or nontherapized groups. But we rarely test the "efficiency" of treatment methods to determine, on a cost-benefit basis, how much time and effort is normally spent by therapists and clients to achieve "effective" results and how pervasive, thoroughgoing, and long lasting these "results" are. Yet, in view of recent efforts to establish suitable criteria for governmental and insurance-company standards for reimbursing "competent" therapists under existing and suggested mental-health plans, a cost-benefit approach to psychotherapy looms as increasingly important (Hogan, 1980; Pottinger, 1980; Strupp, 1980).

What are some of the main goals to strive for in therapy that is efficient as well as effective? After giving this matter serious thought for more than a quarter of a century, and after experimenting in my own practice with several different methods of psychological treatment ranging from classical psychoanalysis to rational-emotive therapy, I have come up with the following hypotheses about "efficient" psychotherapy.

Brevity in Psychotherapy

Although Freud (1965e) himself usually practiced what today would be called brief psychotherapy and saw most of his analysands for only a matter of months (Jones, 1953), psychoanalysis turned to a longer period of treatment, usually taking a minimum of two years in its classic form and often much longer than that. In recent years, however, many analytically oriented therapists have espoused brief treatment (Sifneos, 1970; Small, 1979) and much of today's nonanalytic therapy is relatively short (Ellis & Abrahms, 1978). This obviously has its advantages: since most clients are disturbed when they come for therapy, they function on a low level of competency; they enjoy themselves little; and the longer they take to overcome their disturbances, the more they and their associates are likely to suffer. Psychotherapy, moreover, is usually expensive and time consuming, and if it is possible to achieve effective treatment in a short period of time, more clients will tend to come, stay in it, and benefit from it in various ways. Governmental and other agencies, moreover, will be more enthusiastic about reimbursing therapists for brief rather than for prolonged therapy.

Resistant clients usually require prolonged treatment in order to make significant improvement. But effective therapy—such as RET—sometimes is relatively brief with them for several reasons: (1) It confronts them with their irrational thinking, actively disputes such thinking, and quickly determines that they are not likely to benefit from therapy or that only limited gains are likely to be achieved. (2) It determines that they had better be forcefully approached in only a few major areas—such as self-downing—and it efficiently restricts itself to those areas where progress is likely to be made and deals lightly with other factors (e.g., complex interpersonal relationships) which may not be too improvable. (3) Efficient therapy that is direct and hardheaded may stop resistant clients from being vague and roundabout and induce them to zero in on specific symptoms, what they are doing to create these symptoms, and how to go about changing them. Thus, RET induces these clients to focus on their ABCs and to start with C, their emotional and behavioral Consequences (e.g., severe anxiety or depression). It then helps them see what are their most common and frequent Activating Events (As) (e.g., a boss treating them unfairly or a lover rejecting them). It then encourages them to find their concrete irrational Beliefs (iBs) (e.g., "My boss *must* treat me fairly!" "I *have to* make my lover care for me!"). It then proceeds to detailed Disputing (D). By focusing on this exact specifying of symptoms, inciting situations, iBs, and disputations of these irrationalities, RET helps some of the vaguest and most confused resisters to concentrate on important aspects of their severe disturbances and, in a relatively brief period of time, to gain some degree of self-understanding and make some significant gains.

Depth-centeredness in Psychotherapy

Many modes of therapy, especially psychoanalysis, advocate that psychotherapy be depth centered (Freud, 1965e; Jones, 1956; Kaplan, 1979). They assume that many symptoms, such as phobias, not only have an environmental and experiential core but also have some kind of deep-seated, underlying "cause," and that this has to be thoroughly understood and worked through over a period of therapeutic time before it can really be resolved. In existential and philosophic therapies it is also assumed that a symptom has depth-centered roots. Thus, RET holds that people's phobias laregly stem from a basic absolutistic or *musturba-tory* philosophy—e.g., "I *must* not suffer any form of severe discomfort or failure when I ride in elevators!"—and that it probably will not be resolved unless clients understand their self-invented "needs" for certainty and unless they consistently think and act against these "necessities."

There are many advantages to therapists trying to help clients arrive at their fundamental disturbance-creating ideas and then to surrender these for less disturbing philosophies: (1) They cannot only help reveal the sources of clients' current symptoms, but preferably should also help reveal prior and later ones, so that they obtain a more comprehensive and clearer knowledge of what they do to disturb themselves. (2) Clients may, in addition to eliminating their negative symptoms, show themselves how to lead a more joyous, creative, and fulfilled existence. (3) Depth-centered psychotherapy may promote a general understanding of human "nature" that may be relevant to many aspects of living, including social and political relations, international understanding, and artistic pursuits.

Because some of its formulations and techniques are simple and clear, RET is often accused of being superficial. Actually, it tries to be depth centered by determining *central* philosophies that create disturbance and by showing clients how to modify these *basic* ideas. It assumes that most serious resisters are little aware of their key irrationalities and/or rigidly hold on to them. And it encourages therapists to work hard at revealing, clarifying, and disputing them. By this kind of piercing, deep-thinking approach, it hypothesizes that it reaches many resisters who otherwise would be unreceptive to therapeutic change.

Pervasiveness in Psychotherapy

Pervasiveness in psychotherapy may be defined as the therapist's helping clients to deal with many of their problems, and in a sense their whole lives, rather than with a few present symptoms. Thus, a psychoanalyst who sees a woman who has poor sex with her husband will try to zero in not merely on that particular issue but also on her general relations with her mate and with other significant people in her life. And a rational-emotive therapist may first show this woman that she has great fear of failing sexually with her husband (because of her absolutistic philosophy, "I *have to* do well sexually and *must* win his approval!") but *also* show her how her dire "need" for success and love are interfering with her other marital and nonmarital functions.

Like depth-centeredness, the value of pervasiveness in psychotherapy has distinct benefits: (1) It shows clients how they can easily create several symptoms from the same underlying attitudes and feelings and how, by changing these attitudes, they can deal with or eliminate more than one or two present symptoms. (2) It helps them to understand and relate better to other people. (3) It may enable them, especially if they learn to apply a form of treatment like RET, to learn how to deal therapeutically with their close associates (Ellis, 1957a).

Resistant clients, RET hypothesizes, tend to have more than one presenting symptom and, especially when they are in the borderline range, to be pervasively disturbed. With such clients, therefore, RET particularly looks at several of their emotional and behavioral problems and tries to help them acquire a basic philosophic change that will apply to virtually *all* of them. It aims at specific *and* general alleviation of their disturbability.

Extensiveness in Psychotherapy

Extensiveness in psychotherapy means that clients can be helped not only to minimize their negative feelings (e.g., anxiety, depression, rage, and self-pity) but also to maximize their potential for happy living (e.g., to be more productive, creative, and enjoying). Where "intensive" therapy usually deals with pain, inhibition, panic, and horror, "extensive" therapy also deals with exploring and augmenting pleasure, sensuality, and laughter. "Efficient" psychotherapy, therefore, includes "intensive" as well as "extensive" treatment, provides self-actualizing as well as deinhibiting procedures, and thereby tries to provide additional gains in the cost-benefit issues that are inevitably involved in therapy.

RET attempts intensive therapy with most resistant clients, as indicated above. But because it views many resisters as limited individuals who may never achieve and maintain thoroughgoing change, it realistically concentrates, in some instances, on helping them to achieve more pleasures, and especially a vital absorbing interest, so that even when they still have serious emotional difficulties they can lead a tolerable and often enjoyable existence (Ellis & Abrahms, 1978, 1979a, 1979b; Ellis & Becker, 1982; Ellis & Whiteley, 1979).

Multimodal Techniques

Since what we call "thought," "emotion," and "behavior" are processes that hardly exist in any pure state but significantly overlap and interact, and since "emotional disturbance" has cognitive and behavioral as well as emotional aspects, "efficient" psychotherapy had better consider and often include multimodal techniques (Ellis, 1979f; Ellis & Grieger, 1977; A. Lazarus, 1981; Wachtel, 1978). This does not mean that it will unselectively use any and all available methods; but it will tend to be a comprehensive system that explores several pathways and will test these to see which usually work best and which had better be used minimally with different clients. The more comprehensive a therapist's armamentarium of techniques is, the more likely he or she is to find suitable procedures for especially unique or difficult clients.

With resistant clients, RET particularly uses a wide variety of cognitive, emotive, and behavioral methods—as demonstrated throughout this book. It assumes that if usual methods do not work, some unusual ones may. It also assumes that if one manner of presentation (e.g., vigorous disputing of iBs) does not seem to be effective, a different emphasis (e.g., more laid back and cautious disputing) may work. Like some forms of strategic therapy (Haley, 1963, 1984; Madanes, 1981; Watzlawick, Weakland & Fisch, 1974), RET tries to be creative and wide ranging in its selection of suitable methods of resolving the problem of resisters (Ellis, 1959a; 1962; Ellis & Abrahms, 1979a, 1979b).

Maintaining Therapeutic Progress

Symptom removal, as Wolpe (1982) has stated, may be valuable and may even lead to a real "cure." But it also has distinct limitations: (1) When a given symptom is removed or ameliorated, another may easily spring up later—not necessarily because of symptom substitution but as a derivative of the same basic self-defeating philosophy with which clients create their original symptoms. (2) Many clients feel so relieved by the temporary or partial removal of a painful symptom (e.g., depression) that they leave the core of it (or its close relatives) still standing.

(3) Most clients have some degree of low frustration tolerance (LFT) and therefore will welcome palliative procedures (e.g., tranquilizers or relaxation methods) to quickly alleviate their worst symptoms rather than working at more elegant philosophic changes that will result in more permanent changes.

For reasons such as these, "efficient" therapy does not merely strive for symptom removal but for more lasting therapeutic gain; and, no matter how pleased clients may feel about their "cures," it does not accept these unless there is some evidence that they will be maintained for a period of time and, preferably, unless clients keep improving after formal therapy has ended. In RET, in particular, one of the hallmarks of "elegant" or highly "efficient" psychotherapy is for treated individuals to feel significantly better at the close of therapy than they did at the beginning—but also to keep improving for a considerable period of time after therapy has officially ended (Ellis, 1979e).

RET faces the fact that borderline personalities, psychotics, and other kinds of resistant clients frequently fall back, sometimes to near zero, subsequent to making considerable (and sometimes remarkable) progress. It tries, however, to help them solidly attain an understanding of at least a few basic ideas about disturbance—especially the ideas that they tend to create their own emotional upsets and that they therefore can almost invariably change themselves. It also depth-centeredly shows them (as, again, indicated above) that they can change their basic absolutistic philosophies—their Jehovian shoulds, oughts, and musts. It thereby helps them get a fundamentally new frame of reference that maintains their gains and interferes with permanent retrogression. Even when they fall back to old dysfunctional ideas and behaviors, it gives them a method of quickly acknowledging that *they* redisturbed themselves and that *they* can forthrightly see what they did and can get to work at reducing their disturbance again.

Preventive Psychotherapy

Most modern systems of therapy strive to have their clients free of presenting symptoms at the close of treatment and still free of these same symptoms months or years after therapy has ended.

Another fairly obvious efficiency goal is that of teaching clients to understand themselves so well, to see so clearly how they usually create their own emotional problems, and to understand so solidly what they can do to restore their own emotional equilibrium that they are able to approach the future with a basically unupsetting philosophy. This is not easy, but it is presumably sometimes achievable. Just as medical patients can presumably learn from their physicians how to get over their current ailments and to prevent these from reoccurring, so can psychotherapy clients often learn from their therapists how to ward off future emotional ills and keep themselves from returning to their old disturbed pathways. From a cost-benefit standpoint it seems obvious that any kind of treatment that provides this kind of preventive therapy will provide more gains than symptom-removal treatments (because the results are lasting and cumulative) and also entail less expense (because the nonrecurrence of the symptoms precludes future hours of therapy).

RET specializes in preventive psychotherapy, especially with resistant clients, in several ways: (1) It is highly educational and tries to teach resisters (and others) that they do not merely *get* upset but *also* unduly upset *themselves* and that they do not *have* to do so. (2) It shows them that if they actively and forcefully keep disputing their iBs *after* they feel disturbed, they will eventually automatically learn how to believe rBs *before* they disturb themselves—and will thereby ward off much (though hardly all) maladjustment. (3) It teaches resisters several techniques, such as rational-emotive imagery, through which they can imagine dire happenings in advance of their actually occurring and can train themselves to react appropriately rather than inappropriately when these actually occur (Maultsby, 1975, 1984; Maultsby & Ellis, 1974). (4) It uses a good deal of *in vivo* desensitization and implosive activity homework assignments (including response prevention) which helps train resisters to rehabituate themselves so that they not only overcome current anxieties (e.g., fear of elevators), but lessen the possibility of their acquiring new ones (e.g., fear of subway trains). (5) It particularly works with the resisters who have secondary symptoms—such as anxiety about anxiety and depression about depression. As these clients come to see how they needlessly horrify themselves about their primary symptoms and how they can stop doing this, they often prevent themselves from developing brand-new symptoms to which secondary symptoms commonly lead.

Illustrative Case Presentation

It is interesting to discuss "efficiency" in psychotherapy abstractly, as I have just done, and to hypothesize about its advantages. Let me be more concrete, however, by presenting a clinical case that illustrates how some of these principles may be practiced. Calvin R., a 40-year-old physician, was exceptionally depressed when he came for RET. He damned himself for his medical errors and for his failings as a husband and father. He was extremely hostile toward his wife whenever she disagreed with him about important matters, and he fumed and frothed about even the smallest unniceties of his life, such as a leaky roof or a run in his socks.

Calvin was a resistant client because he came to therapy, at first, only because his sister (who had benefited from RET herself) insisted that he come. He was not psychologically oriented, preferred to believe that his depression only resulted from physical factors, and thought that if therapy helped at all, it had to be psychoanalytic and intensively explore his past and the part that his parents played in making him disturbed. In other words, Calvin did everything to deny the RET view that people's Beliefs (B) largely give them disturbed Consequences (C). He rigidly held the contrary view—that Activating Events (A), including biological factors, caused his depression (C).

I tried to use the main efficiency factors in RET with Calvin, and treated him along these lines:

Calvin's treatment was brief: he was seen for four months on a once-a-week basis, first for one hour and during the last two months for half-hour sessions. His therapy made little inroads into his very busy medical schedule.

In regard to depth-centeredness, he was helped to zero in on three basic *musts*, or absolutistic philosophies, which permeated almost his entire life and largely created his depressed feelings: (1) "I *must* do outstandingly well in my work and be approved by all my patients." (2) "My wife *must* never disagree with me about important things and *has to* do these things my way." (3) "Conditions under which I live *must* be easy and unhassled, and never frustrate me too badly." Although Calvin was at first convinced that his depression was purely biological and endogenous (even though several self-prescribed antidepressants had not lifted it a bit), I was able to show him that every time he felt depressed he was invariably demanding (not wishing) that he do well and castigating himself when he did not perform outstandingly, and that he was frequently commanding that things be better than they were. He soon acknowledged that his *must*urbatory philosophy underlay his depressed and hostile feelings and that, with this Jehovian attitude, *he* was making himself disturbed.

In the area of pervasiveness, although Calvin at first only wanted to discuss his horror of failing at work, and occasionally his anger at his wife, he was shown that his self-downing and his LFT invaded other areas of his life as well, including his sex activities and his social relations. In fact, he responded better at first in these two areas than he did in giving up his work perfectionism and he was partly able to give up the latter by first surrendering the former.

Regarding extensiveness, Calvin was not only taught how to work against his presenting symptoms but to add interests and pleasures to his days—such as music and running—that enhanced his existence, distracted him somewhat from his incessant worrying, and gave him two more vital absorbing interests that made life more enjoyable.

As for multimodal methods, Calvin was not only treated with the highly cognitive methods of RET (Ellis, 1962, 1979f, 1984c, 1984d), but given a number of emotive exercises and *in vivo* activity homework assignments as well. Thus, he especially seemed to benefit from shame-attacking exercises (Ellis, 1979c), rational-emotive imagery (Maultsby, 1975), and deliberately staying in some painful situation (such as visiting with his boring in-laws) and showing himself that he could stand, if not like, the pain (Ellis & Abrahms, 1978).

Best of all, Calvin seemed remarkably able to maintain his therapeutic progress and to do preventive psychotherapy on his own and increase his gains. For he first, after four months of therapy, lost his depression, went back to a full schedule of work, and started getting along remarkably well with his wife and family in spite of some difficulties which they themselves presented. This seemed surprising, considering the brevity of his therapy. But even more surprising was what he reported when he returned to see me two years later to talk about his wife, who was severely panicked about driving a car (after she had previously driven one without trouble for 12 years) and who was going through a period of severe depersonalization. For Calvin was handling this situation remarkably well, in spite of the immense transportation and other difficulties it was causing his entire family.

To make matters worse, Calvin himself had become afflicted, for the past six months, with a rheumatic condition that handicapped him seriously in his practice; one of his sons turned out to be dyslexic and was behaving in a highly delinquent manner; both his parents were dying of cancer; and his economic situation, for a variety of reasons including some poor investments on his part, had deteriorated. In spite of all these adversities, this ex-client's spirits were unusually high. He had virtually no hostility or self-pity in the face of his family frustrations. He was not downing himself for his own economic blunders. And he was doing a reasonably good job using some of the RET principles he had learned to help his wife, his children, and his parents cope with some of the serious emotional troubles that they all were undergoing.

This is the kind of "elegant" therapeutic results that I particularly strive for and like to see effected (Ellis, 1979e). Calvin not only overcame his presenting symptoms and maintained this change. Moreover, he improved significantly after therapy had ended and was at a stage, two years later, where he wouldn't allow virtually any normal kind of setbacks to disturb him too seriously (i.e., to make him depressed, panicked, hostile, or self-pitying).

Other Kinds of Efficiency in Psychotherapy

In addition to the ways previously hypothesized, some other kinds of efficiency in psychotherapy may be obtained in the following ways:

1. Efficient therapy tends to be stated in clear and simple terms, so that it is relatively easily understood both by practitioners and their clients. Abstruse or esoteric modes of therapy may have desirable qualities but they tend to have a limited appeal to therapists and, especially, to the people with whom they are used. Highly mystical and transpersonal forms of therapy, for example, are understood only by a minority of the populace, often aim at contradictory goals, and may easily lead their devotees astray into questionably "healthy" results (Ellis, 1972e).

2. Efficient psychotherapy is fairly easily teachable to therapists and does not require them to undergo years of training and apprenticeship, not to mention years of personal therapy themselves.

3. Efficient therapy is often intrinsically interesting to therapists and clients, and motivates the latter to stay with it and to use it in their outside lives. This aspect of therapy may indeed have boomerang effects: some of the most questionable and potentially harmful forms of psychological treatment—such as fanatical cult therapy like that promulgated by Jim Jones—are intrinsically fascinating to their followers and strongly motivate them to make changes in their lives. But assuming that a form of psychotherapy has healthy and lasting effects, it seems more efficient for it to be intrinsically interesting than dull and to be motivating than unmotivating.

4. Efficient psychotherapy helps clients achieve maximum good with minimum harm to themselves (and others). Many therapies, including some of the most esoteric and bizarre ones, help bring about healthy or beneficial results for clients (Frank, 1975). But it has also been shown that some of these forms of treatment have harmful results as well (Chapman, 1964; Garfield & Bergin, 1978; Gross, 1979; Hadley & Strupp, 1976; Lieberman, Yalom & Miles, 1973; Maliver, 1972; Rosen, 1977). It may also be questioned whether some modes of cultist or mystical therapies (such as shamanism or exorcism) do not create, as well as alleviate, disturbance (Ellis, 1972e, 1975b). Behavioral or emotional change, when effected through psychotherapy, had better be conducive of human survival and happiness, including social as well as individual happiness: if it leads to pernicious as well as beneficial social results, its efficiency had better be examined (Adler, 1964; Ellis, 1983b, 1984k; Zilbergeld, 1983).

5. Efficient psychotherapy favors flexibility, lack of dogma, and provision and encouragement for its own change. It not only tends to help its clients be less absolutistic, rigid, unscientific, and devout but it also endorses scientific falsifiability: that is, it sets up its theories so that they are ultimately falsifiable; it views them skeptically and tentatively; and it constantly strives to check on their errors and invalidities (Popper, 1962; Russell, 1965). In this manner, it not only tries to achieve but does its best to maintain both effectiveness and efficiency.

My work with many clients, and especially difficult and resistant ones, leads me to hypothesize that even when psychotherapy is shown, by controlled studies, to be effective it may still be inefficient; and that unless it includes some of the elements discussed in this chapter, its efficiency remains doubtful.

Psychotherapists, being humanistically oriented and somewhat allergic to hardheaded realities, often neglect the value of efficiency in their work. This is hardly in the best interests of their clients! Efficiency is a distinctly valuable concept for therapists, for their clients, and for the science of psychotherapy itself. Effectiveness is indeed an important aspect of psychological treatment, and we had better strive for therapy that works. But efficiency includes, in addition to effectiveness, several other ingredients such as depth-centeredness, pervasiveness, extensiveness, multimodal procedures, the maintenance of therapeutic progress, and preventive psychotherapy. It also encourages minimization of therapeutic harm and scientific flexibility and falsifiability. All these aspects of efficient therapy can probably be concretized and measured. If this is done, it will probably be found that what we now call "effectiveness," as measured in most contemporary outcome studies of therapy, is significantly correlated with "efficiency," but that the latter involves important aspects of treatment that are commonly neglected in considering the former. Research along these lines would seem to be highly desirable.

8
Overcoming Resistance with Special Clients

In the previous chapters, I have been fairly general about treating various clients. I shall now be more specific and shall show how rational-emotive therapy (RET) and cognitive-behavior therapy (CBT) handle specific kinds of clients who come (or are involuntarily forced to go) for psychotherapy and who frequently resist treatment.

Different Kinds of Resistant Clients

Many kinds of clients are resistant to therapy: some of them are seriously disturbed individuals—e.g., psychotics, borderline personalities, and psychopaths—who are "naturally" or biologically, by the very nature of their problems, resistant; and some of them are less severely disturbed but otherwise limited—e.g., retarded, organic, and senile individuals who have limited intellectual resources and who, with all the will in the world, are not too capable of changing.

Another group may not be too disturbed or intellectually

139

limited but may be called *willful* resisters. Included in this group
are (1) people who insist that they really do not have problems
(e.g., adolescents and adults who are forced to have therapy
when they feel they don't need it); (2) those who think that their
associates are disturbed but that they themselves are not (e.g.,
hostile individuals); (3) people who believe they are hopeless, that
they cannot change, and that they therefore might as well not
try to improve (e.g., severely depressed individuals); (4) those
who "enjoy" their symptoms and therefore don't want to give
them up (e.g., alcoholics, drug addicts, and overtly hostile people);
(5) those who acknowledge that they have emotional problems
but feel that working at surrendering these problems is too hard
and not worth the effort (e.g., people with abysmally low frustration tolerance [LFT] who won't work at therapy); (6) moralistic
and dogmatic individuals who think that they are absolutely
right and that other people are utterly wrong, and that therefore
they *should* keep pursuing their disturbed ways (e.g., members of
fanatic cults or political groups, such as the Jim Jones cult, who
commit mass suicide or who kill others to achieve salvation). RET
(and to some extent, CBT) deal with specific types of resistant
clients as follows:

Treatment of Psychotics

RET assumes that many individuals with schizophrenia, manic-
depressive disturbance, psychotic depression, and other major
psychoses are born vulnerable to severe disturbance and are
precipitated into psychotic states by uncomfortable life situations. They bring their disturbability to their childhood and ado-
lescence and therefore tend to experience significantly more
"traumatic events" at these times, and they frequently have
severely disturbed parents who treat them in a blaming, cruel,
and unduly frustrating manner—so that they actually lead unfortunate early lives. When finally seen for therapy, they are still
exceptionally vulnerable and disturbable, and therefore overreact
to both past and present events, as well as to their therapist (Ellis,
1962, 1977f).

RET usually first attempts to help psychotic individuals unconditionally accept themselves *with* their severe vulnerability and disturbance. It shows them, realistically, that they *are* somewhat different from nonpsychotics and that their mental condition *is* bad or unfortunate, but that they never have to blame or condemn *themselves* for their serious deficiencies and failings. It especially teaches them full self-acceptance—as it teaches less difficult clients as well—and it ideally tries to help them to stop rating their essence, self, or being at all but *only* to keep rating their acts and traits (Ellis, 1962, 1972a, 1973, 1976a; Ellis & Abrahms, 1978, 1979a; Ellis & Becker, 1982; Ellis & Harper, 1975).

Because of the high degree of crooked thinking and the disordered emotionality of most psychotics, RET heavily stresses full self-acceptance and strongly persists at teaching it. The therapist works hard at unconditionally accepting psychotics, in spite of their resistance and their limitations, and forcefully tries to show them that they are never damnable, no matter how badly they behave. As a case in point, I recently saw a 25-year-old male who had had five hospitalizations for schizophrenic breaks, who treated his family very badly (though they had accepted him fairly well), who hated his brother and once tried to kill him, who had a scholarship at a leading art school, was not studying, and who was contemplating quitting school and going back to live with, and be dependent on, his retired (and economically marginal) parents. He blamed himself severely for being mentally ill, thought that he was hopelessly disturbed, and insisted that he could not work at getting better. He also damned himself for not studying and for hating and being dependent on his family.

I spent three months strongly arguing with this client and insisting that he could accept himself in spite of his failings and despite his refusing to work at his emotional problems. I showed him that, as a presumably good Christian, he could always give himself grace and could totally accept himself, and he finally agreed that he could do so and that he didn't *have* to improve his behavior in order to be self-accepting. Ironically, once he decided to accept himself *with* his hatred of his brother, father, and mother, he was able to accept them, too, and became nonhating and, at times, actually loving.

As he gave up his hatred of himself and others, this client was able to plan a practical approach to his school work and to economic independence. Although his feelings of alienation and detachment never completely vanished, his behavior improved considerably and he acted in a borderline rather than a schizophrenic manner. He was able to function without therapy and with minimal medication after two years of once-a-week RET; and he is still making a reasonably good life adjustment five years later, though he is hardly leading a happy, symptom-free existence. He finished school, is working as an art director, and has a steady woman friend. He swears that RET has saved his life, and is especially grateful that I vigorously attacked his self-downing for being mentally ill, and because I strongly insisted that he was not hopeless and that he could lead a good life.

Another psychotic person who now swears by RET is a 30-year-old male computer programmer, diagnosed manic depressive, who has been hospitalized six times since the age of 15 and who was severely depressed when he first came to see me. He could not work, couldn't maintain any long-term relationships, was very guilty about sex, and kept bouncing from compulsive abstinence to compulsive promiscuity. After seeing him for six months, I helped him accept the RET view that humans are never damnable no matter what foolish acts they do, and he then rarely depressed himself and remained depressed for only a day or two when he did. After ten months of RET, he had a severe manic attack, bore up very well under it, accepted himself with his breakdown, and with some increase in medication was not too seriously disturbed. He was able to get along better than ever with his family and was able to return to work and resume his regular life.

When attempting to help psychotic clients to fully accept themselves, I usually am quite strong, assume that they have great difficulty in stopping their self-derogation, and insist that they definitely can do so. Other RET therapists frequently take a milder stand than I do in this respect, and research studies might well test my hypothesis that often the best way to reach seriously disturbed individuals is through strong positive suggestion that they *can* think differently and *can* work hard to overcome their self-downing.

Treatment of Borderline Personalities

Defining borderline personalities is sometimes difficult. They include, as it were, a multitude of sins—some of them self-contradictory. Thus, an individual with borderline personality may be schizoid and avoidant or may be overactive and overimpulsive. He or she may be narcissistic and grandiose, or may be abysmally shy and self-downing (Applebaum, 1979; Giovacchini, 1971; Glazer, 1979; Kernberg, 1975; Kohut, 1971; Masterson, 1976; Spitzer, 1980).

I have described some of the main—but not the only—characteristics of borderline personalities as follows (Ellis, 1977f, 1983c):

They severely condemn themselves for relatively minor imperfections and peccadillos.

They cling rigidly to their dysfunctional thoughts, affects, and behaviors.

They frequently make gross logical errors, and have more difficulty than neurotics in giving them up.

They tend to overreact mightily and to continue their self-defeating reactions frequently and at length.

They tend to have abysmal LFT—and consequently to do little about conquering their basic problems.

They often have trigger-happy hostility and seem to anger themselves "automatically" at the drop of a hat.

Although they may do well at complicated tasks, in many ways they resist understanding themselves and others and resist new emotional teaching.

They often listen poorly to therapists and others.

When they improve during therapy, they easily and often fall back—sometimes to near zero.

They devoutly and powerfully hold on to irrational, self-defeating beliefs and refuse to surrender them even when they clearly see and acknowledge them.

They often are almost completely absorbed in themselves and react in a highly autistic manner.

They frequently display major inefficiencies and disorganization even whey they do well in certain specific areas.

They are often obsessive-compulsive and are easily addicted to harmful substances.

You may treat borderline personalities—as well as psychotics, organics, and other highly resistant clients—in two basic ways, which in some respects are opposite but which also may be amalgamated. The first of these is a warm, easy-going approach. Using this aproach, you may emphasize the following methods:

1. Fully accept your clients no matter how difficult, obnoxious, or annoying they behave.

2. Be patient: assume that therapy will take quite a period of time and freely give your clients that time.

3. If you feel blocked or desperately frustrated, look for and actively dispute your own iBs such as: "My client *should* work harder at therapy." "He *must* not sabotage my great therapeutic efforts." "I *must* be a rotten therapist if I fail with this client."

4. Encourage, encourage, encourage! Show your clients that you know that they *can* change—and keep firmly, patiently pushing them to do so.

5. Give graduated homework assignments, planned so that your clients succeed and thereby get reinforced for continuing to do them.

6. Teach clients to give themselves positive reinforcements for doing their homework.

7. Show clients that you empathize with their difficulties in changing, that you expect them to have problems in this regard, that you accept avoidances and setbacks, and that you accept them with their difficulties.

8. Help your clients with practical problem-solving suggestions when they experience school, job, family, relationships, sex, and other difficulties.

9. Ask clients what they would like to accomplish in therapy and try to help them in these respects. If you think they are choosing too easy, unimportant, or harmful goals, try to tactfully talk them into some harder ones as well.

10. Sometimes, placing clients in a supportive therapy group will encourage and help them. Self-help groups, such as Alcoholics Anonymous, Recovery, and I'Act Rationally may be useful in this respect.

11. Teach borderline clients rational techniques and rational coping self-statements over and over, until they finally tend to internalize them. Steadily show them the differences between

appropriate and inappropriate feelings, rational and irrational beliefs, and self-helping and self-defeating behaviors.

In addition to, and sometimes instead of, the foregoing mild and gentle methods, you may sometimes use the following firmer and harder RET techniques with borderline clients:

1. You may show them that just they are severely disturbed and have probably been so from childhood, they had better work *harder* than others to change themselves.

2. You may strongly emphasize the disadvantages of their indulging in their disturbed tendencies and highlight the endless pains of their doing so. Get them to make a list of these disadvantages and regularly review it.

3. You may heavily stress that unfortunately there's rarely any gain without pain—but that the pains of working at therapy are, in the long run, well worth it.

4. You may give them steady homework assignments if they will accept them—including implosive desensitization of their irrational fears—and closely monitor their performance of these assignments. In having them use specific reinforcements when they perform and clearcut penalties when they don't perform these assignments, you may actively participate—e.g., by burning money or sending it away to a cause they find obnoxious when they fail to carry out their assignments.

5. You may very forcefully dispute their iBs. For example: "You seem to be telling yourself that you can keep overeating and drinking without affecting your high blood pressure. Well, that's most unlikely. You *need* that extra food and drink like you need poison! And it's most likely you *can't* get away with consuming it!"

6. Try using forceful rational and coping statements with your borderline clients and encourage their using them on their own. For example: "It's a pain in the ass if I write up my business reports but it will be a much greater pain if I *don't*! The hassle of writing them up is only a *hassle*, never a *horror*! *Horror* is a devil that I foolishly invent!" Work out strong positive self-statements with your borderline clients and have them carry them around and forcefully go over them several times a day. For example: "I am *never* a bad person or an incompetent no matter how stupidly I act! As long as I fully accept *myself* with my failings, I can do

better and often finally succeed!" Bauer (1979) reports that using trance states to get borderline clients to repeat strong positive self-statements to themselves is quite helpful, and I have sometimes had success with a similar hypnotic method (Ellis, 1962, in press-c).

7. Take on the role of your clients, role play their iBs, and have them try to strongly talk you out of these irrationalities. Have them make tape recordings in which they try to talk themselves out of their irrationalities and listen to these recordings, to see how sensibly and how powerfully they contradict their iBs (Ellis, 1979d; Ellis & Abrahms, 1978).

8. Have your borderline clients actively use RET to help their friends, relatives, and associates, and show them how they can do so more efficiently. Let them select some difficult customers like themselves to work with in this respect.

9. Often encourage your borderline clients to do a number of shame-attacking exercises (Ellis, 1969a, 1972c; Ellis & Abrahms, 1978; Ellis & Becker, 1982). But first work with them to show them that no matter how foolishly they act they are never foolish, shameful *people*.

10. Sometimes, giving borderline clients paradoxical assignments—e.g., making themselves blush when they are afraid of blushing—shows them that they have much more control over their thoughts and feelings than they think they do (Dunlap, 1928; Frankl, 1960; Haley, 1976; Weeks & L'Abate, 1982). But don't be taken in by the spectacular successes of paradoxical intention often reported in the literature, as they are sometimes exaggerated. Use paradox with caution and selectivity, especially with borderline personalities who may easily misinterpret it and confuse themselves about it.

11. Borderline personalities who may always remain deficient and somewhat bizarre can sometimes be considerably helped by their becoming devoted to some interest, hobby, or cause. Unfortunately, they often tend to select fanatical and antisocial causes (such as Naziism and terrorism) and are most preoccupied—and "happy"—devoting their lives to these pursuits. But you can sometimes help them to become absorbed in saner and more constructive causes—such as ecological preservation or helping the handicapped—which will hardly eliminate

their disturbances but which may distract them from some of their emotional problems and help them live more happily.

12. Borderline personalities may sometimes be helped to feel better by strong, pollyannaish, and perfectionistic suggestions from some authority figure or from themselves. Thus, Coué (1923), Hill (1944), Peale (1952), and other advocates of "positive thinking" give them suggestions like, "Day by day in every way I'm getting better and better" or "Think and grow rich!" Workshops, intensives, and seminars sponsored by est, Lifespring, Insight, and other "human potential" groups tell their participants, "You are perfect the way you are," "You can take full charge of your life," "You can rid the world of starvation by thinking correctly about it," and similar pollyannaish slogans. Because people who swallow these kinds of perfectionistic suggestions are frequently borderline personalities who *want* to think in this unrealistic way, these autosuggestions often temporarily work, and those who follow them actually feel better and are more productive. In the long run, they lead to failure and disillusionment and not only boomerang back against people, but often prejudice them against effective therapy. So they are to be used, if at all, with great caution.

13. Devout and fanatical religious appeal and organizations are often attractive to borderline personalities and may sometimes help them. Thus, they may give up their addictions to drugs or alcohol by becoming addicted to Born Again Christianity, Transcendental Meditation, the Moonies, Jews for Jesus, or other sects and cults. The dangers of such fanaticism are fairly obvious and it has been held that dogmatic devotion to certain theistic religions and to secular religions (e.g., Naziism and Stalinism) are themselves forms of mental illness and are personally and socially dangerous (Ellis, 1983b, 1984h, 1984k).

14. Borderline personalities, as shown by the events of the last 20 years, often are quite attracted to mystical creeds, rituals, and organizations (Kilbourne & Richardson, 1984), and there is evidence that they sometimes feel better and act more effectively because of this attraction. Because mysticism is vague, unfalsifiable, and antiscientific, it may be questioned whether this kind of "cure" is worth it (Ellis, 1972e, 1984k).

15. Even bright borderline personalities may resist new ra-

tional ideas and resist disputing their iBs. Therefore, often go over rational and irrational Beliefs many times in simple language and test their responses to see if they can accurately discriminate between them. Steadily show them their *musts* in simple terminology and keep pushing them to dispute their absolutistic and unrealistic ideas.

Treatment of Psychopaths and Sociopaths

Psychopaths and sociopaths, as Cleckley (1950) showed many years ago, wear the mask of sanity and are either basically psychotic or are borderline personalities. They keep unrealistically thinking that they *can* get away with antisocial behavior and/ or that it doesn't make any difference if they get caught and convicted for their crimes. Some clinical results and some outcome studies using RET and CBT have been effective with these very difficult clients (Ellis, 1962, 1984i; Ellis & Gullo, 1972; Fink, 1980; Maultsby, 1975; Patterson, 1982; Chamberlain, Patterson, Reid, Kavanaugh, & Fogatch, 1984; Smith, Jenkins, Petko & Warner, 1979; Snyder & White, 1979; Templeman & Wollersheim, 1979; Yochelson & Samenow, 1977), but much more material on their peculiar nature and how best to treat them is desired.

Because psychopathic individuals are usually severely disturbed, the techniques described in this book that are effective for psychotics, borderline personalities, and other difficult clients are often useful. More specifically, my own experience in treating a good many sociopaths has led to the following treatment recommendations:

1. Whatever their criminal and heinous behavior has been, you can still unconditionally accept *them* while pointing out the immorality and irrationality of their behavior. They are highly fallible, messed-up, *humans* who often can be and always deserve to be helped just because they are human. You can therefore be, and had better be, critical of their *acts* without trying to demean *them*.

2. It is often best to speak to them honestly and directly, in down-to-earth (including "obscene") language, to show them

that you are not a moralistic, ultraconventional individual who does not really understand nor can comfortably relate to them (see Chapter 5). Don't insist, of course, on strong language with moralistic clients who object to it.

3. Try to show psychopaths the real risks and dangers of their antisocial behavior—which they frequently put out of mind. Show them that if they want to risk these dangers, they can choose to do so—as long as they are willing to take the consequences. Stress what the consequences truly are.

4. Try to show them that they cannot, in the long run, get away with their crime, that they almost inevitably will have to "pay the piper"; and that the penalties for their acts are rarely worth it. Keep forcefully but undamningly bringing them back to grim reality.

5. Show them alternative non-self-defeating actions they *can* take. They *are* capable of leading constructive, social, enjoyable lives. They *have* the ability to change and do better—if they will choose to work at doing so.

6. Show them that their hostility to others is largely *self-induced*: that it stems from their unrealistic demands and commands that these others *must* not be the way they indubitably are. Lean over backwards to agree with them that others' *behavior* is often poor or rotten, but that this does not make them bad *people* (Ellis, 1984i).

7. Try to help them see the pains and troubles of others and to become more empathic. Dramatize what some of these victims go through and how pained they may be. Show them some of the social ramifications of their acts—how they lead to widening rings of human suffering.

8. With some of the brighter and more receptive psychopaths, explain to them what the sociopathic personality is, how it includes crooked thinking, how it involves LFT, and how it can be changed (Ellis, 1962; Ellis & Gullo, 1972). Train them how to look at their thinking and fantasizing and how to change it (Yochelson & Samenow, 1977).

9. In some cases, you may be able to show psychopaths how autistic they are and how their lack of empathy and social interest is sick and handicapping. You may teach them the values of social involvement and the joys of helping others and may pos-

sibly even influence them to engage in some cooperative and altruistic behavior. They can sometimes be induced to help other criminals, as they do in organizations such as the Fortune Society.

10. You may be able to do problem solving and skill training with sociopaths and thereby show them how to get more of what they want out of life without engaging in antisocial acts.

11. If psychopaths are seen in prison or when they are on parole or probation, you may show them how to act better to remove the present limitations that are placed on them. This kind of training may help them to adjust better to later life situations that are also restricting.

12. Psychopaths can sometimes be helped to see the underlying feelings of inadequacy and self-downing that encourage them to defensively resort to antisocial behavior. If you induce them to accept themselves fully with their inadequacies, they may not have to resort to crimes to cover up their feelings of inferiority.

The Treatment of Alcohol and Drug Abusers

Some of the most resistant clients are addicted to alcohol, drugs, and other injurious substances. RET and CBT specialize in treating these individuals and often help them recover from their addictions (Ellis, 1962, 1982b; Ellis & Abrahms, 1978; Ellis & Grieger, 1977; Grau, 1977; Higbee, 1977; Maultsby, 1978, 1984; Wolfe, 1979). RET has a unique view of serious addiction. It sees alcoholics as having a biological predisposition to becoming hooked on alcohol. Psychologically, it hypothesizes that, on level one, alcoholics frequently make themselves anxious and depressed by going to Activating Events (A), such as business or social affairs, with the goal of succeeding and being approved and of actually failing and being rejected. After failure or rejection occur (or when they may occur) at point A, they irrationally tell themselves at point B, their Belief System, "I *must* not fail or be rejected. How *awful* if I do! What a *rotten person* that makes me!" They then experience the emotional Consequence (C) of anxiety and/or depression.

Once this occurs, they proceed to level two, where they take their feeling of anxiety, C, and make it into a new Activating Event, A. They then have these ABCs:

A: "I see that I am anxious."
B: "I *must* not be anxious! How awful!"
C: To submerge their terrible feelings of anxiety and to imme-
diately feel no pain, they drink—and drink and drink.

As a result of these second level ABCs and of their biological predispositions, they addict themselves to alcohol. Once they drink steadily and experience the bad effects of alcoholism (e.g., loss of jobs, friends, and health), they often proceed to level three:

A: "I see that I am alcoholic."
B: "I *must* not drink too much! I am no damned good for being an
alcoholic!"
C: To submergee their horrible feelings of self-downing about
their compulsive drinking, they frequently drink more and
become more alcoholic.

RET, then, sees alcoholics and drug addicts as usually (not always) starting with anxiety and depression; as then using their LFT to quell these feelings by temporarily dissolving them in alcohol; and as then creating, often, feelings of self-damnation for compulsive drinking. So RET usually tries to get at these Consequences in reverse order: first, to help addicts accept themselves with their addiction; second, to stay with their original feelings of anxiety and depression and to work on their LFT by seeing that anxiety is only painful and not horrible or intolerable; third, to get back to the original anxiety and self-downing by changing their demands that they *must* do well and *have to* be approved by significant others.

Because alcoholics, drug addicts, and other serious substance abusers are frequently borderline personalities, are sometimes psychopathic, and are usually DCs (difficult customers), you will often find the techniques previously outlined in this chapter helpful. In addition, you may try the following methods:

1. If seriously addicted, alcoholics and substance abusers

often require hospitalization or residency at a treatment center for several weeks so that they may fully dry out and receive appropriate psychotropic medication during this process. If not institutionalized, they may also require medical care during the withdrawal process.

2. Don't trust drug addicts to withdraw when living in their regular setting, since virtually all their friends and associates may be similarly addicted and will often try to keep them on drugs. Some addicts require from several months to a full year of residency in a special center so that they can train themselves for nonaddictive living.

3. Alcohol and drug addicts often benefit considerably from a self-help program such as that of Alcoholics Anonymous or (if they are nonreligious or antireligious) American Atheist Addiction Recovery Groups (2136 S. Birch St., Denver, CO 80222). Such support groups enable them to associate with others who have conquered and are conquering their addiction and may give them a cause and an organization to work for.

4. Substance abusers spend so much time and energy at their addictions that they frequently have few or no other interests. If you can, encourage them to occupy a good portion of their time at some constructive pursuit that helps them stay off alcohol and other harmful substances.

5. Using RET, you can first work with addicts' second-level LFT and third-level self-downing. But you had better also help them get in touch with the original anxiety, depression, anger, or other disturbance that they used their addiction to "solve." Only if you get to these feelings and show them how to deal with and minimize them are you likely to help them achieve what RET calls the "elegant solution" to their emotional problems (Ellis, 1979e, 1982b).

6. Alcoholics and drug addicts frequently have a "need" for excitement and are consequently willing to take great risks to lead a "thrilling" existence. You can sometimes help them alleviate this "need" by (a) strongly emphasizing the great disadvantages they go through to fulfill it and by (b) working with them to make their days exciting in more constructive ways (Ellis, 1982b).

7. Using skill training and educational resources to help addicts increase their abilities and possibility of achievement will sometimes help them to enhance their sense of self-efficiency and to overcome their feelings of inadequacy (Bandura, 1977; Ellis, 1962; Ellis & Becker, 1982; Ellis & Harper, 1975).

Treatment of Other Kinds of Resistant Clients

Most other resistant clients can be treated by RET and CBT with the kinds of methods mentioned previously in this book. Some techniques you can use with other kinds of special clients include the following.

Involuntary Clients

Involuntary clients who insist that they are not disturbed and who deliberately resist treatment may sometimes be persuaded that they can use help in certain areas. Thus, adolescent delinquents frequently won't acknowledge or work on their underlying feelings of inadequacy, but often will admit that they are hostile (particularly against authorities). You can then show them that their hostility has got them into trouble—as demonstrated by the fact that they have been forced against their will to come for therapy—and that you can teach them how to deal better with their anger and keep out of future difficulty. If, in such cases, you particularly tend to agree with unwilling clients that the world may well be treating them badly or unfairly, you can often win their cooperation and get them to allow you to help them change.

Elderly Clients

Lewis and Johansen (1982), in studying the resistance of elderly clients to psychotherapy, find that this resistance involves two main factors: (1) Therapists do not understand the normal coping mechanisms of the aged, and wrongly believe that their aggression, irritating behavior, narcissism, and demandingness is pathological, when these traits are often effective forms of adjustment to the restrictions of their lives. (2) Many therapists themselves are afraid of aging and of death and therefore are empathically blocked in listening to the problems of the elderly (Becker, 1973).

From an RET viewpoint, Lewis and Johansen are at least partly wrong, for RET does not greatly favor the coping mechanisms of aggression, irritating behavior, narcissism, and demandingness and tries to help older (as well as younger) clients ameliorate these reactions. It also views anxiety about their own death, detachment from others, considerable rumination about the past, increased focusing on themselves, preoccupation with physical health, and continuous grieving about the loss of physical health or the fading of life dreams—all of which Lewis and Johansen tend to accept as presenting phenomena associated with normal aging, and therefore nonpathological—as tendencies toward depression, and hence good material for psychotherapy.

RET recognizes that elderly clients come for treatment seldomly and tend to come only a few times when they do accept to come. Because of the rigidity of their thinking, of their reluctance to change, and of their limited abilities to actively engage in pleasurable pursuits, you may find the following RET tactics suitable when working with the elderly: (1) Be very clear and strong about their having iBs and about their ability to change these ideas. (2) Use coping statements and rational philosophies, often, rather than self-disputing, and encourage them to apply these in a forceful, repetitive way. Strongly push the philosophy of acceptance of unfortunate things that realistically cannot be changed. (3) Encourage them to engage in interests and hobbies, both inside and outside the home. (4) Realistically, expect limited gains and a considerable amount of retrogression. (5) Work on accepting your own distaste for the aging process, and if you have any great anxiety about death, honestly acknowledge it and work on it by using RET on yourself (Ellis, 1972g, 1983d). (6) If elderly clients are afraid of death and dying—which many of them, I have found, are not—you can sometimes induce them to accept the elegant RET philosophy which holds: (a) Nothing is *awful* or *horrible*—only highly inconvenient. (b) Even if we die unfairly, justice and fairness are highly *preferable* but do not *have to* exist. (c) We can *stand* what we don't *like*, and even dying is *tolerable* and *bearable*. (d) The state of death, exactly like the state we are in before we are born, is completely insensate, painless, and free of problems. (e) Worrying about how or when our demise will occur only *adds* to our woes and lessens the value of the one life we shall probably ever have. (f) Even when we are crippled, blind, or otherwise seriously handicapped, we can almost always find *some* ways to enjoy ourselves—if we do not insist that we can't (Ellis, 1981b).

Mentally Deficient Clients

Mentally deficient adolescents and adults have a low mental age and are therefore similar in some respects to normal children of eight to twelve years of age. You can therefore use many of the RET and CBT methods that are effective with young children (Bernard & Joyce, 1984; Bingham, 1982; Ellis & Bernard, 1983; Gerald & Eyman, 1982; Merrifield & Merrifield, 1980). In using RET with children and with mental retardates, you would do well to use simple language, considerable repetition or rational coping statements, and games, exercises, stories, and other materials specially designed for youngsters.

Severely Depressed Clients

Severely depressed and inactive clients may require considerable support and bolstering (Beck, 1967, 1976; Beck, Rush, Emery & Shaw, 1979; Dryden, 1984; Ellis, 1982d; Ellis & Abrahms, 1978, 1979b; Hauck, 1973; Walen, DiGiuseppe & Wessler, 1980; Wessler & Wessler, 1980). You may find it desirable to keep pushing and encouraging them, to plan and promote on-going activities, and to strongly show them that they *can* accept themselves unconditionally and that they *can* change.

I find it particularly useful to get my severely depressed clients *active*. If I can help them get involved in some steady work or play activities, they become significantly distracted from their constant negative thoughts, and they also see that they can enjoy themselves. Pleasures, such as those I list in *A Guide to Personal Happiness* (Ellis & Becker, 1982) may be of considerable help if clients can be induced to participate in them. Inducing them to acquire a vital absorbing interest sometimes does more good than virtually any type of treatment (Ellis & Harper, 1975).

Placing severely depressed individuals in a support group at regular group therapy is frequently quite effective in overcoming their resistance to treatment. But sometimes this method boomerangs, because they see themselves as so different from the other group members that they begin to feel more hopeless and more depressed. If a wide variety of RET methods are used with severely depressed individuals there is a good chance that a few of them will work. Referring them for antidepressive medication sometimes is quite helpful—but sometimes is not.

Willfully Resistant Clients

Willfully resistant clients, who rebel against treatment and who sometimes want to play games with the therapist and to win the "battle" with him or her, can often be persuaded to become cooperative in these ways: (1) You can show them that your own ego is not involved in winning the therapeutic game and that you won't feel especially defeated or hurt if they beat you and win it. (2) You can tell them frankly that they are entitled to play resistant games but they'd better accept the consequence: *they* and not *you* will thereby suffer. (3) You can show them that they usually battle you (or their associates who want them to improve) because they (a) believe that they *must* win, even in therapy, or they will rate themselves as worthless individuals, (b) think that they angrily *have to* resist to spite others who want to "force" them to help themselves and (c) because they have LFT and therefore find it *too* hard to work at therapy and find it "easier" (in the short run) to play games and resist changing. Willfully resistant clients almost invariably have decidedly irrational Beliefs that spark their self-defeating willlfulness, and you can often quickly show them these iBs and scientifically dispute them.

Moralistic and Dogmatic Clients

Moralistic and dogmatic clients, who are certain that they are right and undisturbed when there is much evidence that they are wrong and distinctly disturbed, are often impossible to reach. Thus, I have been unsuccessful with a 25-year-old female, a devoted follower of Ayn Rand, who felt that she was legitimately hostile (practically murderous) toward all liberal males who had less than 100% procapitalist views; and I failed completely with a handsome 30-year-old male attorney who felt that he justifiably hated all women because he claimed that they at first liked him for his looks but then as soon as they discovered he had a very small penis—less than four inches when fully erect—they nastily rejected him. You can occasionally help these "righteously" hostile individuals in the following ways.

1. You can seem to agree with their dogmatic premises but induce them to draw different conclusions (Young, 1984). Thus, I seemed to agree with an Irish Catholic male that no suitable Jewish woman would marry him when she discovered he was not Jewish, but I got him to conclude that he had better go through a large sample of Jewish women while perhaps pretending he had a Jewish grandmother to test his hypothesis. He soon saw that out of 20 Jewish women he approached, several didn't care about his gentile background.

2. You can strongly attack bigoted premises and show some clients that unless they surrender them they will continue to suffer indefinitely. When one of my young female clients with one arm insisted that no attractive male would ever love her, I strongly persuaded her to admit that quite a number of women with missing limbs, double mastectomies, or hunched backs gained attractive mates, and I had her advertise her physical deficiency in a Personals column until she received a number of dates and two offers of marriage.

You can sometimes enlist a client's bigoted views to help him or her in an important endeavor. When, in the case of a brilliant 20-year-old female dancer, I could not get her to give up the idea that sex was stupid and evil (because, she held, people became obsessed with it and often mated with others who were inferior),

I largely seemed to agree with her, and I encouraged her to join a fanatical religious group that opposed sexuality. She did so well in this group that she made some close male friends, felt great about her ability to relate to them intellectually and nonsexually, and became so unhostile and undefensive that she finally fell in love with one of the males in her group. Both of them then quit the group, married, and had quite a good sex life.

Cautions About Using Clever Techniques

As can be seen from the points I have just made in regard to some types of resistant clients, you can sometimes use your ingenuity and therapeutic creativity to reach those who are virtually unreachable. Techniques that you devise for one special client, however, may by no means work with another resister. Haley (1984) has devised some clever techniques that worked with unusual clients, and in previous chapters of this book I have described some unusual ones, too. But let me present some caveats about clever and unique techniques, such as mine and Haley's:

1. Almost any method can work once, and practically never again. In everyday life, for example, some lovers curse and scream at their beloveds for not returning their affection, and thereby actually win over a recalcitrant partner. But not very often!

2. Many amusing and fiendishly clever methods are quite often iatrogenic. The paradoxical intention method of telling parents to vociferously agree with their misbehaving children in order to help these children see that they no longer need rebel against the parents may easily persuade many (probably most!) offspring that they are right in behaving obnoxiously!

3. Clever techniques tend to work best when resistant clients are intentionally balking and are deliberately playing games with their therapist. However, most resisters are not playing such games but are finding it genuinely hard to change. They will therefore tend to resist clever techniques even more than they will resist honest work-requiring therapeutic methods.

4. You, as a therapist, can easily become so obsessed with

devising unusually clever techniques of inducing a few unusual resisters to change that you can ignore some of the most powerful bread-and-butter techniques of reinforcement and penalization that usually are more effective. It is interesting to note in this connection that G. R. Patterson (1982), who has spent 20 years researching effective techniques of child rearing and child therapy, has hypothesized that parents often encourage their children to behave badly by refraining from effectively penalizing them as soon as they act disruptively. And Hauck (1984) insists that married individuals frequently train their partners to treat them obnoxiously by not returning their nasty acts in kind after a period of acceptance and forgiveness fails to help. We may similarly hypothesize that unless you somehow arrange for your highly resistant clients to penalize themselves severely each time they refuse to change their self-sabotaging ways, you may encourage many (perhaps most) of them to continue their resistance.

5. Unusually clever and unique methods of combating resistance had better remain just that—unusual and unique. Run of the mill cognitive, emotive, and behavioral techniques that can be used with many clients much of the time will probably prove more economical and useful (Dryden, 1984; Ellis, 1962, 1973; Ellis & Whiteley, 1979; Maultsby, 1975, 1984; Maultsby & Ellis, 1974; Walen, DiGiuseppe & Wessler, 1980; Wessler & Wessler, 1980).

9

How to Deal with the Resistance of Your Most Difficult Client—You

Although the literature on difficult and resistant clients is extensive (Freud, 1912/1965b; Wachtel, 1982; Weiner, 1982), much less attention has been given to the difficult and resistant therapist. Psychoanalytic writers, to be sure, have emphasized the dangers of countertransference (Coltrera & Ross, 1967; Freud, 1912/1965c; Greenson, 1967; Wolstein, 1959), but they have often ignored other problems of the therapist. This chapter will attempt to address some of these problems and make (hopefully) educated guesses about how therapist difficulties arise and what may be done to alleviate them.

Before we can consider what are some of the main blocks to the therapist's effective functioning, it would be nice to have a picture of what a fully functioning therapist is. Unfortunately, we have as yet no real agreement on this point. Freudians, who tend to be relatively passive and who emphasize looking for unconscious determinants of clients' disturbances, stress therapists' listening with their third ear (Fenichel, 1953; Freud, 1965e; Reik, 1948). Rogerians emphasize the therapist's genuiness, accurate empathy and unconditional positive regard (Rogers, 1957,

161

1961) and nonpossessive warmth (Truax & Carkhuff, 1967; Truax & Mitchell, 1971). Behavior therapists and cognitive-behavior therapists recommend that effective therapy also includes several kinds of teaching and persuasive skills (Ellis, 1979d, in press-a; Meichenbaum, 1977; Wessler & Ellis, 1980).

Practices of Effective Therapists

I still take the stand I took many years ago when I objected to Rogers' (1957) seminal paper, "The Necessary and Sufficient Conditions of Therapeutic Personality Change," when I pointed out "that although basic constructive personality change—as opposed to symptom removal—seems to require fundamental modifications in the ideologies and value systems of the disturbed individual, there is probably *no* single condition which is absolutely necessary for the inducement of such changed attitudes and behavior patterns" (Ellis, 1959b, p. 540; 1962, p. 119).

With some amount of temerity, however, let me hazard the guess that when the facts have been more diligently researched, we will find that the most effective therapists tend to practice somewhat as follows:

1. They are vitally interested in helping their clients and energetically work to fulfill this interest.

2. They unconditionally accept their clients as people, while opposing and trying to ameliorate some of their self-defeating ideas, feelings, and behaviors.

3. They are confident of their own therapeutic ability and, without being rigid or grandiose, strongly believe that their main techniques will work.

4. They have a wide knowledge of therapeutic theories and practices and are flexible, undogmatic, and scientific, and consequently open to the acquiring of new skills and to experimenting with these skills.

5. They are effective at communicating and at teaching their clients new ways of thinking, emoting, and behaving.

6. They are able to cope with and ameliorate their own disturbances and consequently are not inordinately anxious, depressed, hostile, self-downing, self-pitying, or undisciplined.

7. They are patient, persistent, and hard working in their therapeutic endeavors.

8. They are ethical and responsible, and use therapy almost entirely for the benefit of the clients and not for personal indulgence.

9. They act professionally and appropriately in a therapeutic setting but are still able to maintain some degree of humanness, spontaneity, and personal enjoyment in what they are doing.

10. They are encouraging and optimistic and show clients that, whatever difficulties they may experience, they can appreciably change. At times, effective therapists forcefully urge and push clients to change.

11. They not only try to help clients feel better and surrender their presenting symptoms, but also try to help them make a profound attitudinal change that will enable them to maintain their improvement, continue to improve, and ward off future disturbances.

12. They are eager to help virtually all their clients, freely refer to other therapists those they think they can't help or are not interested in helping, and try to be neither underinvolved nor overinvolved with clients they retain. They sincerely try to overcome their strong biases for or against their clients that may interfere with their therapeutic effectiveness. They monitor their prejudices (countertransference feelings) that lead to their strongly favoring or disfavoring some of their clients and, if advisable, refer such clients to other therapists.

13. They possess sufficient observational ability, sensitivity to others, good intelligence, and some judgment to discourage their clients from making rash and foolish decisions and from seriously harming themselves.

Assuming that effective therapists tend to behave as just described, which practitioners consistently follow this ideal pathway? Damned few, I would guess! I fully admit that in the 40-plus years I have been practicing psychotherapy, I have by no means fully lived up to this ideal myself. Nor do I think that any of the scores of therapists I have supervised has done so. On the other hand, I have met and supervised many who have fallen far below this ideal.

Although therapeutic infallibility is hardly a realistic goal, we may still ask: How do therapists block their own effectiveness and what can they do to overcome their resistances to seeing and eradicating their blocks? If you are a psychotherapist and are ignoring some of the best rules of the game—including several that you personally endorse and would prefer to follow—how can you understand your own blocks to good practice—and how can you unblock yourself? How can you decrease, if not annihilate, some of your therapeutic fallibility?

Irrational Beliefs of Therapists

✗Ever since I threw off the shackles of psychoanalytic theory some 30 years ago and started to develop a new theory that blossomed out into rational-emotive therapy (RET), I have stubbornly insisted that human disturbance is contributed to by environmental pressures, including our childhood upbringing, but that its most important and vital source is our innate tendency to indulge in crooked thinking. People not only learn or take over unrealistic expectations, absolutistic ideas, illogical conclusions, and irrational beliefs (iBs) from their parents and their culture; but they also have a positive genius for inventing and exacerbating these self-defeating cognitions themselves. They don't *have* to think exaggeratedly, perfectionistically, dogmatically, and unscientifically, but they sooner or later do; and they thereby make themselves—yes, creatively make themselves—emotionally disturbed and behaviorally dysfunctional. Their parents, teachers, and peers appreciably help them in this respect. But, being talented neurotics in their own right, they scarcely need such help and can easily disturb themselves without it (Ellis, 1957a, 1962, 1971, 1973, 1977a, 1982c, in press-a).

Being, in spite of their aspirations to godliness, still human, psychotherapists often indulge in the same kind of irrational absolutistic beliefs that other people hold. After giving this matter some thought, reviewing my experiences with therapists I have supervised, and considering the therapeutic irrationalities that other writers have observed (Grieger & Boyd, 1980; Novaco, 1980; Tosi & Eshbaugh, 1978; Weinrach, 1977; Walen, DiGiuseppe & Wessler, 1980; Wessler & Wessler, 1980), I have come up with several iBs that I hypothesize often lead to therapeutic inefficiency.

1. *"I have to be successful with all my clients practically all the time."* Although, as RET hypothesizes, strong wishes, desires, and preferences will rarely get you into serious emotional trouble, absolutistic necessities and demands frequently will. If you under all conditions *must* succeed with your clients, you will tend to be horrified and depressed when you don't—and still be anxious when you do. For how can you be sure that you will succeed again next time? You can't!

Your dire need to help virtually all your clients all the time leads to several equally pernicious corollaries: (a) "I must continually make brilliant and profound interpretations." (b) "I must always have good judgment." (c) "I must help my clients *more* than I am now helping them." (d) "If I fail with any of my clients, it has to be my fault." (e) "When I fail, as I must not, I am a thoroughly lousy therapist—and a rotten person. (f) "My successes don't count if I have a *real* failure."

When you place golden ideals like these on your therapeutic back, how can you fail to feel inadequate, to interfere with your work, and to make yourself a prime candidate for early burnout? Not very easily!

2. *"I must be an outstanding therapist, clearly better than other therapists I know or hear about."* This is another preferential goal which, when you escalate it to necessity, tends to make you inefficient. Some corollaries of this absolutistic demand include: (a) "I must succeed even with impossible clients." (b) "I must have *all* good sessions with clients." (c) "I must use the best and most prestigious system of therapy and be outstanding at using it." (d) "I must be famous as a therapist." (e) "Because I am a therapist, I should have no emotional problems myself and am disgraced if I do."

Like the first iB mentioned above, this second one leads to frantic endeavor and to the inefficiencies that accompany such franticness. Panic also results when it appears that this unrealistic goal may not be achieved—or may not be constantly reachieved.

3. *"I have to be greatly respected and loved by all my clients."* If and when you have this dire need—instead of preference—you again frequently have several perfectionistic corollaries: (a) "I must not

dislike any of my clients and, especially, must not show that I dislike them." (b) "I must not push my clients too hard, lest they hate me." (c) "I must avoid ticklish issues that might upset and antagonize my clients." (d) "The clients whom I like and who like me must remain in therapy practically forever." (e) "My clients must see that I am thoroughly devoted to them and that I never make serious mistakes." (f) "It's horrible to be disapproved of by any of my clients because their disapproval makes me a bad therapist and a rotten person."

4. *"Since I am doing my best and working so hard as a therapist, my clients should be equally hard working and responsible, should listen to me carefully, and should always push themselves to change."* This iB accompanies low frustration tolerance (LFT) and anger—and leads you to blame your clients for being disturbed. It frequently has several unrealistic corollaries, such as: (a) "My clients should not be difficult and resistant." (b) "They should do exactly what I tell them to do." (c) "They should work very hard in between sessions and always do their therapeutic homework." (d) "I should only have young, bright, attractive, and easy clients!"

5. *"Because I am a person in my own right, I must be able to enjoy myself during therapy sessions and to use these sessions to solve my personal problems as well as to help my clients."* This irrational idea contradicts the nature of paid psychotherapy—which indeed may be of help to therapists but which ethically puts the interests of clients first. The philosophy of self-indulgence that underlies this belief often leads to several corollaries that also sabotage therapy: (a) "I must mainly use therapeutic techniques that I enjoy using, whether or not they are very helpful to clients." (b) "I must only use techniques that are easy and that do not wear me out." (c) "I must make considerable money doing therapy and must not have to work too hard to make it." (d) "If I use some of my clients amatively and sexually that will do both them and me a lot of good." (e) "Because I am so helpful as a therapist, I should be able to get away with coming late to appointments, canceling them at the last minute, sleeping during sessions, and indulging myself in other ways."

Now I am not contending that all therapists frequently and strongly hold many of the above iBs. Some of you may hold none of them or may lightly maintain the few that you do hold. But I am hypothesizing that when you resolve to work at doing effective therapy but then sabotage your own efforts and wind up with severe feelings of anxiety, depression, hostility, guilt, or self-pity about your therapeutic endeavors, you then tend to subscribe to some of these irrationalities. And I am suggesting that you may be resistant to finding and surrendering them. Why? Because, first, you may be reluctant to admit that you, a psychotherapist, really have deep-seated emotional difficulties. Second, you may be so preoccupied with helping others that you rarely think about helping yourself. Third, you may wrongly assume that your authoritative knowledge of disturbance and your self-explorations during your training protect you from being disturbed about the therapeutic process. Fourth, you may have the same kind of LFT—commonly known as laziness—that prevents so many of your own clients from working to change themselves. Fifth, you may be so involved with yourself that you myopically fail to see your shortcomings and emotional difficulties.

How to Deal with Your Own Resistances

For reasons such as these, you may well be your most difficult client. If so, don't despair, bolster your defenses, and run away from facing and dealing with your problems. As a therapist, you often meet clients' resistance and do your best to overcome it. Why not similarly tackle your own?

Having outlined in earlier chapters of this book the RET theory and practice of treating resistance, let me now apply some of these practices to resistant therapists. If you have been consciously or unconsciously subscribing to some of the iBs listed above; if you have consequently felt disturbed about yourself as a therapist; and if your effectiveness has thereby suffered, here are some of the cognitive, emotive, and behavioral techniques you can use to deal with your most difficult client—you.

1. Assume that some strong iBs lie closely behind your therapeutic upsets and that these include one or more absolutistic shoulds, oughts, or musts, such as those listed above.

2. Search diligently for those that specifically apply to you and your therapy. Don't give up until you find a few.

3. Consider these iBs as hypotheses—not facts—that you can dispute and surrender. Use the same scientific methods to challenge them as you would employ to question any other dubious hypothesis. For example: "Where is the evidence that I *have to be* successful with all my clients practically all the time?" "Who says that I *must* be better than other therapists? "Where is it written that *it is necessary* for me to be respected and loved by all my clients?"

4. Carefully think about these hypotheses until you come up with disconfirming evidence and therefore are really willing to give them up.

5. Create alternate rational, preferential statements to substitute for these unrealistic, unconfirmable hypotheses. For example: "I clearly don't *have to be* successful with all my clients, though that would be lovely! Because I would *like to* help most of them, let me work at that goal."

6. Convince yourself that you can unconditionally accept yourself as a person—that is, see yourself as deserving to continue to live and enjoy yourself—*whether or not* you succeed as a therapist and *whether or not* your clients (or other significant people) approve of you. Acknowledge some of your deeds and traits (such as your acting irresponsibly in therapy) as being ineffective and deplorable but refuse to lambaste your *self* or your *being* for these failings.

7. Refuse to awfulize about anything. See that it's most inconvenient and annoying when your clients refuse to do their agreed upon homework. But it's not awful, horrible, or terrible. *Just* annoying! (Ellis, 1979a, 1979d, 1980a).

8. Instead of mainly looking at the ease of staying the way you are and the discomfort of changing, make a comprehensive list of the pains of maintaining your disturbance and the advantages of giving them up. Review and think about this list every day until you are more motivated to change.

9. Give yourself the strong challenge and excitement of doing one of the most difficult and most rewarding things you can do in life—pigheadedly refusing to make yourself needlessly miserable about anything (Ellis & Becker, 1982).

10. Actively talk your clients (and friends and relatives!) out of their irrationalities and thereby help yourself to talk yourself out of your own.

11. Reduce some of your self-defeating ideas to absurdity and see the humor in some of the profound stupidities that you rigidly hold. Tell yourself, for example, "I really *should* do only what I enjoy doing during my therapy sessions. What do you think those blasted clients are paying me for, anyway—to get better?" Sing to yourself one of the rational humorous songs made famous by RET (Ellis, 1977b, 1977c, 1981a), such as:

WHINE, WHINE, WHINE!
(To the tune of the Yale Whiffenpoof
Song, by Guy Scull—a Harvard man!)

I cannot have all of my wishes filled—
   Whine, whine, whine!
I cannot have every frustration stilled—
   Whine, whine, whine!
Life really owes me the things that I miss;
Fate has to grant me eternal bliss!
And since I must settle for less than this—
   Whine, whine, whine!

(Lyrics by Albert Ellis, copyrighted 1977
by the Institute for Rational-Emotive Therapy)

12. Show yourself that so-called intellectual insight into your difficulties is not enough and that what is often called emotional insight consists of at least three major kinds of knowledge: (a) The realization that you, rather than external events, largely create your own disturbance. (b) The understanding that no matter how and when you originally started to think irrationally, you still stubbornly persist in thinking that way today. (c) The insight that only considerable work and practice—yes, *work and practice*—to challenge and dispute your iBs and only persistent *action* against the dysfunctional behaviors that accompany these beliefs will suffice to make and keep you less disturbed (Ellis, 1962; Ellis & Becker, 1982; Ellis & Harper, 1975).

13. You can use rational-emotive imagery created by Maultsby (1975) and adapted by me (Maultsby & Ellis, 1971b, 1974) to change your intensely disturbed feelings. Thus, you can vividly imagine yourself failing miserably as a therapist—letting yourself feel very anxious, depressed, or self-downing—and as

you imagine this, implode this feeling, then (while still imagining this scene) make yourself feel *only* disappointed and regretful (and *not* self-hating). Finally, practice this new appropriate feeling every day for at least 30 days until you automatically begin to feel regretful and disappointed instead of anxious or depressed whenever you think about failing.

14. You can publicly perform one or more of the RET shame-attacking exercises (Ellis, 1969a, 1972c). The purpose of these exercises is to do an act that you normally consider foolish and shameful—for example, sing at the top of your voice while walking down the street—and make yourself feel *unashamed* while performing it. You thereby show yourself that you never *have to* denigrate yourself even when other people clearly disapprove of you; and you help convince yourself that you *prefer* but do not *need* your clients' (and other people's) approval.

15. Whenever you can do so, unequivocally, strongly, and persistently *act* against your iBs. If, for example, you abhor difficult clients and think that you *can't stand* them, deliberately take some on and show yourself that you *can* tolerate what you don't like and that you *can* accept (and learn from) clients who behave obnoxiously. If you find yourself using only the techniques you find easy and enjoyable, force yourself to try more difficult methods and keep trying them until they become familiar—and probably rewarding.

As you can see from the foregoing suggestions, dealing with yourself and your problems as a therapist involves some of the same techniques you would often employ with your own difficult clients (DCs). The difference is that they have you to monitor them in following these techniques while you only have yourself to do the monitoring. Tough—but not impossible. You can, if you deem it desirable, go back into therapy yourself and thereby acquire a paid monitor. But unless you are an unusually difficult customer, it would be better if you go it alone. Why? Frankly, to make things a bit more troublesome for yourself. For if you try to change yourself, at first, without guidance and support from another therapist, you may be able to appreciate better the struggles of your own clients when they strive for self-change; and you may thereby come to accept them with their struggles and their setbacks. In any event, if you find that you do not satisfactorily change on your own, you can always later work with another therapist—and had better!

Therapists are humans—and, believe it or not, fallible humans. Ideally, they are supremely well informed, highly confident, minimally disturbed, extremely ethical, and rarely under- or over-involved with their clients. Actually, they are hardly ideal. If you, as a therapist, find yourself seriously blocked in your work, look for the same kind of iBs, inappropriate feelings, and dysfunctional behaviors that you would investigate in your underachieving clients. When you ferret out the absolutistic philosophies and perfectionist demands that seem to underlie your difficulties, ask yourself—yes, *strongly* ask yourself—these trenchant questions: (1) Why do I *have to be* an indubitably great and unconditionally loved therapist? (2) Where is it written that my clients *must* follow my teachings and absolutely *should* do what I advise? (3) Where is the evidence that therapy *must* be easy and that I *have to* enjoy every minute of it?

If you persist in asking important questions like these and insist on thinking them through scientifically and logically, you may still never become the most accomplished and sanest therapist in the world. But I wager that you will tend to be happier and more effective than many other therapists I could—but charitably will not—name. Try it and see!

10

Additional Methods of Overcoming Resistance

No book is ever complete, particularly when it covers a wide-ranging topic such as that of overcoming psychotherapeutic resistance. As I look back over what I have written in the previous chapters, I see that I could make a good many additional points—and then keep adding to those points, almost *ad infinitum*. Rather than start this never-ending corrective and additive process, let me make some additional remarks on overcoming resistance that, I hope, will suitably wind up this volume.

Style of Therapist's Presentations

Precisely because resisters have special problems in listening to therapists and fully utilizing the help that they offer, their therapists had better give some consideration to the style, tone, and manner in which they present points that they hope will be significantly unblocking. Some of the things that you can heed in this regard are the following:

1. Once in awhile, clients deliberately play games and consciously resist changing in order to put themselves one up on the therapist and show how damnably clever they are. But not too often! Try to remember that their resistance is usually unwillful and unconscious, and that in spite of it they really *would* like to change. In most cases, they have created their emotional problems and the irrational Beliefs (iBs) that go with them without clearly realizing what they were doing; and they have then practiced their disturbed behaviors for a good many years. No wonder, then, that they resist change. It really *is* hard for them to modify their thoughts, feelings, and actions, and you can show them that you fully appreciate how hard it is and that you are not condemning them for having such trouble changing. But you can still forcefully show them that *hard* doesn't mean *impossible*, and that with real effort they *can* change in spite of the difficulty of doing so.

2. When resistant clients say, "I have intellectual insight but don't have emotional insight and therefore I can't seem to change," try to show them that *all* insight is "intellectual" but that they really mean that they have *weak* and *occasional* rather than *strong* and *persistent* insight. They therefore can work at making their "intellectual" insight stronger and more persistent until it becomes "emotional" (Ellis, 1963). "Emotional" or "real" insight, as Schlesinger (1982) points out, includes *action* to implement knowledge and understanding. By helping resistant clients to act on their insight (e.g., by giving them specific activity homework assignments to implement it), you may help them to "feel" what they call "emotional insight."

3. When clients resist interpretations that you are fairly sure are correct and that would probably be helpful to them, ask them to accept these interpretations *tentatively* and *experimentally* and to discover for themselves whether or not they are valid. I once suggested to a female client that she might be horrified at her husband's ogling other women because she herself actually would like to have some brief affairs with other men. At first, she denied this completely. Then I asked her to experiment with this interpretation by frankly asking herself, whenever she met a man she considered to be quite attractive, "Would I really like to have an affair with him if I were sure I wouldn't become too

emotionally involved and that it would not interfere with my marriage?" She came in a week later and acknowledged, to her great surprise, that she had met four men that very week with whom she could easily answer that question in the affirmative.

4. When your interpretations are denied or avoided, experiment with repeating them several times. As Schlesinger (1982) notes, interpretation may work as a process rather than as a one-time affair. However, the more consistently and vigorously that you make the same interpretation to dependent and suggestible clients, the more they may accept them even when they have little validity. So watch it!

5. When clients are trying to avoid discussing unpleasant subjects or experiencing powerful feelings, be careful about your own queasiness and florence-nightingalism. If you have trouble bringing up such topics, for fear that you will offend a client, take an honest look at your own dire need for approval—and make yourself *un*comfortably act against it. You can sometimes say something like this to the client: "I know that what I am about to discuss may be a ticklish area for you, and frankly I am having some problems of my own in bringing it to the fore and risking your disapproval, but nonetheless I would like you to consider my hypothesis that—." Then you can probe for the client's response to this ticklish issue.

6. Try to bring to resistant clients' attention some of the grim consequences of their behavior without being preachy or condemning. You can say, for example: "Yes, I see that you have often got away with borrowing money from your friends and not paying it back; and perhaps you can continue to keep getting away with it. But statistically speaking, and in the long run, some of them will probably tend to resent this, and you will therefore lose them as friends. Now that's all right, if you're willing to take that consequence—for you can always get new friends, and maybe succeed in borrowing from them, too! But you will probably lose out, to some extent. And even if you don't, you may train yourself to keep avoiding facing various responsibilities of life and enhancing your low frustration tolerance. That won't make you a worm or a totally weak individual. But it usually has its distinct disadvantages. So give the matter some thought and see if your behavior is really worth it in the long run."

7. Some therapists—such as Palazzoli, Boscolo, and Cecchin (1978) and Walker and Aycock (1984)—advocate avoiding all arguments with clients, taking a "positive connotation" approach, and finding resistance itself something of a positive or constructive tactic for clients to take. This approach has its advantages because, as I point out in Chapter 2, resistance is so ubiquitous as to be "normal" (albeit self-destructive), and it is good to point this out to some clients. However, if you, as a therapist, are "chicken," as Walker and Aycock advocate, you may easily miss many opportunities for constructive confrontation. No general or universal attitude is likely to be suitable in this respect. Some resistant clients will benefit from a "hard line" and some from a softer approach. Discretion and selectivity would seem to be the better part of valor!

8. Lauver, Holiman, and Kazama (1982) point out that counseling and psychotherapy can be viewed as a battleground, with the client and his or her resistance being the enemy, and with the therapist's language being a rhetoric of warfare rather than one of caring. They quote Vygotsky as observing, "Thought is not merely expressed in words, it comes into existence through them. Every thought tends to connect something with something else, to establish a relationship of things" (1962, p. 125). They therefore advocate that therapists look for some alternative to warfare rhetoric, such as Thorne's (1950) operationism, Carkhuff's (1969) concreteness, and Mager's (1962) tools for consensual meaning. They particularly advocate what they claim is the common denominator of these approaches—action language.

In using action language, you simply describe human events as things that people do instead of adding other and often negative interpretations or connotations to them. Thus, instead of saying to a client, "Your aggression was actively expressed," you say, "You shoved him out of your way," and instead of interpreting, "You sabotaged your plan to confront your boss," you say, "You did not ask your boss for a conference." In RET, we often use action language, and show resistant clients what they actually did instead of making general, and often dubious, interpretations that they may easily resist.

9. Vriend and Dyer (1973) point out that therapists had better have some idea about why their clients are resisting treatment and ask themselves whether their noncompliance is typical of their general reactions or is more specifically related to their interactions with and conceptions about the therapist and about therapy. Assuming that resistance stems from clients' attitudes toward the therapeutic relationship, it is usually best to explore these attitudes and the feelings about therapy to which they lead. Doing this, you can specifically show your clients that (a) you acknowledge and understand their resistant feelings, (b) you think these are an important part of their personality and therefore crucial to discuss in therapy, (c) you and they had better explore any irrational Beliefs (iBs) involved in this kind of resistance, (d) you are strong and competent enough yourself to handle the resistance without being personally threatened, (e) you can unconditionally accept them even when their resistances are sabotaging your therapeutic efforts (Ellis, 1982d).

Vriend and Dyer also indicate that by dealing honestly and openly with clients' resistance, you have a good chance to show them that therapy is not a process in the course of which they merely express their feelings or passively listen to what you have to say, but it is a two-sided effort in the course of which both of you had better face unpleasant facts and work hard to help each other abet the counseling process.

10. Barbara Kerr and her associates have done a series of studies that tend to show that clients may be both positively and negatively affected by two different factors: (a) the expertness of their therapists about the content of the therapy, and (b) the interpersonal influence and social power of the therapists (Kerr & Dell, 1976; Kerr, Olson, Claiborn, Bauers-Gruenler & Paolo, 1983). If their findings are accurate, then when your clients are opposed to the content of counseling or therapy (e.g., when they oppose some of the philosophies you are trying to teach them about accepting themselves, others, and the world), you are wise to approach them in a manner that shows that you are expert and efficient. When, however, your clients are resistant to therapy because of their negative attitudes toward the process of counseling (e.g., when they have negative attitudes toward ther-

apy itself), you are wise to use attractive counseling behaviors
(such as relating to clients more personally and warmly and
making an appearance that they would find attractive). Another
way of stating this is to say that when you discover your clients
are resisting because they are skeptical about some of the teachings of RET, you can try to show them increased expertness and
competence; while when you find them resisting largely because
they have problems with therapy itself or with relating to a
therapist, you can try to make your form and manner of presentation more personable and attractive.

More Points About Therapist Resistance

Therapists are, of course, human, and many of them actually
entered the field of psychotherapy and counseling largely because they had problems of their own and were therefore interested in techniques of working on them. You, as a therapist, may
well resist seeing certain things about some of your clients and
may be myopic in regard to some effective ways to help them
change. You can look for your own resistances and try to work
on them as follows:

1. Assume that although most of your clients in some ways
significantly resist therapy, your *own* thoughts, feelings, and
behaviors may significantly contribute to or encourage their
resistance. Therefore, whenever you encounter serious resistance in a client, actively look for your own possible contributions to it.

2. Investigate how your therapeutic goals and those of your
clients may clash. Is a client aiming for mere symptom removal
(e.g., overcoming social anxiety) while you are aiming for a more
profound personality change (e.g., the client's acceptance of himself or herself in *any* situation)? What goals can the two of you
agree upon and mutually work for?

3. If your therapeutic goals are more pervasive and far
reaching than the client's and you are willing to let this discrep-
ancy exist, at least be aware of it and consider the advisability of
making the client aware of it, too. You can then realistically *expect*
the client to resist some of your methods, and the client can more

fully *acknowledge* resistance—and either work harder to overcome it, choose to live with it, or look for another therapist.

4. Assume that you may well have iBs and inappropriate feelings about your clients' resistances. These iBs of your own will often tend to interfere with your relating well with clients and may help make them *more* resistant than they would otherwise be. Some of your main irrationalities may be: "I *must* succeed with resistant clients and I am a lousy therapist and something of a rotten person if I don't!" "These goddamned clients don't really want to change—as they *should*—and they are lazy people who *deserve* to keep suffering!" "Therapy with this difficult client *shouldn't* be so hard! How *awful* that she keeps resisting! What a crummy life I lead in this blasted profession!"

If, when you feel discouraged as a therapist, you promptly look for your own iBs about resistant clients, and if you use RET to surrender these ideas and then go back to the therapeutic drawing board, you will still have quite a few strong resisters— but I think that you will often do much better with them and actually find some enjoyment in this difficult process. You will also, to your own advantage, be a perennial user of RET on your own problems!

Overcoming Resistance by Using Rational-Emotive Systems Therapy

RET is famous for holding that while Activating Events (As) and environmental factors significantly contribute to and interact with disturbed emotional Consequences (Cs), the more direct and important human processes that "cause" and interact with Cs are peoples' Belief Systems (Bs) (Ellis, 1957a, 1962, 1971, 1973, 1979d, in press-a; Ellis & Harper, 1975). But it has also been pointed out that the As, Bs, and Cs of human behavior inevitably (and biologically) interact with each other, and that changing A significantly affects B and C, changing B affects A and C, and changing C affects A and B. Especially, in regard to working with groups and with families, RET emphasizes a comprehensive system approach to effecting individual and group change (Ellis, 1957a, 1981c, 1982a, 1982c; Ellis & Harper, 1961b).

With highly resistant clients, RET mainly tries to help them change their basic self-disturbing Beliefs (Bs), and thereby more elegantly change their Consequences (Cs) and be better equipped to modify the frustrating Activating Events (As) that they encounter during their lives. But it realistically acknowledges that many resisters will deliberately or unconsciously refuse to work on their iBs and their disruptive feelings (Cs) unless and until they are helped to change the happenings and stimuli that badly affect them. RET, therefore, tries in every feasible cognitive, emotive, and behavioral way to help resisters change their Bs and Cs; but it also does its best to get them to succeed at changing their As.

A 38-year-old male salesman ceaselessly complained about his wife, his children, his boss, and his conditions of work and, although he admitted he was childishly temper ridden and was thereby defeating himself, he kept refusing to accept (and gracefully lump!) grim reality, as I showed him he had damned well better, for the good of his own blood pressure. After six months of forceful (and, I think, excellent) RET, we were making almost no inroads in stemming his frequent angry outbursts.

Giving his case some careful thought, I decided to take a different tack and focus mainly on how he could get a better job and how he could deliberately fog his new boss and customers and *act* less angrily than he felt with them. He cooperated much more readily and energetically in these endeavors than he had ever worked at changing his iBs and his angry feelings. Four months later, he had a new job, was making almost twice as much in commissions as he had previously made, and was getting along almost famously with his boss and his customers.

At first, he still had many temper tantrums with his wife and children. But after he had been on the new job for seven months and he was still doing well, his outbursts at family members decreased significantly and he was much more tolerant of their "stupid" behaviors. His own view of his improved family relations was "because things are going so much better in my business life." Although by working with this irate individual on his relations with the people at his business I was able to help him change some of his iBs and emotional Consequences, I think that without helping him change A (by getting a new job and making more money), his rantings and ravings about the "injustices" of life might well not have appreciably decreased.

A 47-year-old woman with a lifelong history of confusion, indecision, depression, and failure to achieve intimacy with any man, kept clinging, during her first nine months of RET, to her narcissistic need to be everyone's center of attention and her abysmal self-downing whenever she was rejected. In spite of her having graduated from college magna cum laude, she worked as a claims adjuster, made little money, overspent on clothing, and complained bitterly about her poverty.

After getting almost nowhere with this borderline client for almost a year, I focused on helping her to change the Activating Events of her life by marrying a nice "schnooky" man whom she had dated for six years, but whom she found physically unattractive and below her intellectual level. Once she decided that he had more good than obnoxious characteristics and worked on regularly satisfying him sexually (sometimes giving him seven orgasms a week, although she only occasionally had one herself), he fell enthusiastically in love with her and devoted himself to pleasing her (as he had only mildly done before).

Married to him, her life changed radically: she worked only part time, got very involved with fixing up their new home, was busily drawn into her husband's social/business life, and had little time for her previous moaning and wailing. She accepted herself (wrongly, in RET terms) because of her better marital and financial status, and although I would say (and she would agree) that her irrational philosophies had not changed that much, she lived more happily with them. She and her husband frequently come to my famous Friday night workshops at the Institute for Rational-Emotive Therapy in New York (where I demonstrate RET in public with volunteers from the audience), and from talking with them from time to time (as well as from talking with several of her friends whom she has referred to me for therapy), I would say that for the past several years she has been functioning in the modestly neurotic rather than the borderline personality range. And mainly, I hypothesize, because by changing some of her Activating Events she has thereby helped herself change some of her emotional and behavior Consequences—as well as a few of her iBs.

An 18-year-old college student came to see me over 20 years ago and, although I tried very hard to help her overcome her procrastination in her school work and her anxiety in talking with personable males, I got nowhere for 17 months. She almost got thrown out of college several times because of her incompletes and, although she was unusually attractive, she rarely dated (and was horrified because two of her best women friends were already engaged to be married).

Seeing that I was getting nowhere with conventional RET, and that I was not helping her give up her iBs that she shouldn't have to do onerous school work and that she was a no-goodnik if a personable male rejected her, I experimented with a different tack. I encouraged this resistant client to dress beautifully, to indicate to her schoolmates that she was sexually liberal, and to say only flattering things to all the males (as well as females) she encountered. Doing this, she was soon beseiged with dates, even though she did nothing herself (as I vainly tried to get her to do) about going out of her way to meet suitable men.

After a few months of huge social success, this student's confidence in her ability to win males enormously increased; she had immense fun dating; and she gave up her goal of marrying soon because she wanted to keep enjoying playing the field. She was definitely not unconditionally accepting herself with her failures, as RET would prefer, but she was conditionally accepting herself because of her successes. However, she gained such a degree of achievement–confidence (though not *self*-confidence) about her social life that she realized that she could, with effort, get more of the things she wanted from life and that this could apply to her studies as well. So she began to work harder at school, procrastinated much less, and for the first time since she entered college began to get good marks. So her increased confidence in her social ability apparently helped her to see that she could do better in her school work and that it was not *too* hard for her to do it. By inducing her to change some of the As in her life, I presumably helped her to change some of her major Bs and Cs as well.

I find this true for more difficult than nondifficult clients—particularly for those in the borderline range. It is sometimes almost impossible to persuade them to change themselves unless they can also be shown how to change the conditions under which they live and work. So be it. Using RET, you can often show them how to change A—and *therefore* make themselves more likely to change B and C. This, of course, has its distinct disadvantages and dangers, for many resistant clients will only work at modifying their life conditions *rather than* change their disturbance-creating beliefs, feelings, and behaviors *about* those conditions. They are more interested in *feeling* better rather than *getting* better (Ellis, 1972f).

I have seen, for example, literally hundreds of people who temporarily overcame their feelings of anxiety as soon as they formed a (presumably) lasting relationship. When they considered quitting therapy, I advised many of them to continue, but they cavalierly quit anyway. A good many of them later returned, to confess that their leaving had been premature; many others, however, from what I heard from their friends and relatives, were ashamed to return—and admit that they had mistakenly thought that changing some of their important As automatically, and permanently, changed their Bs and Cs.

Nonetheless, part of efficient therapy is helping people to change the Activating Events of their lives as well as their iBs and disturbed Consequences—especially when these people ask for but seriously resist treatment. Rational-emotive systems therapy tries to deal with them and the situations in which they exist, and although it would prefer them to make themselves disappointed and sorry rather than severely anxious and depressed about almost any situation they find undesirable, it often settles for getting them to feel better by modifying the situation itself. Inelegant—but what else can you sometimes effectively do?

Some of the ways in which you can use rational-emotive systems therapy to help resistant clients change the Activating Events of their lives include the following:

1. Instead of giving up their whining and wailing about a partner they seem to be losing, they can increase their efforts to be nice to and possibly win back that partner.

2. Similarly, if they refuse to give up their self-deprecation about their job performances or anger about their conditions of

work, they can put their energies into finding an easier or more enjoyable job. And you can help them do better at their jobs rather than accept themselves when they don't do so well.

3. When they retain their philosophy of addiction—e.g., still believe that they *need* to smoke, overeat, or procrastinate and that they *can't stand* immediate pain to arrive at the future gain of nonaddiction—you can help them switch to a less pernicious addiction—e.g., caffeine rather than cigarettes.

4. When resistant clients won't do their *in vivo* desensitizing homework assignments—e.g., taking elevator rides that they fear—you can let them take toned-down assignments (such as riding on escalators or going in one elevator every month) or can assign them concomitant pleasures (such as only riding in elevators when accompanied by a very nice or attractive partner).

5. When clients won't do a difficult task (e.g., write a book that they want to write), show them how to get a competent collaborator (such as a co-author) to do it with.

6. Give difficult clients a choice of working on an elegant or philosophic solution to their main emotional problems and/or figuring out practical solutions to partially resolve it. But show them that if they pick the less elegant pathway, they have a right to this choice and need never put themselves down for taking it.

7. When resistant clients refuse to give up their philosophy and feelings of anger, you can help them to stay away from people at whom they are angry and to make greater efforts to be with those they can more easily accept and like.

Dealing with Resistant Clients' Low Frustration Tolerance

As noted previously in this book and in some of my other writings (Ellis, 1979a, 1980a), when people have feelings of inadequacy and strong hostility, they have dramatic problems that they fairly clearly see and acknowledge and that are quite visible to others. But when they have discomfort anxiety or low frustration tolerance (LFT), they may undramatically defeat themselves for many years and not be too aware that they are doing so. But LFT is in some ways even more pervasive and pernicious than self-downing or hating others. Some of its main disadvantages are: (1) It gets into many aspects of people's lives—and blocks them in several areas, including that of coming for and working at therapy. (2) It seems like normal "laziness" to millions of people—who therefore do not take it seriously and try to do something about it. (3) It is tied up with a *musturbatory*, grandiose philosophy that is largely unconscious or implicit and therefore not too easy to observe. It is fairly obvious that self-damners are telling themselves, "I *must* do well or I am a thorough failure," and that hostile people are believing, "You *should* treat me correctly or you are no damned good!" But it is not so evident that people with LFT are philosophizing, "Conditions *should* be nice and easy, but the world is a terrible place, so what's the use of my doing anything?" (4) LFT usually accompanies feelings of inadequacy and rage, interacts with them, exacerbates them, and hinders the understanding and alleviation of them. (5) The philosophy behind LFT often seems based on realism and logic and is therefore difficult to surrender. When people suffer many frustrations (e.g., in economic hard times) and are often treated unfairly (e.g., when they are discriminated against), it seems obvious to them that these unusual happenings *absolutely should* not exist and that it is *utterly horrible* that they do. (6) Part of LFT—the frustration part—is beneficial and had better be retained. If people are dealt with unjustly and feel highly displeased about this, they will be motivated to do something about this injustice; so they'd better not feel calm and serene! But if they have LFT, they will tend to rant and rave, *do* very little, and finally have an irrational outburst and do something foolish (and unjust!). (7) LFT frequently leads to depression (Ellis, 1979a), and when people are depressed, they tend to become inert and withdrawn and do *less* than they would normally do to overcome life's frustrations. They feel *hopeless*, have *less* energy, and thereby (ironically) *increase* their frustrations.

I hypothesize that when clients resist therapy in spite of their desire to change and be happier, and in spite of the reasonably competent efforts of their therapist, they frequently have considerable LFT, and that this largely stems from their iBs (Ellis, 1962, 1973, 1976d, 1979a, 1980a; Ellis & Whiteley, 1979; Nolan, Boyd & Grieger, 1980; Janis & Mann, 1979). Some effective means you can use to help them alleviate their LFT and thereby overcome their resistance include the following:

1. Show them that their resistance to change frequently involves LFT and the iBs which lie behind it. These iBs might include the following: "I must find *easy* and *quick* ways to overcome my disturbance. It's too hard for me to *keep* working to relieve it. I *can't stand* having my symptoms and also *can't stand* having to work so hard to alleviate them."

2. Show clients that their LFT about the efforts of changing trap them in a no-win situation: If they *must* get rid of their uncomfortable symptoms, presumably by working at doing so, and if they *must* not work too hard to do this, they reach an impasse and practically assure that, barring a miracle, they will retain their symptoms and perhaps get worse.

3. Agree with your clients that, yes, it is hard for them to keep working at changing themselves—but keep showing them, forcefully and graphically, that it is much harder if they don't do this work.

4. Keep showing clients that no matter how bad it is for them to change, they *can* do so. Because they (consciously or unconsciously) *choose* to think irrationally, emote inappropriately, and act dysfunctionally, they can (with work and effort!) also consciously choose to think, emote, and behave self-helpingly.

5. Show clients that although it is often very difficult for them to overcome their inertia and start working to change, if they make themselves uncomfortable for awhile, they usually become much more comfortable—and eventually enjoy life more.

6. Work out plans with clients to break their homework into reasonable doable chunks and to reinforce themselves for working on these chunks (and perhaps penalize themselves when they fail to work at them) (Ellis & Knaus, 1977).

7. Encourage resistant clients to take on the *challenge* of working at changing themselves, so that they have additional incentives to enjoy the change process. Thus, if a bulemic client is shown that she may become one of the *few* people to stop food binging and regurgitating and to prevent herself from falling back, she may work harder to achieve this relatively *rare* result.

8. When you discover that resisters will not do their thera-

peutic homework (such as encountering potential love partners or stopping their compulsive drinking), you may arrange to accompany them or get an assistant therapist or a friend to accompany them to see that they actually carry out this homework.

In all these respects, perhaps the main thing to keep in mind is that resisters (and virtually all clients) frequently have some degree of LFT: showing them this fact and helping them work against it is often crucial to successful therapy (Ainslie, 1974; Ellis, 1979a, 1979g, 1983c, 1984d; Ellis & Knaus, 1977; Mischel & Baker, 1975; Mischel & Ebbesen, 1970; Mischel & Gilligan, 1964; Mischel & Mischel, 1975; Mischel & Moore, 1973; Patterson & Mischel, 1976).

Inadvisable Techniques of Overcoming Resistance

As I have noted several times in this book, some techniques of helping clients overcome their resistance actually work—and sometimes quickly—but have their own serious limitations and disadvantages, and some are inherently dangerous and antitherapeutic (Ellis, 1983a, 1984f; Hadley & Strupp, 1976; Strupp, Hadley, & Gomes-Schwartz, 1977). Some of them can even be considered as emotional disturbances in their own right. Thus, if I convince a male client that he has a fairy godmother who will always take care of him and make sure that everyone loves him, he may therefore help himself become less inhibited, shy, withdrawn, and self-hating and may start making therapeutic progress when he previously was consciously or unconsciously resisting. Or if I convince another client that I am really the devil and that unless she follows what I say and compulsively does her therapeutic homework (e.g., diet rigorously or always go in the elevators that she foolishly fears) I will make sure that she roasts in hell for eternity, she may well significantly improve—but at what cost!

Although, therefore, RET fully acknowledges the efficacy of certain change tactics, it avoids many of them or uses them only in exceptional cases because it holds that they commonly do more harm than good. With this caveat in mind, let me list several techniques that may distinctly motivate clients—including difficult and resistant clients—to change for the "better," but that you are only to use, if at all, with great caution:

1. Induce clients to become devoutly and dogmatically religious or cultish.

2. Induce clients to follow secular dogmas and bigotries—e.g., rigid and absolutistic views on communism, utopianism, capitalism, patriotism, or scientism.

3. Use magical rituals, such as shamanism, witchcraft, voodooism, and necromancy.

4. Convince clients that they are immortal or will doubtless experience some kind of afterlife.

5. Convince them that they will undoubtedly wind up in heaven—or hell.

6. Convince them that they undoubtedly have mystical ties to the universe—e.g., are at one with the universe, can tap into universal energy, or have a perfect soul.

7. Convince them that they have supernatural powers by which they can achieve miracles, such as perfect extrasensory perception, psychokinesis, or mediumship.

8. Induce clients to dogmatically believe in and to run their lives by antiscientific doctrines, such as astrology, astral visions, phrenology, superstitions, and other unvalidated "sources of knowledge."

9. Get clients to rigidly follow arbitrary rituals that will supposedly protect them from harm—such as wearing phylacteries, killing sacrificial animals or humans, resorting to circumcision or clitoridectomy, or eating sacred wafers.

10. Teach clients that they are members of some superior race, ethnic group, religion, or therapy group and that by virtue of their being born or inducted into this group they will be favored and protected, and will make outstanding achievements.

11. Teach clients that no matter what they do they are perfect and will therefore always do well and will triumph. Also, teach them that they are God.

12. Teach clients that they are not responsible for their poor, bad, or antisocial acts because some external source—e.g., their parents, culture, society, or god—makes them do whatever they do.

13. Convince clients that their past experiences, and particularly their early childhood experiences, utterly determine the way they behave today and that by fully understanding these experiences they will gain insight that will easily and automatically get them to make great personality changes.

14. Induce clients to blame and hate someone else—e.g., their parents or some political tyrant—for their immoral acts and disturbances, and thereby help them accept themselves as "good" people.

15. Show people that if they fully know themselves—i.e., know what all their motives, ideas, feelings, and behaviors are—they will automatically and spontaneously change their disturbances and their dysfunctional behaviors.

16. Induce clients to fully express all their feelings—especially their feelings of hostility—and thereby permanently rid themselves of these uncomfortable and self-defeating feelings.

17. Show clients that you, their therapist, have very warm feelings for them and that they can greatly depend on you for support and direction.

18. Induce clients to devote themselves to pleasing the therapist—e.g., by giving you gifts, money, or sexual favors—and thereby win great support and help with their problems from you.

19. Often and strongly threaten to throw clients out of therapy if they don't do exactly what you—the therapist—want them to do.

20. Intimidate clients with your own authority and power, to force them to follow your therapeutic rules.

21. Show clients that you distinctly despise them because they are resisting your great efforts and are stubbornly refusing to do what you are trying to get them to do.

All the above techniques of trying to overcome resistance may work at certain times and under special circumstances. You may therefore, in a pinch, and when you think that all other methods will fail (or that clients may commit suicide or seriously harm others), consider using them. But with due consideration and caution! These techniques will be used, I strongly hope, rarely!

Additional Points on Maintaining
Therapeutic Change

Let me return to the important point with which I briefly dealt in Chapter 6: the maintenance of therapeutic change. RET, somewhat similarly to psychoanalysis and existential therapy, too cavalierly assumes that, if clients make a profound philosophic or attitudinal change, they will not only lose their presenting symptoms, but also maintain their therapeutic gains. This is often true: in fact, I am often delighted to learn that some of my most difficult clients not only see life much more healthfully after therapy has ended, but also make remarkable continuing improvement during the following years because of their steady use of RET principles in their daily lives.

But some do not! Many clients who have "successfully" undertaken all kinds of therapy sooner or later fall back to their old symptomatic levels—or on to worse feelings and behaviors than they exhibited before therapy (W. Miller, 1980; Stokes & Baer, 1977; Stunkard, 1980).

Therapy of all clients, and particularly of resistant ones, had therefore better give serious consideration to the problems of maintenance of personality change. A number of behavioral and cognitive-behavioral therapists have made specific suggestions which you can incorporate in your therapeutic procedures to encourage your clients to maintain their therapeutic gains:

1. Recognize the complex nature of the skills you are teaching clients and the transactional elements in their accepting and using these skills (Kendall, 1984b; Meichenbaum, 1984). Emotive as well as cognitive and behavioral methods are important in facilitating generalization and maintenance of change (Ellis, 1962, 1973; Ellis & Abrahms, 1978; Ellis & Becker, 1982).

2. Performance-enhancement procedures are fine, but a focus on cognitive and affective processes that go beyond more behavioral methods is also quite important (Bandura, 1977; Bowers & Meichenbaum, 1984; Ellis, 1973, 1984d, 1984e; Meichenbaum, 1977; Olson & Dowd, 1984).

3. When feasible, include the client's relevant social environment in making therapeutic decisions, and encouarge and teach family members and other close associates to help him or her

achieve and maintain changes (Bierman, 1981; Ellis, 1957a, 1965; Haley, 1976; Lazarus, 1981; Lazarus & Fay, 1984; Meichenbaum, 1984). As I. Miller (1984, p. 12) notes: "In order to maximize maintenance for some patients, we have attempted to modify the patient's environment in relatively direct ways. . . . For some patients these types of changes in life situations are necessary in order to make and/or maintain treatment gains."

4. Assume that your treatment of difficult clients will not necessarily lead to generalization and maintenance and try to train them specifically for this (Meichenbaum & Gilmore, 1982; Meichenbaum & Jaremko, 1983; Stunkard, 1980).

5. Keep in mind the RET principle that all the insight in the world will help little if clients do not steadily *work and practice* healthy thoughts, feelings, and behaviors they have learned in therapy—and continue this practice for the rest of their lives (Ellis, 1962, 1973; Lazarus & Fay, 1984; Maultsby, 1975, 1984). As Lazarus and Fay (1982) have emphasized, try to see that clients appreciate the value and rationale behind homework exercises; that agreed-upon homework is viewed as cost effective and relevant to the clients' problems; and that assigned tasks are not too difficult.

6. Encourage clients to use cassette recorders (and sometimes video equipment) to listen to therapy sessions, to forcefully talk themselves out of their iBs, and to remind themselves to keep working at their problems (Ellis, 1979b, 1984d, 1984e; Lazarus & Fay, 1984; Maultsby, 1975, 1984).

7. By using behavior rehearsal, coping imagery, and rational-emotive imagery, clients can continually work on their problems even when they are not specifically under stress (Lazarus, 1981; Maultsby, 1984; Maultsby & Ellis, 1974).

8. Clients can be encouraged to return for booster sessions after regular therapy has ended (Ellis, 1962; Lazarus & Fay, 1984; W. Miller, 1980; Stunkard, 1980).

9. The more comprehensive therapy is, and the more cognitive, emotive, and behavioral techniques it includes, the less likely clients may be to fall back to their old symptoms and the more likely to use some of the methods they have learned to once again overcome their symptoms (Bernard & Joyce, 1984; Ellis, 1962, 1969b, 1970b, 1984d, 1984e; Ellis & Bernard, 1983; Ken-

dall, 1984; Lazarus, 1981; Meichenbaum & Jaremko, 1983; Shelton & Ackerman, 1974).

10. I. W. Miller (1984) and his associates have found that if clients are instructed to practice their newly acquired coping skills beyond a "competence" level they are more likely to maintain therapeutic gains. Having clients review these coping skills toward the end of therapy also helps.

11. When Carl Rogers and Jerry Berlin listened to some of my tape recordings in 1959, they noted (personal communication, July, 1959) that I was very active and directive during the first session, and frequently talked much more than the client, but that as the sessions progressed the client assumed greater responsibility and became more in charge of the therapy. This has always been one of the main techniques of RET—to use the first few sessions largely for active-directive teaching and then to encourage clients to take over, assume responsibility for their own self-teaching and change, and to become independent of the therapist. I. W. Miller (1984) also finds that giving increased responsibility to clients and having them participate fully in the last few sessions in the direction of their own treatment, significantly helps them maintain progress once treatment ends.

12. Rational-emotive and cognitive-behavior therapies usually focus on between-session cognitive and behavioral activity by clients, especially as therapy comes to a close. This between-session activity helps clients maintain therapeutic change (Ellis, 1962, 1973, 1984e; Ellis & Grieger, 1977; Ellis & Whiteley, 1979; Lazarus & Fay, 1984; I. Miller, 1984).

13. You can often help clients by informing them, both at the beginning and the end of therapy, that they are only likely to help themselves by hard work, that they are likely to relapse after improving, and that they therefore had better continually work at preventing relapse (Ellis, 1962, 1984e, in press-a; Lazarus & Fay, 1984; I. Miller, 1984; Walen, DiGiuseppe & Wessler, 1980; Wessler & Wessler, 1980).

14. Generalization and maintenance of therapeutic gains may be enhanced if you use reinforcers with clients that have already worked in their natural environment and if you maximize the similarity between the training situation and the natural situation. Thus, you may help train your clients in their

natural setting or you may structure the therapeutic situation so that it is similar to the natural situation (L. Miller, 1980; Olson & Dowd, 1984; Stokes & Baer, 1977). This is why RET usually favors *in vivo* desensitization homework assignments rather than imaginal systematic desensitization (Ellis, 1962, 1983a, 1984e, in press-a; Ellis & Abrahms, 1978; Ellis & Becker, 1982; Ellis & Harper, 1975).

15. You can help clients program new and healthy responses for a number of difficult settings in the presence of a diversity of individuals (Olson & Dowd, 1984; Stokes & Baer, 1977).

16. If you help clients to have a greater sense of self-efficacy, so that they believe that they *can* keep maintaining their gains and *can* keep themselves minimally disturbed in the future, they will be more likely to generalize and continue therapeutic successes (Bandura, 1977; Franks & Wilson, 1978; Meichenbaum, 1977; Olson & Dowd, 1984). RET especially tries to help clients increase their feelings of self-efficacy but not of ego inflation or self-worth. It shows them that they *can* take charge of themselves and that it is good for them to control their own emotional destiny; but it discourages their false and dangerous conclusion that they are *therefore* good or estimable *persons* (Ellis, 1962, 1972a, 1973, 1976a, 1984e). But RET emphasizes performance accomplishments—which are probably the best way most clients can see that they are now capable of mastering and succeeding in previous threatening problem situations (Bandura, 1977; Olson & Dowd, 1984).

17. You may specifically encourage generalization of therapeutic advances, as Wilson and Franks (1982) have pointed out, in two ways: (a) Conceptualize therapy as an educational or skill-training process and help clients see it this way. (b) Encourage clients to analyze and understand exactly how they brought about changes and how they can presumably continue to do so (Ellis & Abrahms, 1978; Ellis & Becker, 1982). Particularly help clients to attribute their changes to themselves and not to outside forces or to mystical or magical influences (Ellis, 1984f, 1984k).

18. You can discuss with clients and help them predict in advance when stressful times are likely to occur and when they

may fall back to old dysfunctional thinking and behavioral patterns. Plans can then be made to cope with these stressful occasions and to resist reverting to unhealthy responses (Krantz, Hill, Foster-Rawlings & Zeeve, 1984; Stuart, 1980). You can also encourage clients to bring up new situations, and can get them to imagine the worst possible situations that could occur, as is done in the RET technique Disputing Irrational Beliefs (DIBS) (Ellis, 1974a; Ellis & Harper, 1975). They can then prepare themselves, in advance, to create and maintain appropriate feelings and behaviors in these situations (Ellis & Abrahms, 1978; Ellis & Becker, 1982).

19. You can provide clients with handouts, such as the one quoted in Chapter 6, that explain to them the problems of maintaining and generalizing therapeutic gains and that instruct them how to help themselves in this respect (Ellis, 1984g).

In a study of cognitive-behavioral therapists' use of strategies for maintenance and generalization of therapeutic results, Krantz, Hill, Foster-Rawlings, and Zeeve (1984, p. 21) found the five most popular strategies to be: (1) Promote internal attributions of change. (2) Train general strategies. (3) Identify barriers to maintenance. (4) Transfer directiveness from therapist to client. (5) Discuss need for continuing change efforts.

These all seem like effective techniques, but research to confirm their usefulness is as yet almost nonexistent. And all generalization and overgeneralization, as Baer (1984) notes, is hard to maintain—if you really think about it. Helping clients, therefore, to generalize and to maintain their therapeutic gains is exceptionally difficult and requires persistent work by themselves and their therapists. So be it.

Conclusions and Caveats

Resistance, whether we like it or not, is one of the most important aspects of almost all psychotherapy. Even when clients are unusually cooperative and hard working, they still reach plateaus of improvement, fall back, and resist getting better or improving as effectively as they could. Whether their resistance is largely their own fault (Coltrera & Ross, 1967; Ellis, 1962, 1979a, 1980a, in press-a; Freud, 1912/1965b, 1912/1965c; Greenson, 1967, Wolstein, 1959), or whether it stems mainly from therapists' deficiencies (Lazarus & Fay, 1982), the fact remains that it had better be handled and at least partly overcome.

It is assumed in this book that clients, because of their biological tendencies, social learning, and own negative practice and self-reinforcement, naturally and easily resist acknowledging disturbance, going for therapy, and fully working at benefiting from therapy. But it is also assumed that therapists often consciously and unconsciously resist being efficient and overcoming client resistance. I have presented a number of cognitive, emotive, and behavioral RET and CBT methods of understanding and handling resistance in the foregoing chapters. None of these, nor all of them collectively, work well in many instances, and research studies specifically investigating the effectiveness of various methods of overcoming resistance have been rarely done. In fact, the controlled study of antiresistance techniques is in its infancy: considerable research in this area is overdue and could well supplement the large number of clinical outcome studies of RET, CBT, and behavior therapy that have already been done.

Until this kind of research is published, let me give some caveats to therapists who want to deal with the problems of resistance more effectively:

1. Clients resist making therapeutic changes for various reasons at various times. Therefore, don't dogmatically assume that you clearly *know* why a given client resists and are *sure* what to do about his or her resistance.

2. A client, you, or both of you may be the main contributor to resistance. Remain open minded to all three possibilities.

3. Whatever your main theory of psychotherapy, don't assume that it fully explains and will help you deal effectively with *every* client's resistance. Explore possibilities, as well, that are not especially covered by your regular theory and practice.

4. If one cognitive, emotive, or behavioral technique doesn't help you (and the client) overcome serious resistance, try another and another. Experiment—use several methods, if necessary, with a single resistant client.

5. Persist! Just because your chosen methods of helping clients overcome resistance do not work for awhile, don't as-

sume that they are totally ineffective and will never work. By definition, serious resistance *is* difficult, for you and the clients, to conquer. Expect that it will be—and persist!

6. If you think that a client's resistance is impossible to alleviate and are ready to abandon therapy with this individual, consider consulting with other therapists to check out your hypothesis and to consider their suggestions about how you might successfully continue.

7. Closely monitor your own feelings with resistant clients to see whether you are only appropriately disappointed with and regretful about their *behavior* or inappropriately angry at *them*. If you see that you are enraged, or impatient, at resistant clients, look for your Jehovian shoulds, musts, and demands, and do your best to change them to desires and preferences. If you think you can change, but have trouble changing, consider personal therapy.

8. If you have feelings of anxiety, depression, or self-downing about your inability to reach resisters, check your iBs about yourself and the supposed *necessity* of your being helpful to them. Work hard to surrender these beliefs. If you don't succeed, consider going for therapy (preferably RET, of course!) yourself.

9. If you fail completely to help some clients overcome their resistance, first work on acknowledging your failures. But refuse to down yourself as a therapist, or as a person, because of these failings. Try to see whether your clients would have probably resisted any therapist and accept that possibility. But even if you think you personally are responsible for the failure, unconditionally accept *you* in spite of your *failing*. And consider going for more supervision and training.

10. You don't *have* to continue to be a therapist just because you have had considerable training and experience as one. Some therapists rationally decide, after awhile, that overcoming resistances and the other hassles of therapy are not sufficiently enjoyable or are too much of a hassle; and you may agree with them. If so, you can unashamedly take your degrees and talents elsewhere—into some other area that strikes your fancy. But don't quit too soon! Just because you enjoy helping people, don't think that you *must* do so as an individual or group therapist. One of my therapist clients decided to give up individual treatment and

only do workshops and write self-help books. Another therapist I know left the field of psychology completely to become a stockbroker. Both these ex-therapists are happy about their new choices and are making out well in following them.

11. Try to be honest with yourself about your therapeutic failures and about the ineffectuality of psychotherapy in general. As I point out in the final chapter of *Reason and Emotion in Psychotherapy* (Ellis, 1962), and in some of my other writings (Ellis, 1979e, 1982c, 1983a, 1983c, 1984g), therapy has distinct limitations and shortcomings—yes, all psychotherapy, including RET. Don't be grandiose! Acknowledge the possible harm (as well as good) you do as a therapist—and try to be less iatrogenic. Psychotherapy is distinctly a two-way process. Therapist, heal thyself!

References

Adler, A. (1968). *Understanding human nature.* Greenwich, CT: Fawcett World. (Work originally published in 1927)

Adler, A. (1964). *Social interest: A challenge of mankind.* New York: Capricorn.

Ainslie, G. (1974). Specious reward: A behavioral theory of impulsiveness and impulse control. *Psychological Bulletin, 82,* 463–496.

Alberti, R. E., & Emmons, M. L. (1982). *Your perfect right* (4th ed.). San Luis Obispo, CA: Impact.

Albin, R., & Montagna, D. D. (1977). Mystical aspects of science. *Humanist, 37*(2), 44–46.

Alexander, F., & French, T. M. (1946). *Psychoanalytic therapy.* New York: Ronald.

Alperson, B. I. (1976). On shibboleths, incantations, and the confusion of the I-thou and the Oh-wow. *Humanist, 36*(1), 12–14.

Applebaum, S. A. (1979). To define and decipher the borderline syndrome. *Psychotherapy, 16,* 364–370.

Araoz, D. L. (1982). *Hypnosis and sex therapy.* New York: Brunner/Mazel.

Baer, D. M. (1984). It's hard to maintain generalization if you think about it. *Cognitive Behaviorist, 6*(1), 22–24.

Bandura, A. (1969). *Principles of behavior modification.* New York: Holt, Rinehart & Winston.

Bandura, A. (1977). *Social learning theory.* Englewood Cliffs, NJ: Prentice-Hall.

Bard, J. A. (1980). *Rational-emotive therapy in practice.* Champaign, IL: Research Press.

Bartley, W. W. (1962). *The retreat to commitment.* New York: Knopf.

Basch, M. J. (1982). Dynamic psychotherapy and its frustrations. In P. L. Wachtel (Ed.), *Resistance* (pp. 3–24). New York: Plenum.

Bauer, R. (1979). The use of trance in working with the borderline personality. *Psychotherapy, 16,* 371–380.

Beck, A. T. (1967). *Depression.* New York: Harper-Hoeber.

Beck, A. T. (1976). *Cognitive therapy and the emotional disorders.* New York: International Universities.

Beck, A. T., Rush, J., Emergy, G., & Shaw, B. (1979). *Cognitive therapy of depression.* New York: Guilford.

Becker, E. (1973). *The denial of death.* New York: Free Press.

Benson, H. (1975). *The relaxation response.* New York: Morrow.

Bernard, M. E., & Joyce, M. R. (1984). *Rational-emotive therapy with children and adolescents.* New York: Wiley.

Berne, E. (1964). *Games people play.* New York: Grove.

Bernheim, H. (1947). *Suggestive therapeutics.* New York: London Book Company. (Original work published in 1886)

Bierman, K. (1981). *Enhancing generalization of social skills training with peer involvement and subordinate goals.* Paper presented at the biennial meeting of the Society for Research in Child Development, Boston.

Bingham, T. R. (1982). *Program for affective learning.* Blanding, UT: Metra.

Blatt, S. J., & Erlich, H. S. (1982). Levels of resistance in the psychotherapeutic process. In P. L. Wachtel (Ed.), *Resistance* (pp. 69–91). New York: Plenum.

Bowers, K., & Meichenbaum, D. (1984). *The unconscious reconsidered.* New York: Wiley.

Brehm, S. S. (1976). *The application of social psychology to clinical practice.* Washington, DC: Hemisphere.

Burns, D. (1980). *Feeling good.* New York: Morrow.

Burton, A. (Ed.). (1969). *Encounter.* San Francisco, CA: Jossey-Bass.

Campbell, J. (1975). Seven levels of consciousness. *Psychology Today, 9*(4), 77–78.

Carkhuff, R. R. (1969). *Helping and human relations.* 2 vols. New York: Holt, Rinehart & Winston.

Casriel, D. (1974). *A scream away from happiness.* New York: Grosset and Dunlap.

Chamberlain, P., Patterson, G., Reid, J., Kavanagh, K., & Forgatch, M.

(1984). Observation of client resistance. *Behavior Therapy, 15,* 144–155.

Chapman, A. H. (1964, Sept.). Iatrogenic problems in psychotherapy. *Psychiatry Digest,* pp. 23–29.

Cleckley, H. (1950). *The mask of sanity.* St. Louis, MO: Mosby.

Coltrera, J. R., & Ross, N. (1967). Freud's psychoanalytic technique—from the beginnings to 1923. In B. J. Wolman (Ed.), *Psychoanalytic techniques* (pp. 13–50). New York: Basic Books.

Comfort, A. (1972). *The joy of sex.* New York: Crown.

Coué, E. (1923). *My method.* New York: Doubleday, Page.

Crawford, T. (1982), October). Paper presented at the Workshop on rational-emotive therapy and communication, Los Angeles, CA.

Danysh, J. (1974). *Stop without quitting.* San Francisco, CA: International Society of General Semantics.

Dewald, P. A. (1982). Psychoanalytic perspectives on resistance. In P. L. Wachtel (Ed.), *Resistance* (pp. 45–68). New York: Plenum.

Dewey, J. (1922). *Human nature and conduct.* New York: Modern Library.

Dryden, W. (Speaker). (1981). *Annotated therapist tapes* (Cassette recording, No. C2029). New York: Institute for Rational-Emotive Therapy.

Dryden, W. (1982). The therapeutic alliance: Conceptual issues and some research findings. *Midland Journal of Psychotherapy, 1*(6), 14–19.

Dryden, W. (1984). *Rational-emotive therapy: Fundamentals and innovations.* London: Croom Helm.

Dubois, P. (1907). *The psychic treatment of nervous disorders.* New York: Funk & Wagnalls.

Dunlap, K. (1928). A revision of the fundamental law of habit formation. *Science, 67,* 360–362.

D'Zurilla, T. J., & Goldfried, M. R. (1971). Problem solving and behavior modification. *Journal of Abnormal Psychology, 78,* 107–126.

Duffy, A. (1975, June 2). Esalen: Slow death. *Village Voice,* pp. 8–9.

Elkin, A., Ellis, A., & Edelstein, M. (Speakers). (1974). *Recorded sessions with RET clients* (Cassette recording, No. C2025). New York: Institute for Rational-Emotive Therapy.

Ellenberger, H. F. (1970). *The discovery of the unconscious.* New York: Basic Books.

Ellis, A. (1956). The effectiveness of psychotherapy with individuals who have severe homosexual problems. *Journal of Consulting Psychology, 20,* 191–195.

Ellis, A. (1957a). *How to live with a "neurotic."* (Rev. ed., 1975). New York: Crown.

Ellis, A. (1957b). Outcome of employing three techniques of psychotherapy. *Journal of Clinical Psychology, 13,* 334–350.

Ellis, A. (1958a). Rational psychotherapy. *Journal of General Psychology, 59,* 35–49.

Ellis, A. (1958b). Hypnotherapy with borderline psychotics. *Journal of General Psychology, 59,* 245–253.

Ellis, A. (1959a). Comments on cases. In S. W. Standal & R. J. Corsini (Eds.), *Critical incidents of psychotherapy (passim).* Englewood Cliffs, NJ: Prentice-Hall.

Ellis, A. (1959b). Requisite conditions for basic personality change. *Journal of Consulting Psychology, 23,* 538–540.

Ellis, A. (1962). *Reason and emotion in psychotherapy.* Secaucus, NJ: Citadel.

Ellis, A. (1963). Toward a more precise definition of "emotional" and "intellectual" insight. *Psychological Reports, 13,* 125–126.

Ellis, A. (1965). *The art and science of love.* (Rev. ed.). Secaucus, NJ: Lyle Stuart.

Ellis, A. (Speaker). (1966a). *Recorded sessions with clients with a study problem, with dating anxiety and with anger.* (Cassette recording, C2003). New York: Institute for Rational-Emotive Therapy.

Ellis, A. (Speaker). (1966b). *Recorded sessions with child and adolescent clients* (Cassette recording, No. C2011). New York: Institute for Rational-Emotive Therapy.

Ellis, A. (1969a). A weekend of rational encounter. In A. Burton (Ed.), *Encounter* (pp. 112–127). San Francisco, CA: Jossey-Bass.

Ellis, A. (1969b). A cognitive approach to behavior therapy. *International Journal of Psychiatry, 8,* 896–900.

Ellis, A. (1970a). *The essence of rational psychotherapy: A comprehensive approach.* New York: Institute for Rational-Emotive Therapy.

Ellis, A. (1970b). *Homework report.* New York: Institute for Rational-Emotive Therapy.

Ellis, A. (1971). *Growth through reason.* North Hollywood, CA: Wilshire Books.

Ellis, A. (1972a). *Psychotherapy and the value of a human being.* New York: Institute for Rational-Emotive Therapy.

Ellis, A. (Speaker). (1972b). *Twenty-one ways to stop worrying* (Cassette recording). New York: Institute for Rational-Emotive Therapy.

Ellis, A. (Speaker). (1972c). *How to stubbornly refuse to be ashamed of anything* (Cassette recording). New York: Institute for Rational-Emotive Therapy.

Ellis, A. (1972d). *How to master your fear of flying.* New York: Institute for Rational-Emotive Therapy.

Ellis, A. (1972e). What does transpersonal psychology have to offer to the art and science of psychotherapy? *Voices, 8*(3), 10–20. (Rev. version: *Rational Living, 8*(1), 20–28).

Ellis, A. (1972f). Helping people get better rather than merely feel better. *Rational Living, 7*(2), 2–9.

Ellis, A. (1972g). Psychotherapy without tears. In A. Burton (Ed.), *Twelve Therapists* (pp. 103–126). San Francisco, CA: Jossey-Bass.

Ellis, A. (1973). *Humanistic psychotherapy: The rational-emotive approach.* New York: McGraw-Hill.

Ellis, A. (1974a). *Disputing irrational beliefs (DIBS).* New York: Institute for Rational-Emotive Therapy.

Ellis, A. (Speaker). (1974b). *I'd like to stop but . . . Overcoming addictions* (Cassette recording). New York: Institute for Rational-Emotive Therapy.

Ellis, A. (Speaker). (1975a). *RET and assertiveness training* (Cassette recording). New York: Institute for Rational-Emotive Therapy.

Ellis, A. (1975b). Comments on Frank's "The limits of humanism." *Humanist, 35*(5), 43–45.

Ellis, A. (1976a). RET abolishes most of the human ego. *Psychotherapy, 13*(4), 343–348. (Reprinted: New York: Institute for Rational-Emotive Therapy).

Ellis, A. (1976b). *Sex and the liberated man.* Secaucus, NJ: Lyle Stuart.

Ellis, A. (1976c). The biological basis of human irrationality. *Journal of Individual Psychology, 32*, 145–168. (Reprinted: New York: Institute for Rational-Emotive Therapy)

Ellis, A. (Speaker). (1976d). *Solving emotional problems.* (Cassette recording). New York: Institute for Rational-Emotive Therapy.

Ellis, A. (1977a). *Anger—how to live with and without it.* Secaucus, NJ: Citadel Press.

Ellis, A. (1977b). Fun as psychotherapy. *Rational Living, 12*(1), 2–6. (Also: Cassette recording. New York: Institute for Rational-Emotive Therapy)

Ellis, A. (1977c). *A garland of rational songs.* (Songbook and cassette recording). New York: Institute for Rational-Emotive Therapy.

Ellis, A. (Speaker). (1977d). *Conquering low frustration tolerance* (Cassette recording). New York: Institute for Rational-Emotive Therapy.

Ellis, A. (Speaker). (1977e). *Conquering the dire need for love* (Cassette recording). New York: Institute for Rational-Emotive Therapy.

Ellis, A. (1977f). Characteristics of psychotic and borderline individuals. In A. Ellis & R. Grieger (Eds.), *Handbook of rational-emotive therapy* (pp. 177–186). New York: Springer.

Ellis, A. (1977g). Religious belief in the United States today. *Humanist,* *1977, 37*(2), 38–41.

Ellis, A. (1977h). Why "scientific" professionals believe mystical nonsense. *Psychiatric Opinion, 14*(2), 27–30.

Ellis, A. (1979a). Discomfort anxiety: A new cognitive behavioral construct (Part I). *Rational Living, 14*(2), 3–8.

Ellis, A. (1979b). The issue of force and energy in behavioral change. *Journal of Contemporary Psychotherapy, 10,* 83–97.

Ellis, A. (1979c). *The intelligent woman's guide to dating and mating.* Secaucus, NJ: Lyle Stuart.

Ellis, A. (1979d). The theory of rational-emotive therapy. In A. Ellis & J. M. Whiteley (Eds.), *Theoretical and empirical foundations of rational-emotive therapy* (pp. 33–60). Monterey, CA: Brooks/Cole.

Ellis, A. (1979e). Rejoinder: Elegant and inelegant RET. In A. Ellis & J. M. Whiteley (Eds.), *Theoretical and empirical foundations of rational-emotive therapy* (pp. 240–267). Monterey, CA: Brooks/Cole.

Ellis, A. (1979f). The practice of rational-emotive therapy. In A. Ellis & J. M. Whiteley (Eds.), *Theoretical and empirical foundations of rational-emotive therapy* (pp. 66–100). Monterey, CA: Brooks/Cole.

Ellis, A. (1979g). Rational-emotive therapy: Research data that support the clinical and personality hypotheses of RET and other modes of cognitive-behavior therapy. In A. Ellis & J. M. Whiteley (Eds.), *Theoretical and empirical foundations of rational-emotive therapy* (pp. 101–173). Monterey, CA: Brooks/Cole.

Ellis, A. (1980a). Discomfort anxiety: A new cognitive behavioral construct (Part II). *Rational Living, 15*(1) 25–30.

Ellis, A. (1980b). The value of efficiency in psychotherapy. *Psychotherapy, 17,* 414–419.

Ellis, A. (1980c). Psychotherapy and atheistic values: A response to A. E. Bergin's "Psychotherapy and religious values." *Journal of Consulting and Clinical Psychology, 48,* 635–639.

Ellis, A. (1981a). The use of rational humorous songs in psychotherapy. *Voices, 16*(4), 29–36.

Ellis, A. (1981b). The rational-emotive approach to thanatology. In H. J. Sobel (Ed.), *Behavior therapy in terminal care: A humanistic approach* (pp. 151–176). Cambridge, MA: Ballinger.

Ellis, A. (1981c). Rational-emotive family therapy. In A. M. Horne & M. M. Ohlsen (Eds.), *Family counseling and therapy* (pp. 302–327). Itasca, IL: Peacock.

Ellis, A. (1982a). Rational-emotive group therapy. In G. M. Gazda (Ed.), *Basic approaches to group psychotherapy and group counseling* (pp. 381–412). Springfield, IL: Thomas.

Ellis, A. (1982b). The treatment of alcohol and drug abuse: A rational-emotive approach. *Rational Living, 17*(2), 15–24.

Ellis, A. (1982c). Must most psychotherapists remain as incompetent as they now are? *Journal of Contemporary Psychotherapy, 13*, 17–28.

Ellis, A. (1982d). Intimacy in rational-emotive therapy. In M. Fisher & G. Striker (Eds.), *Intimacy* (pp. 203–217). New York: Plenum.

Ellis, A. (1983a). The philosophic implications and dangers of some popular behavior therapy techniques. In M. Rosenbaum & C. M. Franks (Eds.), *Perspective on behavior therapy in the eighties* (pp. 138–151). New York: Springer.

Ellis, A. (1983b). *The case against religiosity.* New York: Institute for Rational-Emotive Therapy.

Ellis, A. (1983c). Failure in rational-emotive therapy. In E. Foa & P. M. Emmelkamp (Eds.), *Failures in behavior therapy* (pp. 159–171). New York: Wiley.

Ellis, A. (1983d). The origins of rational-emotive therapy (RET). *Voices, 18*(4), 29–33.

Ellis, A. (1984a). Rational-emotive therapy (RET) and pastoral counseling: A reply to Richard Wessler. *Personnel & Guidance Journal, 62,* 266–267.

Ellis, A. (1984b). How to deal with your most difficult client—you. *Psychotherapy in Private Practice, 2*(1), 25–35. (Also: *Journal of Rational-Emotive Therapy, 1*(1), 2–8, 1983)

Ellis, A. (1984c). *Intellectual fascism.* New York: Institute for Rational-Emotive Therapy.

Ellis, A. (1984d). Foreword to W. Dryden's *Rational-emotive therapy: Fundamentals and innovations* (pp. vii–xxvi). London: Croom Helm.

Ellis, A. (1984e). Rational-emotive therapy. In R. J. Corsini (Ed.), *Current psychotherapies.* (3rd ed., pp. 197–238). Itasca, IL: Peacock.

Ellis, A. (1984f). The place of meditation in cognitive-behavior therapy and rational-emotive therapy. In D. H. Shapiro & R. N. Walsh (Eds.), *Meditation: Classic and contemporary perspectives.* New York: Aldine.

Ellis, A. (1984g). Maintenance and generalization in rational-emotive therapy (RET). *The Cognitive Behaviorist, 6*(1), 2–4. (Revised and reprinted, *How to use RET to maintain and enhance your therapeutic gains.* New York: Institute for Rational-Emotive Therapy)

Ellis, A. (1984h). Responsibility of counselors and psychologists in preventing nuclear warfare. *Personnel and Guidance Journal, 63,* 75–76.

Ellis, A. (1984i). Treating the abrasive client with rational-emotive therapy (RET). *The Psychotherapy Patient, 1*(1), 21–25.

Ellis, A. (1984j). Intellectual fascism. *Journal of the Institute for the New Man,* *1*(1), 39–54. (Reprinted, New York: Institute for Rational-Emotive Therapy)

Ellis, A. (1984k, August). *Rational-emotive therapy and transpersonal psychology.* Paper presented at the 92nd Annual Convention of the American Psychological Association, Toronto, Ontario, Canada.

Ellis, A. (in press-a). *Rational-emotive therapy and cognitive-behavior therapy.* New York: Springer.

Ellis, A. (in press-b). (Introduction to special issue on the contributions of Howard Young). *British Journal of Cognitive Psychotherapy.*

Ellis, A. (in press-c). The use of hypnosis with rational-emotive therapy (RET). In E. T. Dowd & J. Healy (Eds.), *Case studies in hypnotherapy.* New York: Guilford.

Ellis, A. (in press-d). Expanding the ABCs of RET. In A. Freeman & M. Mahoney (Eds.), *Cognition and psychotherapy.* New York: Plenum.

Ellis, A. (in press-e). Case presentation of rational-emotive therapy. In I. L. Kutash & A. Wolf (Eds.), *Psychotherapist's casebook.* San Francisco, CA: Jossey-Bass.

Ellis, A. (in press-f). Application of rational-emotive therapy (RET) to love problems. In A. Ellis & M. E. Bernard (Eds.), *Applications of rational-emotive therapy.* New York: Plenum.

Ellis, A. (in press-g). A rational-emotive approach to acceptance. In J. Francek, S. Klarreich & E. Moore (Eds.), *The human resources management handbook.* New York: Praeger.

Ellis, A. (in press-h). Jealousy: Its etiology and treatment. In D. C. Goldberg (Ed.), *Contemporary marriage: Special issues in couple therapy.* Homewood, IL: Dorsey.

Ellis, A., & Abrahms, E. (1978). *Brief psychotherapy in medical and health practice.* New York: Springer.

Ellis, A., & Abrahms, E. (Speakers). (1979a). *Rational-emotive therapy in the treatment of schizophrenia* (Cassette recording). New York: BMA Audio Cassettes.

Ellis, A., & Abrahms, E. (Speakers). (1979b). *Rational-emotive therapy in the treatment of severe depression* (Cassette recording). New York: BMA Audio Cassettes.

Ellis, A., & Becker, I. (1982). *A guide to personal happiness.* North Hollywood, CA: Wilshire Books.

Ellis, A., & Bernard, M. E. (Eds.). (1983). *Rational-emotive approaches to the problems of childhood.* New York: Plenum.

Ellis, A., & Bernard, M. E. (in press). What is rational-emotive therapy (RET)? In A. Ellis & M. E. Bernard (Eds.), *Applications of rational-emotive therapy.* New York: Plenum.

Ellis, A., & Grieger, R. (Eds.). (1977). *Handbook of rational-emotive therapy.* New York: Springer.

Ellis, A., & Gullo, J. (1972). *Murder and assassination.* Secaucus, NJ: Lyle Stuart.

Ellis, A., & Harper, R. A. (1961a). *A guide to rational living.* Englewood Cliffs, NJ: Prentice-Hall.

Ellis, A., & Harper, R. A. (1961b). *Creative marriage.* Secaucus, NJ: Lyle Stuart. (Paperback edition retitled: *A guide to successful marriage.* North Hollywood, CA: Wilshire Books)

Ellis, A., & Harper, R. A. (1975). *A new guide to rational living.* North Hollywood, CA: Wilshire Books.

Ellis, A., & Knaus, W. (1977). *Overcoming procrastination.* New York: New American Library.

Ellis, A., & Whiteley, J. M. (Eds.). (1979). *Theoretical and empirical foundations of rational-emotive therapy.* Monterey, CA: Brooks/Cole.

Epictetus. (1890). *The works of Epictetus.* Boston: Little, Brown.

Epstein, S. (1984). Emotions from the perspective of cognitive self-theory. In P. Shaver (Ed.), *Review of personality and social psychology* (pp. 1–59). Beverly Hills, CA: Sage.

Erikson, M. H., & Rossi, E. L. (1979). *Hypnotherapy: An exploratory casebook.* New York: Irvington.

Eysenck, H. J. (1964). *Experiments in behavior therapy.* Oxford: Hawthorn.

Farrelly, F., & Brandsma, J. M. (1977). *Provocative therapy.* Fort Collins, CO: Shields.

Fay, A. (1978). *Making things better by making them worse.* New York: Hawthorn.

Fenichel, O. (1945). *Psychoanalytic theory of neurosis.* New York: Norton.

Fenichel, O. (1953). *The collected papers of Otto Fenichel.* New York: Norton.

Ferenczi, S. (1952). *Further contributions to the theory and technique of psychoanalysis.* New York: Basic Books.

Ferguson, M. (1980). *The Acquarian conspiracy.* Los Angeles: Tarcher.

Fink, E. R. (1980). *A cognitive-behavioral group therapy program for problems of anger and aggression in adult male offenders.* Unpublished Psy.D. dissertation, Rutgers University, New Brunswick, New Jersey.

Finney, B. C. (1972). Say it again: An active therapy technique. *Psychotherapy, 9,* 128–131.

Flew, A. (1976). Parapsychology revised. *Humanist, 36*(3), 28–30.

Foreyt, J. P., & Goodrick, G. R. (1984). Cognitive behavior therapy. In R. J. Corsini (Ed.), *Encyclopedia of psychology* (pp. 231–234). New York: Wiley.

Frank, J. D. (1973). *Persuasion and healing* (2nd ed.). Baltimore: Johns Hopkins University Press.

Frank, J. D. (1975). The limits of humanism. *Humanist, 35*(5), 40–52.

Frankl, V. (1960). Paradoxical intention: A logotherapeutic technique. *American Journal of Psychotherapy, 14,* 520–535.

Frankl, V. (1966). *Man's search for meaning.* New York: Washington Square.

Frankl, V. (1975). *Psychotherapy and existentialism.* New York: Simon and Schuster.

Franks, C. M., & Wilson, G. T. (1978). *Behavior therapy: Theory and practice.* New York: Brunner/Mazel.

Freud, A. (1946). *The ego and mechanisms of defense.* New York: International Universities Press.

Freud, S. (1965a). The interpretation of dreams. In J. Strachey (Ed. and Trans.), *The standard edition of the complete psychological world of Sigmund Freud* (Vol. 5). New York: Basic Books. (Original work published 1900)

Freud, S. (1965b). The dynamics of transference. In J. Strachey (Ed. and Trans.), *The standard edition of the complete psychological works of Sigmund Freud* (Vol. 1, pp. 97–108). New York: Basic Books. (Original work published 1912)

Freud, S. (1965c). Recommendations to physicians practicing psychoanalysis. In J. Strachey (Ed. and Trans.), *The standard edition of the complete psychological works of Sigmund Freud* (Vol. 12, pp. 109–120). New York: Basic Books. (Original work published 1912)

Freud, S. (1965d). Inhibitions, symptoms and anxiety. In J. Strachey (Ed. and Trans.), *The standard edition of the complete psychological works of Sigmund Freud* (Vol. 21). New York: Basic Books. (Original work published in 1926)

Freud, S. (1965e). *The standard edition of the complete psychological works of Sigmund Freud.* New York: Basic Books.

Friedman, M. (1975). *Rational behavior.* Columbia, SC: University of South Carolina.

Garfield, S. L., & Bergin, A. E. (1978). *Handbook of psychotherapy and behavior change.* New York: Wiley.

Gerald, M., & Eyman, W. (1982). *Thinking straight and talking sense: An emotional education program.* New York: Institute for Rational-Emotive Therapy.

Giovacchini, P.L. (1971). Character disorders: With special reference to the borderline state. *Journal of Psychoanalytic Psychiatry, 127,* 867–871.

Giovacchini, P. L., & Boyer, I. B. (Eds.). (1982). *Technical factors in the treatment of the severely disturbed patient.* New York: Aronson.

Glasser, W. (1965). *Reality therapy.* New York: Harper and Row.

Glazer, M. W. (1979). The borderline personality diagnosis: Some negative implications. *Psychotherapy, 16,* 376–380.

Golden, W. L. (1983a). Rational-emotive hypnotherapy: Principles and techniques. *International Journal of Eclectic Psychotherapy, 1*(2), 47–56.

Golden, W. L. (Speaker). (1983b). *Self-hypnosis: The rational-emotive approach* (Cassette recording). New York: Institute for Rational-Emotive Therapy.

Golden, W. L. (1983c). Resistance in cognitive behavior therapy. *British Journal of Cognitive Psychotherapy, 1*(2), 33–42.

Goldfried, M. R. (1982). Resistance and clinical behavior therapy. In P. L. Wachtel (Ed.), *Resistance* (pp. 94–114). New York: Plenum.

Goldfried, M. R., & Davison, G. C. (1976). *Clinical behavior therapy.* New York: Holt, Rinehart & Winston.

Greenson, R. R. (1967). *The technique and practice of psychoanalysis.* New York: International Universities Press.

Greenwald, H., & Rich, E. (1984). *The happy person.* New York: Stein & Day.

Grau, A. F. (1977). Dealing with the irrationality of alcoholic drinking. In J. L. Wolfe & E. Brand (Eds.), *Twenty years of rational therapy* (pp. 225–230). New York: Institute for Rational-Emotive Therapy.

Grieger, R., & Boyd, J. (1980). *Rational-emotive therapy: A skills-based approach.* New York: Van Nostrand Reinhold.

Grieger, R., & Grieger, I. Z. (Eds.). (1982). *Cognition and emotional disturbance.* New York: Human Sciences.

Gross, M. L. (1979). *The psychological society.* New York: Simon and Schuster.

Guidano, V. F., & Liotti, G. (1983). *Cognitive processes and emotional disorders.* New York: Guilford.

Hadley, S. W., & Strupp, H. W. (1976). Contemporary view of the negative effects in psychotherapy. *Archives of General Psychiatry, 33,* 1291–1302.

Haley, J. (1963). *Strategies of psychotherapy.* New York: Grune & Stratton.

Haley, J. (1976). *Problem-solving therapy.* San Francisco: Jossey-Bass.

Haley, D. (1984). *Ordeal therapy.* San Francisco: Jossey-Bass.

Harrell, D. E. (1976). *All things are possible.* Bloomington, IN: Indiana University Press.

Hauck, P. A. (1973). *Overcoming depression.* Philadelphia: Westminster.

Hauck, P.A. (1984). *The three faces of love.* Philadelphia: Westminster.

Herzberg, A. (1945). *Active psychotherapy.* New York: Grune & Stratton.

Heidegger, M. (1962). *Being and time.* New York: Harper & Row.

Higbee, J. (1977). Dealing with alcohol-dependent persons. In J. L. Wolfe & E. Brand (Eds.), *Twenty years of rational therapy* (pp. 231–233). New York: Institute for Rational-Emotive Therapy.

Hill, N. (1944). *Think and grow rich.* North Hollywood, CA: Wilshire Books.

Hobbs, N. (1962). Sources of gain in psychotherapy. *American Psychologist, 17*, 741–747.

Hogan, D. B. (1980, September). *Defining what a competent psychotherapist does.* Paper presented at American Psychological Association Convention, Montreal, Canada.

Horney, K. (1937). *The neurotic personality of our time.* New York: Norton.

Houston, J. (1982). *The possible human.* Los Angeles: Tarcher.

Hovland, C. I., & Janis, I. L. (1959). *Personality and persuasibility.* New Haven, CT: Yale University Press.

Ingalls, J. D. (1976). *Human energy: The critical factor for individuals and organizations.* Reading, MA: Addison-Wesley.

Jacobsen, E. (1942). *You must relax.* New York: McGraw-Hill.

Janis, I. L., & Mann, L. (1979). *Decision making.* New York: Free Press.

Janov, A. (1970). *The primal scream.* New York: Delta.

Johnson, C. H., Sehnov, R. S., & Gilmore, J. D. (1983). Thought-stopping and anger induction in the treatment of hallucinations and obsessional ruminations. *Psychotherapy, 20*, 445–448.

Johnson, N. (1980). Must the rational-emotive therapist be like Albert Ellis? *Personnel & Guidance Journal, 59*, 49–51.

Johnson, W. (1981). *So desperate the fight.* New York: Institute for Rational-Emotive Therapy.

Jones, E. (1953). *The life and work of Sigmund Freud.* New York: Basic Books.

Jones, M. C. (1924a). Elimination of children's fears. *Journal of Experimental Psychology, 7*, 382–390.

Jones, M. C. (1924b). A laboratory fear: The case of Peter. *Journal of Genetic Psychology, 31*, 308–311.

Kaplan, H. S. (1979). *Disorders of sexual desire.* New York: Brunner/Mazel.

Kelly, G. (1955). *The psychology of personal constructs.* New York: Norton.

Kelly, G. (1966). *The selected papers of George Kelly.* New York: Wiley.

Kendall, P. C. (1984a). Cognitive processes and procedures in behavior therapy. In C. M. Franks, G. T. Wilson, P. C. Kendall, & K. D. Brownell (Eds.), *Annual review of behavior therapy.* Vol. 8 (pp. 122–148). New York: Guilford.

Kendall, P. C. (1984b). On miracles, magic, and good tricks: Toward generalization in cognitive-behavioral self-control therapy with children. *Cognitive Therapist, 6*(1), 5–7.

Kernberg, O. (1975). *Borderline conditions and pathological narcissism.* New York: Aronson.

Kerr, B. A., & Dell, D. M. (1976). Perceived interviewer expertness and attractiveness. *Journal of Counseling Psychology, 23*, 553–556.

Kerr, B. A., Olson, D. H., Claiborn, C. D., Bauers-Gruenler, S. J., &

Paolo, A. M. (1983). Overcoming opposition and resistance. *Journal of Counseling Psychology, 30,* 323–331.

Kilbourne, B., & Richardson, J. T. (1984). Psychotherapy and new religions in a pluralistic society. *American Psychologist, 39,* 237–251.

Knaus, W. (1974). *Rational emotive education.* New York: Institute for Rational-Emotive Therapy.

Knaus, W. (Speaker). (1975). *Overcoming procrastination* (Cassette recording). New York: Institute for Rational-Emotive Therapy.

Knaus, W. (1982). *How to get out of a rut.* Englewood Cliffs, NJ: Prentice-Hall.

Kohut, K. (1971). *The analysis of self.* New York: International Universities Press.

Krantz, S. E., Hill, R. D., Foster-Rawlings, S., & Zeeve, C. (1984). Therapists' use and perceptions of strategies for maintenence and generalization. *Cognitive Behavoirist, 6*(1), 19–22.

Krippner, S., Davidson, R., & Peterson, N. (1973). Psi phenomena in Moscow. *Journal of Contemporary Psychotherapy, 6,* 79–88.

Kurtz, P. (1976, Spring). Gullibility and nincompoopery. *Religious Humanism,* 1–7.

Lange, A., & Jakubowski, P. (1976). *Responsible assertive behavior.* Champaign, IL: Research Press.

Langs, R. (1981). *Resistances and interventions.* New York: Aronson.

Lauver, P. J., Holiman, M. A., & Kazama, S. W. (1982). Counseling as battleground: Client as enemy. *Personnel & Guidance Journal, 61,* 99–101.

Lawrence, C., & Huber, C. H. (1982). Strange bedfellows?: Rational-emotive therapy and pastoral counseling. *Personnel & Guidance Journal, 61,* 210–212.

Lazarus, A. A. (1978). *In the mind's eye.* New York: Rawson.

Lazarus, A. A. (1981). *The practice of multimodal therapy.* New York: McGraw-Hill.

Lazarus, A. A., & Fay, A. (1975). *I can if I want to.* New York: Morrow.

Lazarus, A. A., & Fay, A. (1982). Resistance or rationalization? A cognitive-behavioral perspective. In P. Wachtel (Ed.), *Resistance* (pp. 115–132). New York: Plenum.

Lazarus, A. A., & Fay, A. (1984). Some strategies for promoting generalization and maintenance. *Cognitive Behaviorist, 6*(1), 7–9.

Lazarus, R. S. (1966). *Psychological stress and the coping process.* New York: McGraw-Hill.

Lazarus, R. S. (1984). Coping. In R. J. Corsini (Ed.), *Encyclopedia of psychology* (pp. 294–296). New York: Wiley.

Lembo, J. (1976). *The counseling process.* New York: Libra.

Lewis, J. M., & Johansen, K. H. (1982). Resistance to psychotherapy with the elderly. *American Journal of Psychotherapy, 36,* 497–504.

Lieberman, M. A., Yalom, I. D., & Miles, M. B. (1973). *Encounter groups: First facts.* New York: Basic Books.

Losoncy, L. E. (1980). *You can do it.* Englewood Cliffs, NJ: Prentice-Hall.

Lowen, A. (1970). *Pleasure.* New York: Lancer.

Luria, A. R. (1976). *Cognitive developments: Its cultural and social foundations.* Cambridge, MA: Harvard.

Madanes, C. (1981). *Strategic family therapy.* San Francisco: Jossey-Bass.

Mager, R. F. (1962). *Preparing instructional objectives.* Palo Alto, CA: Fearon.

Mahoney, M. J. (1974). *Cognition and behavior modification.* Cambridge, MA: Ballinger.

Mahoney, M. J. (1976). *The scientist.* Cambridge, MA: Ballinger.

Mahoney, M. J. (1977). Personal science: A cognitive learning theory. In A. Ellis & R. Grieger (Eds.), *Handbook of rational-emotive therapy* (pp. 352–366). New York: Springer.

Mahoney, M. J. (1980). Psychotherapy and the structure of personal revolution. In M. J. Mahoney (Ed.), *Psychotherapy process.* New York: Plenum.

Maliver, B. L. (1972). *The encounter game.* New York: Stein & Day.

Marcus Aurelius (1890). *Meditations.* Boston: Little, Brown.

Marks, I. M. (1972). Flooding (implosion) and allied treatments. In W. S. Agras (Ed.), *Learning theory applications of principles and procedures to psychiatry.* Boston: Little, Brown.

Maslow, A. (1962). *Toward a psychology of being.* Princeton: Van Nostrand.

Masters, W., & Johnson, V. A. (1970). *Human sexual inadequacy.* Boston: Little, Brown.

Masterson, J. F. (1976). *Psychotherapy of the borderline adult.* New York: Brunner/Mazel.

Maultsby, M. C., Jr. (1971a). Systematic written homework in psychotherapy. *Psychotherapy, 8,* 195–198.

Maultsby, M. C., Jr. (1971b). Rational emotive imagery. *Rational Living, 6*(1), 24–27.

Maultsby, M. C., Jr. (1975). *Help yourself to happiness.* New York: Institute for Rational-Emotive Therapy.

Maultsby, M. C., Jr. (1978). *A million dollars for your hangover.* Lexington, KY: Rational Self-help Books.

Maultsby, M. C., Jr. (1984). *Rational-behavior therapy.* Englewood Cliffs, NJ: Prentice-Hall.

Maultsby, M. C., Jr., & Ellis, A. (1974). *Technique of using rational-emotive imagery.* New York: Institute for Rational-Emotive Therapy.

May, R. (1969). *Love and will.* New York: Norton.

McGovern, T. E., & Silverman, M. S. (1984). A review of outcome studies of rational-emotive therapy from 1977 to 1982. *Journal of Rational-Emotive Therapy, 2*(1), 7–18.

Meehl, P. E. (1962). Schizotaxia, schizotype, and schizophrenia. *American Psychologist, 17,* 827–838.

Meichenbaum, D. (1977). *Cognitive-behavior modification.* New York: Plenum.

Meichenbaum, D. (1984). Fostering generalization: A cognitive-behavioral approach. *Cognitive Behaviorist, 6*(1), 9–10.

Meichenbaum, D., & Gilmore, J. B. (1982). Resistance from a cognitive-behavioral perspective. In P. L. Wachtel (Ed.), *Resistance* (pp. 133–156). New York: Plenum.

Meichenbaum, D., & Jaremko, M. E. (Eds.). (1983). *Stress reduction and prevention.* New York: Plenum.

Merrifield, C., & Merrifield, R. (1980). *Call me RETman.* New York: Institute for Rational-Emotive Therapy.

Miller, I. W. (1984). Strategies for maintenance of treatment gains for depressed patients. *Cognitive Behaviorist, 6*(1), 10–13.

Miller, L. K. (1980). *Principles of everyday behavior analysis.* Monterey, CA: Brooks/Cole.

Miller, T. (1983). *So you secretly suspect you're worthless, well . . .* Manlius, NY: Tom Miller.

Miller, W. R. (Ed.). (1980). *The addictive behaviors.* Elmsford, NY: Pergamon.

Mischel, H. (1984). Unpublished personal communication.

Mischel, W., & Baker, N. (1975). Cognitive appraisals and transformations in delay behavior. *Journal of Personality and Social Psychology, 31,* 251–264.

Mischel, W., & Ebbesen, E. G. (1970). Attention in delay of gratification. *Journal of Personality and Social Psychology, 16,* 329–337.

Mischel, W., & Gilligan, C. (1964). Delay of gratification, motivation for the prohibited gratification, and response to temptation. *Journal of Abnormal and Social Psychology, 69,* 411–417.

Mischel, W., & Mischel, H. (1975). A cognitive social learning approach to morality and self-regulation. In T. Lickana (Ed.), *Morality: A handbook of moral behavior.* New York: Holt, Rinehart & Winston.

Mischel, W., & Moore, B. (1973). Effects of attention to symbolically presented reward on self-control. *Journal of Personality and Social Psychology, 28,* 172–179.

Morris, K. T., & Kanitz, J. M. (1975). *Rational-emotive therapy.* Boston: Houghton Mifflin.

Mowrer, O. H. (1964). *The new group therapy.* Princeton, NJ: Van Nostrand.

Noland, E. J., Boyd, J. D., & Grieger, R. M. (1980). Influences on irrational beliefs and expectancy of success on frustration tolerance. *Rational Living, 15*(1), 14–20.

Novaco, R. (1975). *Anger control.* Lexington, MA: Lexington.

Novaco, R. (1980). Training of probation counselors for anger problems. *Journal of Counseling Psychology, 27,* 385–399.

Olson, D. H., & Dowd, E. T. (1984). Generalization and maintenance of therapeutic change. *Cognitive Behaviorist, 6*(1), 13–20.

Osgood, C. E. (1971). Exploration in semantic space. *Journal of Social Issues, 24,* 5–6.

Ostrander, S., & Schroeder, L. (1974). *Psychic discoveries behind the Iron Curtain.* New York: Bantam.

Palazzoli, M., Boscolo, L., & Cecchin, G. (1978). *Paradox and counter paradox.* New York: Aronson.

Paris, C., & Casey, B. (1983). *Project you.* North Hollywood, CA: Wilshire Books.

Patterson, C., & Mischel, W. (1976). Effects of temptation inhibiting and task facilitating plans on self-control. *Journal of Personality and Social Psychology, 33,* 209–217.

Patterson, G. R. (1982). *Coercive family process.* Eugene, OR: Castalia.

Peale, N. V. (1952). *The power of positive thinking.* Greenwich, CT: Fawcett.

Perls, F. (1969). *Gestalt therapy verbatim.* Lafayette, CA: Real People Press.

Phadke, K. M. (1982). Some innovations in RET theory and practice. *Rational Living, 17*(2), 25–30.

Pomerleau, O. F. (1979). Behavioral medicine. *American Psychologist, 34,* 654–663.

Popper, K. R. (1962). *Objective knowledge.* London: Oxford.

Pottinger, P. S. (1980, September). *Certifying competence, not credentials.* Paper presented at American Psychological Association Convention, Montreal, Canada.

Pulvino, C. J. (1975). Psychic energy: The counselor's undervalued resource. *Personnel & Guidance Journal, 54*(1), 28–32.

Raimy, V. (1975). *Misunderstandings of the self.* San Francisco, CA: Jossey-Bass.

Reik, T. (1948). *Listening with the third ear.* New York: Rinehart.

Redl, F. (1966). *When we deal with children.* New York: Free Press.

Rimm, D., & Masters, J. C. (1974). *Behavior therapy.* New York: Academic.

Rogers, C. R. (1942). *Counseling and psychotherapy.* Boston: Houghton Mifflin.

Rogers, C. R. (1951). *Client-centered psychotherapy.* Boston: Houghton Mifflin.

Rogers, C. R. (1957). The necessary and sufficient conditions of therapeutic personality change. *Journal of Consulting Psychology, 21,* 459–461.

Rogers, C. R. (1961). *On becoming a person.* Boston: Houghton Mifflin.

Rogers, C. R., & Berlin, J. (1959 July). Unpublished personal communication.

Rorer, L., & Widiger, T. A. (1983). Personality structure. *Annual Review of Psychology, 34,* 101–123.

Rosen, R. D. (1977). *Psychobabble.* New York: Atheneum.

Rosenbaum, M. (1983). The long haul of psychotherapy. [Review of M. F. Weiner, The psychotherapeutic impasse.] *Contemporary Psychology, 28,* 136–137.

Russell, B. (1950). *The conquest of happiness.* New York: New American Library.

Russell, B. (1965). *The basic writings of Bertrand Russell.* New York: Simon and Schuster.

Salter, A. (1949). *Conditioned reflex therapy.* New York: Creative Age.

Saltmarsh, R. E. (1976). Client resistance in talk therapies. *Psychotherapy, 13,* 34–39.

Santayana, G. (1946). *The life of reason.* New York: Scribner's.

Schlesinger, H. J. (1982). Resistance as process. In P. L. Wachtel (Ed.), *Resistance* (pp. 25–44). New York: Plenum.

Schutz, W. C. (1971). *Here comes everybody.* New York: Harper & Row.

Schwartz, R. M. (1982). Cognitive-behavior modification: A conceptual review. *Clinical Psychology Review, 2,* 267–293.

Shapiro, D., & Walsh, R. N. (Eds.). (1984). *Meditation.* New York: Aldine.

Shelton, J., & Ackerman, J. M. (1974). *Homework in counseling and psychotherapy.* Springfield, IL: Thomas.

Sichel, J., & Ellis, A. (1984). *Self-help report form.* New York: Institute for Rational-Emotive Therapy.

Sifneos, P. (1979). *Short-term dynamic psychotherapy.* New York: Plenum.

Small, L. (1979). *The brief psychotherapies.* New York: Brunner/Mazel.

Smith, R. F. (1976). *Prelude to science.* New York: Scribner's.

Smith, R. R., Jenkins, W. O., Petko, C., & Warner, R. (1977). An experimental application and evaluation of rational-behavior therapy in a work release setting. *Journal of Clinical Psychology, 46,* 348–349.

Snyder, J. J., & White, M. J. (1979). The use of cognitive self-instruction in the treatment of behaviorally disturbed adolescents. *Behavior Therapy, 10,* 227–235.

Sperry, R. W. (1977). Bridging science and values: A unifying view of mind and brain. *American Psychologist, 32,* 237–245.

Spinoza, B. (1901). *Improvement of the understanding, ethics and correspondence.* New York: Dunne.

Spitzer, R. L. (Ed.). (1980). *Diagnostic and statistical manual of mental disorders* (3rd ed.). New York: American Psychiatric Association.

Spivak, G., & Shure, M. (1974). *Social adjustment in young children.* San Francisco, CA: Jossey-Bass.

Stampfl, T. G., & Lewis, D. J. (1967). Essentials of implosive therapy. *Journal of Abnormal Psychology, 72,* 496–503.

Standal, S. W. (1954). *The need for regard: A contribution to the client-centered theory.* Unpublished Ph.D. thesis, University of Chicago, Chicago, IL.

Stanton, H. E. (1977). The utilization of suggestions derived from rational-emotive therapy. *Journal of Clinical and Experimental Hypnosis, 25,* 18–26.

Stewart, R. (Ed.). (1981). *East meets west: The transpersonal approach.* Wheaton, IL: Theosophical Publishing House.

Stokes, T., & Baer, D. (1977). An implicit technology of generalization. *Journal of Applied Behavior Analysis, 10,* 345–367.

Strupp, H. H. (1980, September). *Toward the measurement of therapists' contributions to negative outcomes.* Paper presented at American Psychological Association Convention, Montreal, Canada.

Strupp, H. H., Hadley, S. W., & Gomes-Schwartz, B. (1977). *Psychotherapy for better or worse: Analysis of the problem of negative effects.* New York: Aronson.

Stuart, R. B. (1980). *Helping couples change.* New York: Guilford.

Stunkard, A. J. (Ed.). (1980). *Obesity.* Philadelphia: Saunders.

Sullivan, H. S. (1956). *Clinical studies in psychiatry.* New York: Norton.

Targ, R., & Puthoff, R. (1977). *Mind-reach.* New York: Delacorte.

Tart, C. T. (1975). *States of consciousness.* New York: Dutton.

Templeman, T. L., & Wollersheim, J. P. (1979). A cognitive-behavioral approach to the treatment of psychopathy. *Psychotherapy, 16,* 132–139.

Thorne, F. C.. (1950). *Principles of personality counseling.* Brandon, VT: Journal of Clinical Psychology Press.

Tillich, P. (1953). *The courage to be.* New Haven, CT: Yale University Press.

Tosi, D., & Eshbaugh, D. (1978). A cognitive experiential approach to the interpersonal development of counselors and therapists. *Journal of Clinical Psychology, 34,* 494–500.

Tosi, D., & Henderson, G. W. (1983). Rational stage-directed therapy: A cognitive experiential system. *Journal of Rational-Emotive Therapy, 1*(1), 15–20.

Tosi, D., & Marzella, J. N. (1977). Rational stage-directed therapy. In J.

L. Wolfe & E. Brand (Eds.), *Twenty years of rational therapy*. New York: Institute for Rational-Emotive Therapy.

Tosi, D., & Reardon, J. P. The treatment of guilt through rational stage-directed therapy. *Rational Living, 11*(1), 8–11.

Truax, C. B., & Carkhuff, R. R. (1967). *Toward effective counseling and psychotherapy*. Chicago, IL: Aldine.

Truax, C. B., & Mitchell, K. M. (1971). Research in certain therapist skills in relation to process and outcomes. In A. E. Bergin & S. L. Garfield (Eds.), *Handbook of psychotherapy and behavior change*. New York: Wiley.

Turkat, D., & Meyer, V. (1982). The behavior-analytic approach. In P. L. Wachtel (Ed.), *Resistance* (pp. 157–184). New York: Plenum.

Vriend, J., & Dyer, W. W. (1973). Counseling the reluctant client. *Journal of Counseling Psychology, 20*, 240–246.

Vygotsky, L. S. (1962). *Thought and language*. New York: Wiley.

Wachtel, P. L. (1978). *Psychoanalysis and behavior therapy*. New York: Basic Books.

Wachtel, P. L. (Ed.). (1982). *Resistance*. New York: Plenum.

Walen, S. R., DiGiuseppe, R., & Wessler, R. L. (1980). *A practitioner's guide to rational-emotive therapy*. New York: Oxford.

Walker, J. R., & Aycock, L. The counselor as "chicken." *Personnel & Guidance Journal, 62*, 424–426.

Watson, J. B., & Rayner, P. (1920). Conditioned emotional reactions. *Journal of Experimental Psychology, 3*, 1–14.

Watzlawick, P., Weakland, J., & Fisch, R. (1974). *Change*. New York: Norton.

Weeks, G., & L'Abate, L. (1982). *Paradoxical psychotherapy*. New York: Brunner/Mazel.

Weil, A. (1973). *The natural mind*. Boston: Houghton Mifflin.

Weimer, W. B. (1979). *Psychology and the conceptual foundations of science*. Hillside, NJ: Erlbaum.

Weiner, M. F. (1982). *The psychotherapeutic impasse*. New York: Free Press.

Weinrach, S. (1973). Even counselors have irrational ideas. *Personnel & Guidance Journal, 52*, 245–247.

Weinrach, S. (1977). Review of five-day intensive practice in rational-emotive psychotherapy by Albert Ellis and staff. *Personnel & Guidance Journal, 55*, 558–559.

Wessler, R. A., & Wessler, R. L. (1980). *The principles and practice of rational-emotive therapy*. San Francisco: Jossey-Bass.

Wessler, R. L. (1982, November). *Alternative conceptions of rational-emotive therapy and their integration with the cognitive-behavior therapies*. Paper presented at the 13th Annual Conference of the Psychological Society of Ireland, Sligo, Ireland.

Wessler, R. L., & Ellis, A. (1980). Supervision in rational-emotive therapy. In A. K. Hess (Ed.), *Psychotherapy supervision* (pp. 181–191). New York: Wiley.

Wessler, R. L., & Ellis, A. (1983). Supervision in counseling: Rational-emotive therapy. *Counseling Psychologist, 11*(1), 43–49.

Wicks, E. (1983). Psychotherapy focus: Old and new. *Voices, 18*(4), 34–38.

Wilson, T., & Franks, C. M. (1982). *Contemporary behavior therapy.* New York: Guilford.

Wolberg, L. R. (1948). *Medical hypnosis.* New York: Grune & Stratton.

Wolberg, L. R. (1967). *The technique of psychotherapy.* New York: Grune & Stratton.

Wolfe, J. L. (Speaker). (1977). *Assertiveness training for women* (Cassette recording.) New York: Institute for Rational-Emotive Therapy.

Wolfe, J. L. (1979). A cognitive-behavioral approach to working with women alcoholics. In V. Burtle (Ed.), *Women who drink* (pp. 197–216). Springfield, IL: Thomas.

Wolfe, J. L., & Fodor, I. G. (1975). A cognitive/behavior approach to modifying assertive behavior in women. *Counseling Psychologist, 5*(4), 45–52.

Wolfe, J. L., & Fodor, I. G. (1977). Modifying assertive behavior in women: A comparison of three approaches. *Behavior Therapy, 8,* 567–574.

Wolpe, J. (1958). *Psychotherapy by reciprocal inhibition.* Stanford, CA: Stanford University Press.

Wolpe, J. (1982). *The practice of behavior therapy* (3rd ed.). New York: Pergamon.

Wolpe, J., & Lazarus, A. A. (1966). *Behavior therapy techniques.* New York: Pergamon.

Wolstein, B. (1959). *Transference and countertransference.* New York: Wiley.

Yates, A. J. (1975). *Theory and practice of behavior therapy.* New York: Wiley.

Yochelson, S., & Samenow, S. E. (1977, 1980). *The criminal personality.* (2 Vols.). New York: Aronson.

Young, H. (1974). *A primer of rational counseling.* New York: Institute for Rational-Emotive Therapy.

Young, H. (1977). Counseling strategies with working class adolescents. In J. L. Wolfe & E. Brand (Eds.), *Twenty years of rational therapy* (pp. 187–202). New York: Institute for Rational-Emotive Therapy.

Young, H. (1984). *The work of Howard S. Young.* Special issue of the *British Journal of Cognitive Psychotherapy, 2*(2), 1–98.

Zilbergeld, B. (1983). *The shrinking of America.* Boston: Little, Brown.

Index

Index

Date Due